Fiction and Incarnation

Fiction and Incarnation

RHETORIC, THEOLOGY, AND LITERATURE IN THE MIDDLE AGES

Alexandre Leupin

Translated by David Laatsch

University of Minnesota Press
Minneapolis / London

This work, published as part of a program of aid for publication, received support from the French Ministry of Foreign Affairs and the Cultural Services of the French Embassy in the United States.

Cet ouvrage, publié dans le cadre d'un programme d'aide à la publication, bénéficie du soutien du Ministère des Affaires étrangères et du Service Culturel de l'Ambassade de France aux Etats-Unis.

First published in France as *Fiction et incarnation: Littérature et théologie au moyen age.*

Published by the University of Minnesota Press
111 Third Avenue South, Suite 290
Minneapolis, MN 55401-2520
http://www.upress.umn.edu

Library of Congress Cataloging-in-Publication Data

Leupin, Alexandre, 1948–
[Fiction et incarnation. English]
Fiction and incarnation : rhetoric, theology, and literature in the Middle Ages / Alexandre Leupin ; translated by David Laatsch.
p. cm.
Includes bibliographical references and index.
ISBN 0-8166-3724-5 (HC : alk. paper) — ISBN 0-8166-3725-3 (PB : alk. paper)
1. Literature, Medieval—History and criticism. 2. Theology—History—Middle Ages, 600–1500. 3. Incarnation in literature. 4. Religion and literature.
I. Title.
PN673 .L4813 2002
809'.93382—dc21

2002011519

Printed in the United States of America on acid-free paper

12 11 10 09 08 07 06 05 04 03 10 9 8 7 6 5 4 3 2 1

Mendacia poetarum inserviunt veritati. [The lies of poets serve truth.]
—John of Salisbury

With the arrival of the first stampeders, Bonanza Creek woke up, and thereupon began a long-distance race between unveracity and truth, wherein, lie no matter how fast, men were continually overtaken and passed by truth. When men who doubted Carmack's report of two and a half to the pan, themselves panned two and a half, they lied and said that they were getting an ounce. And long ere the lie was fairly on its way, they were getting not one ounce but five ounces. This they claimed was ten ounces; but when they filled a pan of dirt to prove the lie, they washed out twelve ounces. And so it went. They continued valiantly to lie, but the truth continued to outrun them.
—Jack London, *Burning Daylight*

The truth verifies itself in fiction.
—Jacques Lacan

Contents

Acknowledgments

The author wishes to thank Edouard Glissant and Peter Haidu for their friendly suggestions.

The writing of this book was made possible in part by a semester sabbatical granted by Louisiana State University in 1990 and by a grant from the Center for French and Francophone Studies located at the same institution, as well as by a grant from the Eliot Dow Healy Memorial Fellowship.

Introduction
The Christian Epistemological Break

Procrustes the Thief (whose name implies "he who strikes first") has a relentless desire to reject the stranger at the door. No person arriving from elsewhere is welcome in his home. The stranger must conform to the bed that is offered to him, either by having his legs cut off because the bed is too short or by being stretched to death because it is too long. The stranger is always made to fit. Procrustes' henchmen, however, do not understand. They find this show useless for their survival, and they could just as easily do without it. Beds represent an affectation whose very nature dilutes the terrifying ferocity of pillage by making it equivocal and indirect. The band of robbers disapproves of this obliqueness but they do not dare to communicate their dissatisfaction to the chief. Why this refinement, this mediation? But the rite continues; right or wrong, Procrustes cannot communicate with the stranger without the subterfuge of the beds. And he must keep this to himself, for his band would never forgive him. In his fevered and perverse imagination, Procrustes believes that only the foreigner in the bed understands him. His gang of thieves, who are happy to emulate him by repeating him, can never articulate what he thinks he hears in the screams of the other.

The kingpin's legend falls silent at a crucial moment. One day, an exceedingly rich stranger arrives at the door. To his good fortune, he fits the bed perfectly. What does Procrustes do, against the advice of his band? Careful to respect the rules that he himself has declared, and faithful to what he takes to be his profound calling, he lets the stranger go unharmed. This incident has only one result: Reassured by this one exception, more and more travelers make the voyage from Athens to Megara, thinking that Procrustes' thesis has been negated. The brigand, however, never feels the need to question his system. As he continues to strip these credulous travelers of their belongings, he patiently awaits the day when once again a stranger will fit the great bed so that once again he can set him free.

A thesis, shattered by its antithesis, reunited in a synthesis (so that nothing escapes it), is always a Procrustean bed. In it, the particular becomes general. It neglects everything that does not conform to it. A thesis thus has a common measure, a bottom layer that accepts only what miraculously fits its imperious demands and rejects everything that differs from them. And yet what would a critic or a theoretician be without a thesis? He would be a maniac, obsessively devoted to a diffuse account of imagination and to a narcissism (both his and the text's) of the minute detail. The book without a thesis eludes a common measure and so is destined to be undone in every way by thought.

My goal is to relieve this torture inflicted by models. I will not repudiate them, however, for it is not necessary to repudiate a model to eliminate its persecution. Rather, I will look at the spaces these models leave open: the space between the foreigner and Procrustes, between the particular and the general, between the other and the same. This requires us to pay careful attention to the dialectical movement of an infinite back-and-forth, to the tension that arises between the concentric themes of texts and their uncentered diversity. This may require letting the texts be, so that without diminishing their own alterity, they may reflect, at one moment or another, the shape of the thesis.

Western Europe is unique because of the character of the Middle Ages. Of the other great civilizations of the time (China, India, Israel, the Islamic world, the Kingdom of Benin), none experienced the essential phenomenon of the European medieval era. Medieval Europe undertook a concerted global effort to break from the very roots of its culture: classical antiquity (although it reassimilated ancient culture almost immediately, having reworked and modified it). This shake-up is unique in history because it was internal, voluntary, and conscious. Indeed, that Western civilization is discontinuous owes almost nothing to historical, economic, or natural events (invasions, catastrophes, decline). On the contrary, it owes everything to a book, the New Testament, a mental event that cannot be downplayed with a diachronic interpretation.

In two fundamental books, René Girard reveals how Christian discourse brings about a rupture on the level of ethics, ethnology, and anthropology. This discourse destroys the idolatry of founding violence, brings the mechanisms of persecution to light, and puts them on trial. It demonstrates that the scapegoat is innocent, and it makes the transcendent call for a society finally founded on nonviolence and love for all people.[1] However, Girard never questions language, representation, or the concept, despite his refined ear for the New Testament signifier. I will try to make up a little for this lack. If Christian discourse is as revolutionary as Girard claims, then it must necessarily question everything I have just mentioned.

So what is this phenomenon that we call the Middle Ages? This is an enormous question, but epistemology can answer it on the conceptual level. A preliminary response comes from Alexandre Kojève's brief but dense article "L'Origine chrétienne de la science moderne."[2] He starts with a factual observation: The starting point of what is called "modern science" is geographically and temporally located, even though today science extends all over the world without distinctions of class, sex, race, or religion. Modern science first appears in the Christian West, and nowhere else in the world. In the seventeenth century, Copernicus, Galileo, and Descartes first outline a science that is both quantifiable and empirical (which is to say, modern).

Certainly the Greeks, Arabs, Maya, and Egyptians all developed an astronomy/astrology whose refinement was based on a mathematics well beyond anything in the Christian West. For them, however, the heaven of gods and Ideas was unchanging, and they certainly did not consider projecting into it the fluctuation and change that is the eternal essence of the here-below. This change was conceived as random, as the *chaosmos* (the uncreated world ruled by chance). A double projection only began to take place with Copernicus and Galileo. From them comes our modern vision of a universe (both the sublunar realm and the heavens) ruled by mathematical laws and nonrandom variables.

This break occurs only in the Western, Christian world. Is this a coincidence? Or does Christian dogma contain an element that explains the necessity of this event? If the break is predetermined, the cause must lie with an article of Christian faith that no other religion, mythology, or cosmology shares, an article that would define what is unique to Christianity. Kojève isolates this element:

> Monotheism itself is obviously not responsible for this, given that it can be found in advanced paganisms, as well as with the Jews and the Muslims, who were late to come to scientific ideas. As for creationism, because one also finds it equally in Judaism and Islam in an authentic form, it certainly is not responsible for modern science. Nor, again, is the doctrine of the Trinity. Pagan (neo-)Platonism knew something of it. Even for Christians, this doctrine leads more to "mystic" introspection or "metaphysical" speculation than to using the bodily senses to observe phenomena or to experimentation. There remains, then, only the doctrine of the Incarnation, which is furthermore the only great Christian dogma to be both authentically and specifically Christian from the point of view of historical reality. It is the only one that belongs to Christianity and to it alone. So if Christianity is responsible for modern science, this responsibility comes exclusively from the doctrine of the Incarnation.[3]

The Incarnation is nothing other than the conjunction of man with God, the particular with the general, the empirical with the abstract, history with the eternity of what Kojève calls, in quotation marks, "logic":

> In fact, the Incarnation is the possibility for the eternal God to be truly present in the temporal world in which we live, without his falling from his absolute perfection. . . . If, as believing Christians say, a worldly (human) body can at the same time be God's body, and thus divine, and if, as the Greeks thought, divine (celestial) bodies correctly reflect eternal relations among mathematical entities, then nothing prevents us from exploring these relations on earth as well as in heaven.[4]

Nor does anything prevent us from projecting, as did Kepler, the fluctuations and nonrandom variables of our sublunar world into the superlunar heaven, the heaven of mathematical ideas, which then loses its unchanging eternity.

For Kojève, the Incarnation as a concept and as an event is a sign of a major epistemological break. As such, it affects all systems and subsystems of thought, and after a delay of seventeen centuries, it produces modern science. Alexandre Koyré proposes[5] that the emergence of modern science begins with a break in the seventeenth century—that it begins with Galileo and the effects of his work. The break must be pushed back in time and rechristened. It can now be said to have occurred at the beginning of our era, when the dogma of Incarnation (a dogma that the Greeks and pagans thought of as "crazy") developed. As for terminology, the key opposition becomes the one between "pagan" and "Christian" notions of science. These terms replace Koyré's "ancient" and "modern" sciences. On this point, the concept of modernity is absolutely equivalent to that of Christianity, and the adjective "ancient" replaces "pagan."[6]

From this starting point, we need to find a method that will allow us to apply this observation to each text or context we choose to study, so that we can determine whether it belongs to the pagan or the Christian side of the break (or failing this, to disclose its duality). Jean-Claude Milner has formulated the underlying premise for this, calling it "Kojève's theorem": *There is never any synonymy between a notion belonging to antiquity and a modern notion.*[7]

If we suppose a realism of language and notions, the criterion for this distinction is both linguistic and referential. The only difference occurring within a system of language, the diacritical, binary, and fictional distinction internal to that system, can never be enough to found a real distinction. In other words, real synonyms exist, and real homonyms are also possible where a single word designates different ideas and things in a conceptual reapportionment.[8] Tertullian's efforts, for example, are nothing less than a vast attempt to homonymize the words used by ancient rhetoric so as to make them say something else: the reality/truth of the Incarnation.

Kojève's theorem allows one both to find the (rare) major epistemological breaks in the histories of civilizations and to distinguish them from illusory or minor breaks. Concepts on one or another side of a break readily take on the same terminology (this is most often the case), but if a particular term designates a new notion, then there is homonymy. If notions change terms, then there is a break. For example, Kepler's term "orbit" no longer means a sphere (or a circle, as it meant for Copernicus). For ancient science, it carried the connotation of a material object made of crystal, and it indicated symbolic notions of uniformity and perfection. Since Kepler, "orbit" indicates an irregular ellipse, definable only in mathematical terms.

In contrast, a new terminological grouping, a fortiori a previously unknown name, can never function by itself as the decisive index of a major break (the notion of the "Renaissance" is one example among others).

The usefulness of this criterion to indicate homonymy is not limited to the exact sciences. It can be seen, for example, at the center of the Christian religious innovation. The name "Jesus" designates the notion of the God-man, a notion that has no synonym in any thought, system, religion, or mythology that preceded it. This is what Boethius demonstrates around A.D. 512 when he writes his treatise against two heresies, those of Nestorius and Eutyches. The Nestorians refuse to grant divinity to Christ, calling him a human prophet. Eutyches denies him his humanity, calling him God in the simulacrum of a human body. These two heretics look back to the pagan conception of a radical antithesis between man and god(s) and unite in a common denial of the Incarnation. Nestorius claims that two distinct persons correspond to the separate divine and human substances (and thus the name "Jesus" is a complete homonym). In contrast, Eutyches states that there is just one substance, one person (God); Christ's body, then, is no more than the form in which this single divine substance shows itself to man. Boethius placed these two heresiarchs in the same box by reaffirming the Incarnation as "a place of honour midway between two extremes. For if it stands beyond or below where it should, it ceases to be virtue. And so virtue holds to a middle place."[9]

Boethius's work thus maintains that the person (the name) "Jesus" indicates two substances at once, both human and divine. This logical paradox makes a homonym of the name: "The name of Christ is equivocal *[aequivocum]* and cannot be comprised in one definition."[10] Not only does Boethius seize upon an ineffable mystery, he is also clearly conscious of an innovation so radical that no ancient term can grasp it: "For how great and unprecedented a thing it is—unique and incapable of repetition in any other age—that the nature of him who is God alone should come together with human nature which was entirely different from God to form from different natures by conjunction a single Person!"[11] Because there are heresies, dogma must completely think through its own novelty, and this leads to impressive consequences. One can find the starting point of the great debate over universals in Boethius's commentaries.

Kojève's thesis ties the emergence of modern science to the Western Christian tradition. Those who hold to a certain *doxa,* or firm belief, will feel their bile rise at these words. The very formulation of this theorem seems to be a classic reaffirmation of cultural imperialism. However, the very idea that there is a "Western" thought in any area is denied by this theorem, which follows Koyré's epistemology. For thought to be "Western" requires there to be a continuity of tradition from ancient Greece to Western modernity. Kojève's break sends this continuity back to the warehouse of comforting fantasies. The onset of a Christian way of knowing breaks the "Western tradition" in two.

This is not to deny that fantasies are endowed with historical power. "Western thought," for example, was used by imperialism so successfully that no domain of thought or practice seemed able to elude it. But the imperialist dream supported by this fantasy must be completely distinguished from modern science's global expansion. Science must not be confused with a scientism that uses the notion of science in an attempt to legitimate itself. There never was a "Soviet science," and there is no "Western science." To call science "Western" runs directly counter to the very meaning of the word.

Kojève emphasizes that there is no contradiction between Galilean science and institutional ecclesiastic dogma, and the facts have proven him correct:

> Whether one likes it or not, those who founded modern science were not pagans, nor were they atheists, or even anti-Catholic as a general rule (or were so only to the degree that they saw the Catholic Church as mired in paganism). What these scientists were fighting against was the contemporary form of Scholasticism—an Aristotelianism that had returned to its authentic pagan form. Its incompatibility with Christian theology had been clearly seen and demonstrated in the very opening moments of the new philosophy.[12]

This is not to assert that modern science continues Christian discourse, but it is necessary to understand that Christian discourse clears the epistemological ground where science will take root and supplant it.

If Kojève is right, and we hold his proof to be irrefutable, then the Christian epistemological break is a major break and leaves no system of thought untouched. As a result, not only is science profoundly affected, but also art, literature, philosophy, aesthetics, linguistics, and so on.

The problem of the break has been carefully explored by science and art history;[13] this book explores the consequences of the Christian epistemological break for literature. Because we have moved from one field of study to another, epistemology can no longer be the basis of our inquiry; not even the most hypothetical objects of science can be applied to literary texts, so we are compelled to refer to a very different discipline. Everything here begins with Jacques Lacan's distinction between *letter* and *signifier;*[14] the letter depends on a "matheme," a form of scientific writing; it can represent itself (for example, "+" in a mathematical equation); the signifier, on the other hand, "represents [a subject] for another signifier."[15] Its value comes from its placement in a diacritical, symbolic order, and so literature falls within the signifier's domain. Rather than producing objects, literature proposes *projects* that reveal the symptoms of a unique desire to write: *idiograms.* These are encoded on the page and preserved for unforeseen future readers. Literary works produce names and words that have never been heard before (radical, and singular, homonyms), and so literature appears to be the one field that most obstinately resists the general processes of homonymy. The idea of progress, which is that of a historical break, is utterly foreign to literature, just as it is to all artistic activity.[16] In certain respects, each literary text is an absolute beginning that renews itself at every reading through the centuries and across all breaks, even the epistemological ones.

The two suppositions that I have clarified as being at the heart of my project seem to cancel each other out. On the one hand, if we are to demonstrate the occurrence of an epistemological break, we must examine a dogma that only has meaning for a specific time and place. On the other hand, literature breaks away from the conditions in which it first appears; this is what defines it *as* literature. Literature is history's other, outside of temporal representation and communicability. The texts commented on here, a small selection from an immense tradition, are examined in two ways: as taking part in a debate that lies outside them (in the exteriority of language and representation—a Real), and simultaneously as movements in search of their own law, a law that would permit them to show a reflection of themselves to an unforeseen reader. My enterprise (itself a project) is not to seek the epistemology of literature but, rather, to seek a theory of "idiogrammatic"[17] literary projects; it is *gnossology.*[18] Gnossology's object is the signifier; not the one of effusive Gnostic discourse, yet it still takes risks with the improbable.

To situate the Christian break in the schema of literary, theatrical, and artistic representation, we must turn both to Moses' Second Commandment (outlawing idols and images) and to that which it negates: the development of the mythological imaginary. In a double movement, the Incarnation produces a totally new relation to representation. On the one hand, because the God-man necessarily presupposes a relation to the human imaginary, ancient Jewish iconoclasm needs to be overcome. On the other hand, Christ and the church fathers who follow him read paganism in such a way that there can be no question that the fascination with, and the violence and inanity of, its idols is pushed aside. These two movements, to revere the physicality of the God-man and to shun physical representations of the divine, only seem to be contradictory. A new law of Christian discourse can be deduced from them: All fictions, every name, each representation (except those that have to do with God) shall from now on refer to a characteristic. The new law rejects the Old Testament's "Thou shalt make no image" and mythology's "Thou shalt only make images." In their place it puts "All images shall be icons." This law contains the contradiction between the particular and the general, so it can account for the unrepeatable case of God become an individual man. The Incarnation thus explained leads Christianity to a new fascination for each individual and each separate figure, no matter what it may be.

Literature only exists to contradict commandments; that is why this book is not a theological treatise. Its function is to determine the status of the literary exception in the seemingly paradoxical gap between its own individuation and the generality of the law. I propose this: *Each work of literature necessarily belongs to the law of the icon and yet is an exception to it.*[19] In this attempt, I intend to follow the call of this maxim, to read texts literally *(à la lettre)* and at the same time to read them as unique moments without logical relation to the historical and conceptual framework that encompasses them. Even in the medieval period of the rhetorical figure, the text's singularity produces a previously unheard music in its perpetual re-beginning. The Christian, and therefore individuating, nature of medieval literature necessarily leads to a theory and practice of the exception.

The generality of commandments and the particularity of each of their many exceptions give themselves to interpretation in the reflexivity of literary texts—that is, through those figures in which the fiction sets a mirror before the theory and practice of its own production. We must distinguish here between reflexivity and *mise en abyme,* a process that is always internal to the text and delimited by it.[20] The reflexivity that reveals the real work of writing is ubiquitous. Everything in the fiction is likely to refer to it. Furthermore, we must draw a line between the literary mirror and the *specula* that were fashionable in the Middle Ages (the "mirrors of the world," "of the prince and the people," "of knowledge," the *Speculum Historial* of Vincent de Beauvais, and so on); these continually appeal to a transcendent exteriority that they reflect. The literary mirror is internal to the text. It is the monument to a desire to write and read, and it calculates these desires without being able to master them completely. For this reason, we must also separate the mirror from medieval allegory, with which it nevertheless has so many affinities.

The apparent paradox is that as the projection of a gnossology, the immanence of the mirror is almost absent and entirely superficial. An almost-nothing that reverses and deforms, its evanescence also gives it the fearsome and derisory power to make the literary monument primary and to redeploy everything (history, society, theology, context, author, reader, the library of knowledge and representations, and so on) in its service. Yet the mirror is; and in each text, it delimits the general law of enunciation as well as the irreducible singularity of an idiogram (a unique reading, dissimilar from all others). This is why I will proceed throughout in synchronic jumps and take the texts in question one by one; to proceed otherwise would be to run the risk of losing the unique flavor of each text. A gnossology of literature, in effect, cannot be happy with generality; with each step it takes, it also confronts the individual question of one and only one text. Here, there can be no theory without a reiterated practice of reading. On the other hand, in nonliterary discourses, and in antiliterary ones as well (theology, for example), reflexivity allows us to see how such discourses are attached to literature in spite of themselves. As the text folds back on itself, two motions occur. First, a space is cleared in which literature can declare its autonomy; this space is groundless, and this hollow opening, at the same time, permits what is particular in literary autotelism to work its way into the general economy of the discourses that surround and oversee it.

Of course, the literary mirror does not date from the medieval era. It exists at least since Homer's siren song. However, biblical symbolism and allegory give it a credibility that will lead to an extraordinary flowering. The Middle Ages were also the golden age of reflexivity. Geoffrey of Vinsauf was its greatest thinker and practitioner, as he shows in the

Poetria nova, written at the beginning of the thirteenth century. This verse treatise, itself a use of the poetic mirror, transforms each manual and intellectual activity into the *specula* of writing.[21] This is nothing new, but Geoffrey is different from his predecessors in his aspiration to universalize and systematize. On the other hand, as the title of his treatise shows, the *Poetria nova* is evidence of a truly lively modernity. His writing is fully conscious of a radical innovation away from classical antiquity, a break that was a long time in preparation and that compels one to read once more all of the culture that came before. This *rejuvenatio,* as he calls it, comes from the central figure of Christ Incarnate (lines 1142, 1163–1165), the historicity of Christ (1205), his nature as both human and divine (1206), his Resurrection (1210), and his virginal conception (1508–1512). Geoffrey declares this to be "a thing miraculous in every sense!" (1513). But all the points of religious dogma refer here, as if in a mirror, to the articles of a new poetic. The virgin birth is a sign for the birth of a radically other culture. The Incarnation, in retaining its status as a mystery, lends the weight of the Real to literature. Death and resurrection are figures for the extinction of classical civilization and its Christian resurrection (and not its rebirth). The good shepherd and his lost lambs are also, explicitly, the writer and his renewed words: "Such a metaphorical use of words serves you like a mirror, for you can see yourself in it, and recognize your own sheep in a strange countryside."[22]

In this way, Geoffrey establishes the Christic mirror as a model for literature, and this, in its turn—and in a much more heretical and secret way—changes into a theological statement.

Furthermore, if Christ is the model for literature, the medieval writer can no longer conceive of his task as an *otium,* that is, an artistic diversion (as it was in classical antiquity). To write is to work in reality, in imitation of Christ the carpenter. For Geoffrey, this brings about an infinite series of references to all the crafts of the artisan. Even the most humble serves as an emblem for the work of the writer.

Literature, in the *Poetria nova,* is a pure surface that reveals (itself as) the being of its thing in reflection; the Incarnation gives this essence a stress that cannot be confused with anything that came before. "Ecce rei speculum; res tota relucet in illo" [Here is a mirror of the subject: *The entire matter shines out from it*].[23]

A break does not affect all the manifestations of a civilization at once. On the one hand, old gnossologies will endure, and it should be understood that these anachronisms, by themselves, in no way empty texts of their meanings. For example, there is *The Marriage of Mercury and Philology,* by Martianus Capella. This doctrinal and poetic treatise was written as the Roman Empire was becoming completely Christianized, yet in it, pagan thought survives intact and uncompromised. On the other hand, medieval texts can never be set firmly in the sphere of Christianity; they contain a continual play of confrontation and redistribution between the ancient and the new. What they bring to light, for the most part, are the elements of a paganism that survived the break. They do this to such a degree that they contradict Christian knowledge on the profound and most important level of their own writing.[24] We must also emphasize that by the very fact of containing pagan elements, the nature of the texts changes, for they now stand in opposition to Christian discourse. This leads me to propose, as a hypothesis, a veritable schizophrenia in medieval culture. It both preserves and rereads the ancient heritage on a large scale, and it devotes itself over the course of fifteen centuries, and often in the same texts, to drawing out all the consequences of the Incarnation for every endeavor. Isidore of Seville is so conscious of this tension that he devotes all his energy to reducing and harmonizing it, demonstrating in the process that Hebraic civilization is the source of every culture in history.

If the Christian break is to be considered a major one, it must have an institution to establish it.[25] In this case, the church has the function of solidifying and universalizing the notion of the Incarnation. Christ founded the church in a play on words ("Thou art Peter, and upon this rock . . ."; Matt. 16: 18). And so, in a continuing dialectic, the community that accepts Christian dogma as true gives it a canonical status, thus breaking with pagan thought and with the Apocrypha. Dogma and the break it brings about are both made legitimate by the institution and give it credibility in return. In this process, the word only has meaning insofar as it becomes an institution through a series of triumphs (the Christian sect becomes a church through the actions of the great councils). The majority on the side of dogma thus wins out over the sectarianism of the heresies, and as a result the latter are marginalized.

What Christianity has to offer is thus *sufficiently true* to create an institution, "a real world in which man lives."[26] Barely two centuries after its emergence, the declaration of the Incarnation becomes an obsession in the etymological meaning of that word (occupying one, or *the,* space).

It profoundly shakes all the necessary conditions for representation and all the hypostases of fiction. Lacan can be modified on this point; the church, affirming the conjunction of the mysterious and the bodily, brings out a plurality of meanings, in contrast to Docetism, in which meaning tends to be reduced to a vanishing point where it no longer has anything to do with humanity.

This position produces a dialectical antithesis. There is an opposition between the entirely positive affirmation of the Incarnation and the action of the Spirit that always says "no" (the devil). This Spirit arises and assumes sole responsibility for negation. It has nothing more to do with the pagan gods, no matter what the church has to say about it. Lucifer's negativity, the powerful action of nonbeing, is itself dialectically determined by and determinant of the Incarnation. Of course, the force of this action is to discredit the Incarnation, by making the incarnated body into nothing more than a fiction created by an artistic and therefore lying God. "Did you think his body unreal?" Geoffrey of Vinsauf asks Satan.[27] Characterized as the controlling god of all falsehood (by Tertullian in particular), Lucifer finds refuge in popular belief, and also, more importantly, in literature. It is with this in mind that the diabolic nature of medieval textuality must be read. The devil in truth is the beingless God of the medieval artist, even more so since he claims to be the spirit of the world, to be the Creator—the creator of an artistic world based on the elimination of divine creation. In the medieval era, artistic creation had a profound rapport with the heresies of Gnosticism and Manichaeism, which persisted throughout almost the entire age. The writer continually confronts the temptation to be a creator against or outside his Creator. Sometimes he succumbs. Tertullian, Saint Augustine, and Alain of Lille repeated this again and again without anyone paying them much attention. Denis de Rougemont in *L'Amour et l'occident* made note of this.[28] In the *Poetria nova,* Geoffrey of Vinsauf assigns Satan to the role of the prideful usurper: "When the angelic host was created in the newborn heaven, Lucifer, of exceeding light, assumed more of the Creator's light than did the others; and in this he presumed. Thereby inflated, he began to encroach on the supreme light."[29]

Whether sided with God or with Satan, with dogma or with heresy, it is always the limits of faith that determine the symbols of medieval culture, even when an unnameable but not divine cause is at work in a real way in civilization. Because of this, the medievalist works in a museum of sorts. Where are today's heresies? Where are the churches? Where is Satan? How do the ancient debates concern us today? Let us say it outright: My research's archaeological side is, in my opinion, only a necessary step that must be overcome. I have no intention of continuing the tradition of a church, nor do I wish to found a new one. Even less do I wish to found a chapel of criticism. If we are to seize the uniqueness of the literary exception in each of its occurrences, we cannot be satisfied merely to study theology—or its reflected image: heresy. If there is something like literature, no doubt it is outside this double paradigm.

What I wish to show is that the Middle Ages, insofar as it worked out the consequences of the Incarnation, is also the birthplace of our own modernity in both literature and science. A new vision of the universe emerges from its bosom, as does the dialectically linked idea of its representation. This idea is at the base of and is the direct (and often repressed) source of all our theories and practices of fiction.

What follows from this is that the very notion of the "Middle Ages," too rarely questioned even by specialists, and the title of "medievalist" are inconsistent on every level, whether historical, conceptual, or critical. It should be understood that I am not denying that we are separated from those texts, or from the conditions of their enunciation and their individual receptions. However, there is no criterion that we can borrow from literary history (even literary history) that is sufficient to define these conditions in their difference from or resemblance to our own era. Recent forays into medieval literature have taken up the themes of the "modernity" and the "alterity" of the Middle Ages with respect to our own. We must conclude, however, that these positions are untenable, unless they are radically inverted. The entire culture must be reread, and the status that it has been given of being somehow intermediary or mediocre must be rejected. Its place, which I understand to be at the forefront, has to be restored.

1
The Be-Seeming: Cicero and Quintilian

Cicero and Quintilian, two of the major agents in the transmission of a certain Greek culture to the West, at the same time handed down the thought of the Sophists. Their names give a legitimacy to this thought that the second generation of Sophists, who wrote in Greek and were therefore inaccessible to the Latin Middle Ages, could not provide for themselves. This is an important moment in the history of culture. The rhetorical model of thought has such historical wealth that it provides a paradigm for an entire segment of medieval culture. Erasmus reactivates this model during the Renaissance to constitute and define, both implicitly and explicitly, a model for all of humanism.[1]

Cicero and Quintilian ennoble an analogical and metaphorical conception of knowledge. The essence of this knowledge is rhetorical, fictional, and literary, and in it, form and thought are only separable through a corrupting interpretive violence. Analogy rules rhetoric to such a degree that it causes all the words of a given language to be increasingly drawn into a metaphorization that detaches them from the thing. Truth and pertinence have no bearing in this domain, where there is only plausibility and persuasion. In other words, rhetoric's very system destroys any real process of homonymy that could substitute one system of thought for another. And so, despite appearances, rhetorical thought comes to speech independent of the circumstances to which it refers. It is fundamentally ahistorical. The baseless base of literature is located here, and so we are forced to declare that literature itself is a name for everything that resists referential and historical homonymy. This resistance to new words explains rhetoric's longevity.[2] And because rhetoric provided the model for education up to and well into the Middle Ages, it was inevitable that the church fathers of late antiquity would all be sophists. For early Catholic thinkers, breaking from the pagan heritage also meant repudiating themselves, insofar as they were formed by sophistic fictions.

However, they did not completely succeed in the homonymy to which they aspired. Rhetorical thought, dominated by similarity and analogy (which is to say, by literature), lived on in the very heart of the Patristic age. If creation *(natura)* is the book in which the will of the divine writes itself, then everything is linked by correspondences of symbol and analogy. One need only read the church fathers to realize that they were great writers also, despite the horrible curses they flung against literature, in the name of the Incarnation.

Rhetorical thought, a living root of the teachings of the medieval schools, stands opposed to Christian thought, which starts from entirely different premises. Medieval culture everywhere shows the signs of its double birth. Before we enter into Christian gnossology, we must first outline what it struggles to break away from: a structure of knowledge that carries the names of Cicero and Quintilian yet cannot be reduced to them.

CICERO

For several reasons, Cicero holds an important place in cultural history. First of all, he produces what he calls a *conversio,*[3] the translation and importation of Greek thought into the Roman world. Through time, his work opens up a certain reading of the Hellenic world for the Middle Ages, where Greek was largely unknown. It is also from him that the medieval era receives the weighty ideal of the *vir bonus dicendi peritus* (the good man who is skilled in speech). Along with Quintilian's *Institutio oratoria* and the *Rhetoric for Herennius,* Cicero's writing is an index of rhetorical models. He himself also is the ideal model dominating all the official teachings of schools in late antiquity and the Middle Ages.

However, my task is not to trace Cicero's influence back from the medieval texts that encode it. A source study (always contradictory and often hypothetical) cannot adequately measure the effects of this determinate force. Too often, literary history disdains the fact that the meaning of a "source" is determined only by the text that uses it. Thus, the cultural intervention of the Ciceronian text could only be measured by a tradition or an influence that lies outside the text, or by the interpretation that a later writing places over it. My questions will thus be, What is eloquence *(oratio)* in Cicero's work? How might we describe the unique position of rhetoric in a discourse that it produces? We will need to trace out a network of words *(dicendium, eloquentia, oratio, orator)* whose meanings come as much from the structure of the text itself as from linguistic genealogy.

Discordant Voices

De oratore resembles the Socratic dialogues, and like them, it leaves critics to ask which character most nearly approaches the "actual opinion" of Cicero/Plato. Which spokesman are we to prefer when the voices contradict one another? To guide our reading and to overcome this problem, I propose the following hypothesis: The interpretation of the dialogue must take its rhetorical framework into account, in the sense that the structure of the fiction controls what is spoken by the different voices, and not the other way around. In the final analysis, *De oratore* defines rhetoric in a way that is both *rhetorical* and *fictional.* Conceptual logic and the precise use of invented voices count less than the persuasiveness of the attractive words that shape ideas. "Cicero" does not have a preferred spokesman. Anthony, Crassus, and the dialogue's other characters are so many orators using the model that fits the moment (what sophistry called *kairos,* "proper") even as they pretend to disdain such a practice. They interweave a large number of rhetorical threads without consideration for a general logic of argumentation. However, it is still possible to locate an overall structure in these seemingly discordant voices.

How is eloquence defined within the framework of this fiction? The narrator offers the first answer in the prologue, addressed to his brother: "I should publish something more polished and complete on these same topics . . . because I hold that eloquence is dependent upon the trained skill of *highly educated men*" (I, ii, 5; emphasis added).[4] The rhetorician must be a philosopher, mathematician, grammarian, musician, poet, historian, actor, and politician all at the same time. He is a living encyclopedia, a walking compilation of ancient *mathesis* (ways of knowing). Cicero's orator is a plastic and protean being occupying all these functions.

The demand for encyclopedic training also needs to be nuanced. One need not master the theoretical principles dear to specialists. One lifetime would not be enough. All that the student must be able to do, is to put into practice what has been developed by those who have mastered each discipline. Crassus proposes this important distinction: "The pursuit of facts is unlimited, and their acquisition easy if study is reinforced by practice" (III, xxiii, 88). According to Crassus, the orator is a "generalist." Anthony, another voice in the dialogue, states the logical conclusions of this position and thus reveals the true nature of rhetorical knowledge. The difference between Crassus and Anthony, it must be remembered, exists only in their names. The encyclopedia is not a science; it is a subtle knowledge of conventional wisdom:

> He said . . . everything with which orators dealt was doubtful and uncertain, since all of the talking was done by men who had no real grasp of their subject, and all the listening by hearers who were not to have knowledge conveyed to them, but some short-lived opinion that was either untrue or at least not clear. (I, xx, 92)

An obvious coherence runs through the apparent discord of voices (or the differing opinions of the dialogue's different voices). What eloquence knows is not things but words and *doxa.* Rhetoric gives the *appearance* of knowledge and is very close to the sophistic *mathesis* as it appears at the very beginning of Western thought in both Gorgias's *Fragment on Non-Being* and Plato's attacks against the Sophists.[5] Eloquence, then, is the keystone of culture and *humanitas* (humanism), but the price is *doxa*'s fundamental vagueness, ambiguity, accord with uncertainty, and even falsehood. It could be that when Anthony reveals the underlying secret of the "generalist," he also brings the most basic meaning of all humanism to light, so long as it always refers, explicitly or not, to Ciceronian *humanitas.*[6]

Unity of Knowledge

The orator's knowledge takes on the outward appearance of the art that produces it, and thus it seems to be unified and coherent. However, this brings about an aporia that lies at the center of and runs throughout *De oratore:* "Form" and "matter" are one. The signifier and the signified unite in a way that undermines these two concepts. Crassus formulates this: "Every speech consists of matter and words" *[re atque verbis]* (III, v, 19).

People think with language, and it is impossible to separate the "concept" from its "expression": "The words cannot fall into place if you remove the matter, nor can the matter have clarity if you withdraw the words" (III, v, 19).

When he joins thought to *latinitas* (the law of correct usage that codifies commonly held *doxa* and the social pact), Crassus makes the cultural context of Cicero's basic project very clear. The goal of this work is to make philosophical, theological, and literary Greek synonymous with Latin. (It is Cicero who introduces the word *philosophia* into the language.)

If language is understood as the means of thought, rhetoric is no longer an ornament. An ornament would be just another related element appended after the fact to meaning and thought. Instead, it is consubstantial with them. In consequence, the discussions of rhetorical technique, the catalog of figures and tropes, all must be read not as examples to aid the beautification of speech but as instructions on how to think. Rhetoric is thought, and conversely, thought is rhetoric. Precisely because rhetoric has a falsely ornamental function, it can overwhelm every other field of knowledge. Anthony, once again, sheds light on the question: "There is not a subject that is not the orator's own, provided only that it is one that deserves elegant and impressive treatment" (II, viii, 34). Since each matter must be communicated persuasively in order to be convincing, rhetoric is everywhere: "It follows that, if the famous natural philosopher Democritus spoke with elegance, as he is reported and appears to me to have spoken, those notable subjects of his discourse belonged to the natural philosopher, but his actual elegance of diction must be put down to the orator" (I, xi, 49).

As a result, there is a *limit* to thought's universality, since it is always linked in time and place to a local state and language. Although the Ciceronian concept contradicts modern rationalism (which holds that a notion is a notion when it can exist outside the conditions in which it is enunciated), it is not a trivial concept. It endures in contemporary literature and philosophy. Cicero's achievement here is to put into words the unspoken credo of any self-respecting author. Even though Saint Augustine opposes this view of language, the Middle Ages retains it in its entirety, as we shall see in chapter 3.

Cicero's treatise presents a series of consequences of the unity of matter and form: the aporia of the sign. He reverses everything, however, and calls the consequences the causes of the aporia. The first such result is the concept of the unity of nature, which derives its authority from the Eleatic philosophers: "There exists no class of things which can stand by itself, severed from the rest, or which the rest can dispense with and yet be able to preserve their own force and everlasting existence" (III, v, 20). Rhetorical thought never takes nature for itself. Instead, nature is an assembly of systematically and organically linked signs whose meanings must be explored. Nature is a lesson in aesthetics, and it is always influenced by culture.

Once again inverting cause and effect, nature's harmonious union brings about the unity of knowledge: "When we grasp the meaning of the theory *[doctrina]* that explains the causes and issues of things, we discover that a marvellous agreement and harmony underlies all branches of knowledge" (III, vi, 21).

The law of homogeneity now comes into play through a metaphorical (*translatio* and its cognates) relation to the fine arts, and above all to eloquence: "[E]loquence is one, into whatever shores or realms of discourse it ranges" (III, vi, 22).

The law of analogy binds the various disciplines in a universal harmony. Under its rule, the joining of form and meaning is linked to that of body and soul. Nature provides the model for this analogy. "Among natural objects, as it seems to me, there is none which does not comprise in its own kind a multiplicity of things that are different from one another and yet are esteemed as having a similar value" (III, vii, 25).

It is necessary to point out that metaphorical thought grounds the doctrine of "natural" similarities in *De oratore.* It is the real substratum. The linguistics of metaphor (*translatio* or *similitudo,* used interchangeably in the text) is the foundation of analogical thought *(similitudo).* It is as if the metaphor, invented in necessity and then practiced through consent (III, xxxviii, 155), continually displaces the proper terms until it completely obliterates them: "For there is nothing in the world the name or designation of which cannot be used in connexion with other things" (III, xl, 161). As the well-beaten path of thought (III, xl, 160), the metaphor compensates for what the proper term cannot say: "When something that can scarcely be conveyed by the proper term is expressed metaphorically, the meaning we desire to convey is made clear by the resemblance of the thing that we have expressed by the word that does not belong" (III, xxxviii, 155).

Well ahead of its time, *De oratore* evokes the Nietzschean possibility of a thoroughly metaphorical language.[7] In such a language, one no longer distinguishes between literal and figurative speech, and a sign does not indicate a thing. The doctrine of *similitudo* is the final metaphor for universal unification. In one move, it assimilates the order of things to the order of both thought and language. This would be an absolute philosophical and linguistic realism if it did not make all realism impossible. The metaphorical essence of eloquence is the subtle and efficient knowledge of words rather than a science of things,[8] yet it functions by seeming to join words to things.

By definition, rhetorical thought is the thought of absolute synonymy, where everything equals everything else. The things that are necessary for homonymy, for a real difference between concepts, cannot be established within this system. Cicero's rhetoric passes the crucial fiction of the thinker-artist on to the Middle Ages. The philosopher and the physician are poets first of all. Metaphors and commonplaces guide them in the observation of phenomena and in the quest for meaning. Once again, this reading does not trivialize or discredit the Middle Ages; without a grasp of this idea, medieval texts become unintelligible.

The understanding of *De oratore* and the study of its influence on the Middle Ages starts with the recognition that it considers the artist, or more accurately, the great artist, to be the model for the thinker.

Crassus introduces a question that can be formulated in this way: Given that an infinity of analogies holds everything together, as if in a hall of mirrors where repetition rules, how are we to find the best (that is, the most beautiful, persuasive, or convincing) similarity? What is the *difference* here, and how can we identify it? What is the thing that surpasses everything else and is a better repetition where everything is a reiteration of harmony and "natural" unity? *De oratore* answers these questions by introducing a tautological and paradoxical notion. We are to seek the *sui similis,* the "similar analogous to itself." The great orator (which means poet, painter, sculptor) repeats analogies and pushes the play of similarity until a new model arises in the work. As he works within a series of analogies, he nevertheless creates a paradigm. In its turn, this becomes the false original source of another series, to which, at first, he can fit his output: "Now turn your attention to consider the people whose department we are investigating. . . . Which of them is not eminent? And yet, which resembles anyone but himself?" *[nisi sui similis]* (III, vii, 28).

Through a leap of logic that defines its own coherence, the doctrine of analogy opens up to difference. The great artist (a category to which Cicero obviously belongs) is a founder and second model of a genre (a generality) that belongs to him only paradoxically and that remains forever indefinable. This conception of artistic activity is paradoxical, but subtly so. The medievals knew how to apply it best in their usage and renewal of commonplaces.[9]

Antiphilosophy

The science of things, which is to say philosophy, is well within the domain of rhetoric. There is an anecdote directed against Aristotle, the philosopher's philosopher, that proves that he himself could not neglect ornamenting his discourse:

> Accordingly, when Aristotle observed that Isocrates succeeded in obtaining a distinguished set of pupils by means of abandoning legal and political subjects and devoting his discourses to empty elegance of style, he himself suddenly altered almost the whole of his own system of training, and quoted a line from *Philoctetes* with a slight modification: the hero in the tragedy said that it was a disgrace for him to keep silent and suffer barbarians to speak, but Aristotle put it "suffer Isocrates to speak"; and consequently he put the whole of his system of philosophy in a polished and brilliant form, and linked the scientific study of facts with practice in style. (III, xxv, 141)

Beginning with this stance, the "science of things," philosophy, is systematically devalued in the treatise. According to Crassus, rhetoric comes before philosophy in the art of dialectic. The specialists in philosophy have appropriated a method that belongs to the rhetor first of all. Crassus declares,

> Antonius, you are . . . gratifying that singular liking of yours for contradiction, in which no one has ever outdone you; the exercise of this power belongs peculiarly to orators, though nowadays it is in regular use among philosophers, and chiefly those who make a practice of arguing at extreme length either for or against any proposition whatever laid before them. (I, lxi, 263)

And further along, he declares,

> The consummate orator possesses all the knowledge of the philosophers, but the range of philosophers does not necessarily include eloquence; and although they look down on it, it cannot but be deemed to add a crowning embellishment to their sciences. (III, xxxv, 143)

Crassus draws a radical conclusion from the subordination of the philosopher to the rhetor. Because philosophical truth busies itself with theory, it has no bearing on the practice either of eloquence or of life, the final criterion of the true in *De oratore:* "However for my part my present inquiry is not which system of philosophy is the truest but which is most fully akin to the orator" (III, xvii, 64).

We are now very close to Greek sophistry, since only the usefulness of discourse, and not its relation to truth, counts here. For this sophistry, a discourse is true when it has a concrete empirical effect. In principle, and by definition, sophistry is antitheoretical. Indeed, the starting point and the utopian goal of Crassus's position both reach back to the golden age of Greek thought. The fictional and ideal orator discussed above is rooted in this period: "For in old days at all events the same system of instruction seems to have imparted education in both right conduct and good speech; nor were the professors in two separate groups, but the same masters gave instruction in both ethics and in rhetoric" (III, xv, 57).

This crucial idea recurs later in the dialogue (III, xix, 72; III, xxxiv, 140). To equate the good with good speech is a pre Socratic move, for Socrates is the thinker who introduces the break between ethics and eloquence. Because he did so, *De oratore* repeatedly assaults his good name:

> Whereas the persons engaged in handling and pursuing and teaching the subjects that we are now investigating were designated by a single title, the whole study and practice of the liberal sciences being entitled philosophy, Socrates robbed them of this general designation, and in his discussions separated the science of wise thinking from that of elegant speaking, though in reality they are closely linked together. . . . This is the source from which has sprung the undoubtedly absurd and unprofitable and reprehensible severance between the tongue and the brain, leading to our having one set of professors to teach us to think and another to teach us to speak. (III, xvi, 60–61).

The Socratic break both transforms philosophy into a specialized discipline and limits eloquence. After Socrates, good speech becomes a mere refinement of style; hereafter, the orator has only to repeat technical models with no ethical dimension; they are models devoid of meaning. On closer reading, it is apparent that Cicero means to stamp the word *philosophia* with a very particular meaning. He transliterates it from Greek, but he gives it an accent that is uniquely Latin (and pre-Socratic). From this point on, philosophy ought only to be a praxis that combines good speech with good living, so as to create a basis for thinking. This meaning of the word endures throughout the whole medieval period, where *philosophia* indicates at once ethics, philosophy, grammar, and rhetoric.

Despite Cicero's seeming Platonism, *De oratore* returns to the ancient debate between sophistry and philosophy, and it greatly rehabilitates what was formerly supressed. Gorgias, as a near-mythical figure, is put to use to bring about this restoration. Just as with Crassus's position discussed above, and the pre-Socratic thought from which it derives, Gorgias's stand is both the starting point for the best of the Roman orators and the ideal that they must strive to achieve. First of all, the appeal to Gorgias allows Socrates to be placed in a malicious self-contradiction—and this within a Platonic dialogue devoted to refuting sophistry in the name of philosophy: "Plato—whose *Gorgias* I read with close attention . . . What impressed me most deeply about Plato in that book was, that it was when making fun of orators that he himself seemed to me to be the consummate orator" (I, xi, 47). This anodyne remark achieves its full impact later in the dialogue, in a demonstration of a self-evident sophistic character.

> Even the famous Gorgias of Leontini, who according to Plato appeared as advocate for the orator when he lost his case against the philosopher,—an adversary who either in reality was never defeated by Socrates and Plato's famous dialogue is untrue, or if defeated he was, obviously Socrates was more eloquent and fluent and . . . a fuller and better orator. (III, xxxii, 129)

Cicero ensnares philosophy in a double bind. On the one hand, *De oratore* is a dialogue and openly assumes the Platonic model.[10] On the other, it claims that the *Gorgias* is fiction. The triumph of philosophy over eloquence is thus completely overturned. Like its model, this argument occurs within a fiction, making its sophistry equally evident. If one claims that the dialogue is authentic, then philosophy's triumph is ambiguous at best; it comes about not through the power of dialectic but through the very means that it condemns in the character of Gorgias. Socrates would no longer be a philosopher. He would be just the most capable of orators, since he uses the rhetorical veil of philosophical seriousness to hide his manipulations of reason. More generally, the use of Platonic dialogue reduces the differences between Plato and Aristotle to a rhetoric of argumentation rather than a conflict between logical or authoritative arguments. What we gain from reading the two greatest philosophers is not the inspiration of their thought but an understanding of the tricks that produce the effects of seriousness, authority, and truth. In contrast to what has often been claimed, Cicero does not reconcile philosophy (Socrates, Plato, Aristotle) and sophistry. The latter assimilates the former into the very tissue of the dialogue.

The Staging of Truth

Eloquence is *semperque dominata,* "always dominant," and it is a theatrical *orthopedia* in the etymological sense of the word ("right teaching"). In Cicero's dialogue, "actor" and "orator" are synonyms. The demands of the cause at hand shape the speaker's actions and attitudes. Physiognomy, gesture, and natural tones of voice must disappear so that a rhetoric of the body can replace them. The *actio,* the actual performance of a speech, only occurs when this process has finished [III, lvi, 213–III, lxi, 288]. The actor does not have a body to call his own. He must leave what is naturally his in the dressing room and put on a series of masks *(personae),* literally appropriate and appropriated to the needs of each individual case. Furthermore, in the same way that he takes possession of philosophy, the orator must also reclaim from the theatrical arts what the actors have taken from him:

> The whole of this department has been abandoned by the orators, who are the players that act real life, and has been taken over by the actors, who only mimic reality. And there can be no doubt that reality beats imitation in everything; and if reality unaided were sufficiently effective in presentation, we should have no need at all for art. (III, lvi, 214–III, lvii, 215).[11]

A second aspect of this trope is carefully excluded from the theatrical dialectic of nature/artifice, truth/fakery. *Actio* obliges the orator to deny his body and his own being and to subsume himself in the language of the commonplace. As a result, what is natural—the body of the speaker—is always concealed. Only by being fully assimilated to the trope can the rhetor find the tautological and sophistic guarantee of his truth and sincerity:

> The power of those reflections and commonplaces, discussed and handled in a speech, is great enough to dispense with all make-believe and trickery: for the very quality of the diction, employed to stir the feelings of others, stirs the speaker himself even more deeply than any of his hearers. (II, xlvi, 191)

One must keep this speech by Anthony in mind when one addresses the issue of the commonplace, particularly when in reference to the tropes of medieval literature. Romantic dogmas of expression and originality hold these tropes to be repetitive and banal clichés. This anachronistic view of commonplaces has nothing to do with the medieval tradition and dates only from the nineteenth century. On the contrary, in medieval tradition, rhetorical tropes are a lively source of thought, holding both speaker and listener under their domination, joining them in the recognition of what is already there.

Literature's assimilation of commonplaces is all the more inevitable because the orator must regain possession of those domains that once were his alone and that he never should have abandoned to his rivals: poetry, theater, and fable. "What can be so unreal *(fictum)* as poetry, the theatre or stage-plays? And yet, in that sort of things, I myself have often been a spectator when the actor-man's eyes seemed to me to be blazing behind his mask, as he spoke these solemn lines" (II, xlvi, 193).

The orator is thus an actor to the *n*th degree, since he does not play a role conceived by another but instead follows a script that he himself has written. In self-production, where all ownership of being has disappeared, the orator is "author of himself," that is, of his own theatrical mask:

> Do not suppose then that I myself, though not concerned to portray and reproduce in language the bygone misfortunes and legendary griefs of heroes, and though presenting my own personality and not representing another's *[neque actor essem alienae personae, sed auctor meae],* did without profound emotion the things I did when closing that famous case. (II, xlvii, 194)

In Alain Michel's formulation, the orator is *actor veritatis,* the truth's actor.[12] Not only is he the "witty histrion of himself" (as Stéphane Mallarmé would say), but he also knows that the truth does not exist beyond his own ornate speech. It is not enough to speak the truth; one must also play it, act it out. It is inseparable from a fictional structure. This concept opposes the philosophical tradition that arises with Socrates.

By the same token, "life," whether individual or human, becomes a trope, a grounds for discourse and rhetoric. Crassus offers this definition: "The genuine orator must have investigated and heard and read and discussed and handled and debated the whole of the contents of the life of mankind, inasmuch as that is the field of the orator's activity, the subject matter of his study" (III, xiv, 54).

Later, Quintilian will use Socrates as an example of irony, changing the philosopher into a trope (*Institutio oratoria,* IX, ii, 46).[13] In this way, he retains this double reading of the production of the self and of truth. The medievals will repeatedly employ this commonplace, whose influence can be seen clearly in two simple examples. One need only refer to the *Vidas* of the troubadours (brief biographies of the troubadours that frame their poems in the manuscripts), which create biography and prose out of the motifs contained in poetry. Also, one should reread Macabru's Song 16, where the choice of the colors of rhetoric becomes a matter of life and death.

Cascuns s'i gart
C'ab art
M'er viure o morir.

One must take care:
by such an art
I will have to live or die.

De oratore's greatest lesson may be how to transform "life" into a persuasive rhetorical discourse and how to transform discourse into "life." Such a lesson lightens the load of life, because the use of the imaginary of a rhetorical mastery over *bios,* that is, over one's life, and language protects one from the painful encounter with the real and the thing.

The Nothingness of Eloquence

In *On the Character of the Orator,* Cicero's final text dealing with rhetoric, he reactivates the concept of eloquence and draws out its logical consequences. The text opens, as does *De oratore,* with the problem of defining its subject. Cicero, the heir of the new academy, declares that the definition of the orator cannot come from his multiple historical incarnations. Rather, it must come by comparison with a Platonic ideal, a model and ruler for all actual or possible eloquence. The text points out carefully that the orator is highly problematic in Plato. The *Gorgias* devalues him as a Sophist peddling speech, but he is glorified as the philosopher's double in the *Phaedrus.* The entire structure of Platonic dialogue is based on the absent figure of the rhetor. He is the locus of a profound equivocation.[14]

The Platonic model's dual structure of philosophy and eloquence is copied by an antithesis that repeats the debate of *De oratore.* Whereas philosophy assures the knowledge of a notion/thing *(res),* it cannot be the foundation of the rhetorical art because the rhetor is the master of the "doctrine" *(disciplina)* of words and not of things (*alia intelligendi alia dicendi disciplina; On the Character of the Orator,* V, 17). The orator must place the science of things—philosophy—in the care of a purely verbal art of persuasion. How then are we to define what Cicero calls the "power of saying" *(vis discendi)* that belongs to oratory (XIX, 16)? There can be no recourse to the models of rhetoric; they are codified, and they can reproduce and change endlessly. They do not provide the definition of grandiloquence (and so all treatises on rhetoric are doomed to fail, in that they cannot define the supreme rhetor), and so Cicero sketches out a purely negative model for his ideal. Let us recall what *De oratore* says of the quest for this ideal orator when the example of existing orators cannot define him. The passage is in the form of an imperative, a command: "Let us search, then, Brutus, if we can, for this man whom Antonius never saw, or who has never existed at all. If we cannot present an exact copy—he said this was scarcely within the power of a god—yet we may be able to say what he ought to be like" (V, 19).[15]

Quite logically, in *On the Character of the Orator,* the paradigm of the rhetor is systematically eroded by this series of negative definitions (XVIII, 62ff.). The orator can be found not by adding together all the fields of knowledge of antiquity but by subtracting them one by one. He is not a philosopher, since his preoccupation is persuasion, not instruction. He is not a sophist, because his goal is to persuade rather than to please; in contrast to the sophist, he puts his formal art on display and does not conceal it. The orator is not a historian, either, since a historian is concerned with facts and not words. He is not a poet, for poets privilege words over ideas (these last two negative definitions are of course contradictory). All these distinctions arise from the greatest of sophistries, since the orator, as Cicero states, must please his listeners, and at the same time he should hide the strings he is pulling.[16]

The goal of this exegesis is not to denounce a seeming incoherence in Ciceronian discourse, an incoherence that makes an indefinable and contradictory class of the orator and simultaneously makes thought into a "figure of style."[17] Instead, the point here is that despite its contradictions and negations, oratory, the highest art of verbal persuasion, subordinates all knowledge to its empty form. The metamorphosis of knowledge and the possibility of adding to it are examined in *De oratore; On the Character of the Orator* gives it an a posteriori and rigorous definition. This definition is negative, however, for Cicero is the worthy heir of the Sophists. Unable to survive at the level of a concept, eloquence, the *maxima vis,* "supreme power," is only omnipotent outside the realm of the positive and specialized sciences. This is why fiction plays a preponderant role in the definition of the model. The ideal orator is an imaginary construct (*summo oratore figendo; On the Character of the Orator,* II, 7). And more important, before bowing to the diverse tastes of each audience, the rhetor in reality must literally invent himself, fashion himself (VIII, 24). He and his discipline both possess an infinite plasticity, so the ideal orator has neither identity, nor thought, nor his own being. His realm is the pure virtuality of the imaginary, awaiting an appearance before an audience that, as if by reflection, gives him the means to let himself be persuaded.

QUINTILIAN

Rhetoric and Ethics

Quintilian's *Institutio oratoria* restates the fundamental theses of Ciceronian rhetoric. In it we find the dominance of eloquence over the arts and sciences (I, ix–x); the reappropriation of good thinking stolen by the philosophers (*Proemium,* I, 13; XII, 2, 5–9 and 26); and the doctrine of tropes and figures. In his reworking of Cicero, Quintilian is not simply reiterating his model; he places his theses in the context of a new writing. If the *bios,* for Cicero, was itself part of the historical stance, Quintilian will take this position even further: The life that one leads is itself the text. The opening paragraphs are set while the future rhetor is still in the cradle, and the text serves as his guide until his death. The art of living is what must be explored, and eloquence is its fundamental discipline: "If . . . we accept the definition which meets with almost universal approval that art consists in perceptions agreeing and cooperating to the achievement of some useful end, we shall be able to show that rhetoric lacks none of these characteristics" (II, xvii, 41).

If the ethics of life are based on rhetoric, then the very life of the orator, his manners, and his conduct must stand witness to the authority of his speech: "There is another point to which I must call attention, namely the credit which accrues to the *statement of facts* from the authority of the speaker. Now such authority should first and foremost be the reward of our manner of life, but may also be conferred by our style of eloquence" (IV, ii, 125).

Thus "no one can be a true orator unless he is a good man" (I, ii, 3), a *vir bonus dicendi peritus* (XII, i, 1). However, this is only the starting point of a circular argument, because it is impossible to be a good man unless one has also mastered good speech, and so there is more to the *Institutio oratoria* than the rules of rhetoric. It is also a treatise on morals that takes up the questions of the ethics of discourse and language and, reflexively, the discourse of ethics. As does Cicero, Quintilian rejects the authority of ethical philosophy—that "experience of life" (*Institutio oratoria,* XII, ii, 8) that has withdrawn from public affairs (and in Roman terms, from "life") in order to lose itself in intellectual speculation. Philosophers, as a race, are incapable of guidance in the art of practical living. Quintilian's definition of the *vir bonus* arises in his rejection of all philosophical models. Good speech finds its legitimacy elsewhere; in natural philosophy (XII, ii, 20), in divine providence (XII, ii, 21), and above all in the concept of *latinitas* (VIII, i, 1–3). Ethics and rhetoric are fused (and confused) in a terminology that equates good speech to morality. Quintilian places everything under the rule of rhetoric; there is no distinction between the virtues and vices (*virtutes* and *vitia*) of discourse and those of manners. Because the system is all-encompassing, there is nothing upon which to base its morality, so just as the orator must find the proper rhetorical formula, he must also find his ethics with help from nobody else—except Quintilian: "There is no reason for an orator to swear allegiance to any one philosophic code" (XII, ii, 26).

The text is unconsciously aware of its paradox, even its dead end, which Lacan describes as follows: "Good speech does not say where the good is."[18] The dilemma comes completely to light in two examples of illustrious, eloquent speakers: Demosthenes and Cicero. The exemplary status of these two inspires and supports all the discourse of the *Institutio oratoria.* Rumor has it, Quintilian writes, that these masters of eloquence were not free from moral faults, and thus they contradict the system that wants to found its ethics on rhetoric:

> I must now proceed to deal with the objections which common opinion is practically unanimous in bringing against this view. Was not Demosthenes an orator? And yet we are told that he was a bad man. Was not Cicero an orator? And yet there are many who have found fault with his character as well. (XII, i, 14).

This irrefutable testimony must, however, be refuted, and Quintilian carries out this task with a rhetor's consummate ability. He cannot contest the attribution of immorality to his models because he cannot demonstrate otherwise. It must be concluded, then, that the two great orators nevertheless sought a moral ideal, even though they fell short of it. This sophistic argument does not develop from logic or empirical fact. Instead, as Quintilian admits, it comes from the rhetoric of the tapping of good will: "What am I to answer? I must first attempt to conciliate my audience" [XII, i, 14].

The rhetorical demonstration in favor of the discourse of truth dismisses the discourse of truth and replaces it with the force of persuasion. The method of argument contradicts the principles being argued for. The profound truth underlying the *Institutio oratoria* is that morality itself is under the omnipotent rule of sophistry.

My goal, then, is not to formulate a discussion of the positive rules of the morality of eloquence; textual criticism has already very competently carried out this task. Instead, I am striving to expose the fundamentally paradoxical nature of Quintilian's project by assembling a set of rules that appear at various locations throughout the treatise.

Obviously, the purpose of a speech is to establish the plausibility of what it says: "There is one point at any rate which no one will question, namely, that the aim of every speech is to convince the judge that the case which it puts forward *appears to be [vidiantur]* good and honorable" (XII, i, 11; emphasis added). This art of appearance whose aim is to persuade is best served by an honest man: "Well then, which will do this best, the good man or the bad? The good man will without doubt *more often* say what is true and honorable" (XII, i, 11; emphasis added).

These propositions themselves necessarily rely on a persuasive rhetoric. Quintilian, carried away with his argument's incontrovertible logic, must use a refined sophistry to found it: "But even supposing that his duty should, as I shall show may sometimes happen, lead him to make statements which are false, his words are still certain to carry greater weight with his audience" (XII, i, 12).

There are times when an honest man has to lie, to draw on a *simulatio*; this makes *simulatio* an essential weapon in rhetoric's arsenal, and like rhetoric, it relies on lying, fakery, and fiction. So what is the difference between an honest man and a charlatan? Quintilian answers: "Bad men, in their contempt for public opinion and their ignorance of what is right, sometimes drop their mask unawares *[excidit ipsa simulatio]*, and are impudent in the statement of their case and shameless in their assertions. (XII, i, 12). The good man and the dishonest man are not different in either essence or act. They both lie, falsify, and draw on fiction. In the final view, the only distinction comes from the *doxa* that calls one "honest" and the other "dishonest." The only thing that separates them is the credibility that comes from their perceived values. Furthermore, the good orator is he who conceals his lies with more skill, not he who never lies. It follows that the dishonest man is merely a clumsy oaf *who lies poorly*. He rejects, or is simply unaware of, the ethical conventions of public opinion, so his words are unmasked as *simulatio*. With a casuistry worthy of the greatest Jesuits, Quintilian discusses all the situations where the eloquent *vir bonus* is forced to lie (XII, i, 36ff.). In defiance of all logic, this casuistry in no way stains the morality of the good man: "My purpose is not to assert that such tasks will often be incumbent on the orator whom I desire to form, but merely to show that, in the event of his being compelled to take such action, it will not invalidate our definition of an orator as a 'good man skilled in speaking'" (XII, i, 44).

The exception invalidates the rule. This is evident in the attention Quintilian brings to bear on the theory/practice of lying for the greater good of the *vir bonus* (IV, ii, 88). The following is a list of Quintilian's conceptions about lying, in which the word *fingere*, "fiction," and its cognate *fictio* return again and again:

- Fiction *(quod fingemus)* must occur within the limits of the possible.
- It must be plausible in both its system and its consequences *(rationam et ordinem habeat).*
- It must be related to an exact, recognized circumstance.
- It must be tied by argument to the speaker's cause.
- It must avoid contradiction.
- It must accord with what is recognized as true *(doxa).*

Incoherence, implausibility, contradiction, and the irrational give the lie to the lie and threaten to reveal its true nature. The effects of a lie must cohere to make a harmonious and smooth unit. This unity, upon closer scrutiny, is the precise sign of a falsehood. Obviously, one could then infer that contradiction and heterogeneity are sometimes signs of the truth. A rhetorical discourse is therefore measured not by the truth but by its success in hiding its fiction. So despite Quintilian's proclamations on the ethics of discourse, rhetoric is sophistry, and all that matters is the effect produced on an audience. The orator must of necessity do homage to appearance and not to truth, since "it is just when an orator gives the *impression* of absolute truth that he is speaking best" (IV, ii, 44).

An Unprofitable Imitation of Art

Quintilian, ever faithful to the Ciceronian paradigm, employs fiction to create the ideal of the *vir bonus dicendi peritus.* Every art of appearance wears the mantle of this ideal: "Cicero himself has failed to find his orator in actual life and merely imagines and strives to depict the ideal" (XII, i, 21). This claim transforms the project of the *Institutio oratoria* into a vast strategy to gain approval for the ideal it posits. Everything said about the art of persuasive plausibility and the coherent necessary lie no longer applies only to the specific cases within the text (the *quaestiones finitae* of the rhetor and philosopher). These are now issues that apply to the whole of the text—to its *quaestio infinita.* The gap between good speech and the good must be bridged. All the tricks of persuasion will be brought into play in the attempt to legitimate this move and to give its results the appearance of truth. This is a strategy of fiction.

In light of the above, we now turn our attention to the definition of rhetoric that appears in book II. Pleading before an imaginary tribunal, Quintilian first exposes the critiques addressed against eloquence; he explicitly attributes them to Platonic thought. According to those philosophers who attack it, eloquence is a "cacopractice," a perverse and evil art (II, xv, 2). Or again, it is an "anapractice," a practice without the theoretical foundations that define any *techné* (productive activity; II, xx, 2). Elsewhere, it is a "pseudopractice," a false art or an art of the false (II, xvii, 19). It is also a vagabond *(circumcurrentum)* art, without place and without possible definition because it encompasses everything (II, xxi, 7). Finally, it is a "mataiopractice," an art of nothing, or as Quintilian says in Latin, *"supervacua artis imitatio,"* [an unprofitable imitation of art] (II, xx, 3). It is not my purpose here to affirm the Platonic denunciation of rhetoric, any more than it is to defend Quintilian. I must emphasize that demonstrative logic has no part in the treatise's arguments against those who disdain the oratory art; everything functions through a series of indemonstrable aporiae. The positive definition of rhetoric is just a negation of its critics. The affirmative description of the oratorical art uses a subtle discursive strategy, worthy of the greatest rhetors, to cover its inverted and negative truth.

Quintilian himself reveals the secret of *simulatio.* The good orator must know this secret; at the same time, it is the key to interpreting the *Institutio oratoria* itself: "Therefore artifice and stratagem should be masked, since detection in such cases spells failure. Thus far, and thus far only, may eloquence hope to enjoy the advantages of secrecy" (XII, ix, 5).

The play of simulation frequently implicates eloquence. It must conceal itself as eloquence and appear natural. Unveiled, it has no power:

> But when we come to consider the choice of words, the weight of essential to general reflections and the elegance demanded by figures, we are confronted by elements which must either strike the attention or be condemned to nonexistence. But the very fact that they strike attention is a reason why they should not flaunt themselves obtrusively. And, if we have to make the choice, I should prefer that it should be the cause, and not the orator, to which we award our praise. (XII, ix, 6)

This principle in its turn must be applied to the fictional structure of the *Institutio oratoria.*

If ornamentation intervenes obliquely and secretly, it remains utterly foreign to the thing/cause at stake in the trial: "Applause must have been evoked by something having no connexion with the case" (XII, iv, 6).

Quintilian classically separates the "adornment" from the "matter."

In this way, he distinguishes himself from Cicero and also calls attention to the paradox of rhetoric. Rhetorical discourse remains separate from what it speaks about, just as there is a rupture between ethics and good speech. Although rhetorical decoration gives the pretense of founding a morality in the sophistic whorls of feigned argument, it nevertheless remains irreparably removed from the meaning and value of the thing, the cause. Because eloquence lies so far outside the cause for which it speaks and outside the *bios* of the speaker, it cannot modify them in any way.

"Mathesis" and the Status of Literature

Just as Cicero does, Quintilian maintains that the rhetor must be a generalist. Grammar, literature, geometry, arithmetic, astronomy, music (*Institutio oratoria,* I, x), ethics, law, and history (XII, i) are all obligatory elements in his education. Obviously, these disciplines are studied not for themselves but only because they are useful to the orator. Eloquence dominates all knowledge, which is seen here not from the viewpoint of science but from that of rhetorical persuasion, and this depends on literature.

At first glance, the *Institutio oratoria* seems to give literature a subordinate role. In opposition to the rhetorical art of persuasion, poetry seeks only pleasure (*solam petit voluptatem;* X, i, 29). Because it is on the side of desire, it is a pure ornament, entertainingly sensual and completely opposed to the masculine and ascetic ideal that the orator must cultivate.[19] The apprentice rhetor in particular must be kept from the seductions of erotic poetry (I, ix). The contrast between the harshness of verbal combat (*asperitus;* XI, iii, 23) and the softness of poetic enjoyment (*volupta;* X, i, 10) seems insurmountable. According to the *Institutio oratoria,* the orator's "book of life," poetry refreshes the orator after the fatigues of the tribunal (I, x, 27).

Since literature has no interest other than pleasure, it must be added that it has no constraints outside the formal limits of rhythm and meter. Literature's poetic license *(licentia poetica)* is the essential difference between it and the lawyer's plea.[20] Poets have a special right (*ius poeticus;* I, v, 12) that exempts them from the rules of the tribunal, which also includes the right to be unbelievable. Unbelievability must be distinguished from error and lies (reserved, as we have seen, to the rhetor). The scope of the poet's permission to modify language and meaning creatively is in inverse proportion to literature's minor status in the *Institutio oratoria:*

> The orator must not follow the poets in everything, more especially in their freedom of language and their license in the use of figures. Poetry has been compared to the oratory of display, and further, aims solely at giving pleasure, which it seeks to secure by inventing what is not merely untrue, but sometimes even incredible. (X, i, 28)

Because rhetoric always has a well-determined practical target (a deed, an advantage) that it must influence, "the only circumstances where the delights of literature are unalloyed are when it withdraws from action" (II, 18, 4).

Literature draws closer to its essence to the same degree that it distances itself from practice and reflects an *otium* close to the pagan philosopher's idle contemplation. Oratory's goal is serious practice. It thus conceals the play of reflections in favor of its cause. In opposition, literature openly admits that it is a mirror: the expression of oratory's repressed desire. It is aristocratically detached from all work, but it is not pointless. As the necessary, symmetrical, and balancing counterweight of rhetorical praxis, literature plays an integral part in rhetoric's economy.

The *Institutio oratoria* places the letter of rhetoric in contrast to that of literature. Could this be one more example of a difference that comes about through a play of sophistry? It is very possible that the literature/eloquence opposition is only a pretend distinction. Because they are both ruled by *grammatica,* literature and rhetoric both have a place in a science of the signifier.

When Quintilian changes his approach and examines literature from the point of view of its origin and no longer in relation to its goal or its function, the status of literature is shaken from top to bottom. To speak of the origin of poetry means to endow what was first, antecedent, and original with the prestige of truth. This requires, in turn, a return to Homer: "He has given us a model and inspiration for every department of eloquence. . . . He has in truth outdistanced all that come after him in every department of eloquence" (X, i, 46–51). Homer gives an example of each and every exercise the rhetor must master:

> For to say nothing of his eloquence, which he shows in praise, exhortation and consolation, do not the ninth book containing the embassy to Achilles, the first describing the quarrel between the chiefs, or the speeches delivered by the counsellors in the second, display all of the rules of art to be followed in forensic or deliberative oratory? . . . Again,

> in the few lines with which he introduces both of his epics, has he not, I will not say observed, but actually established the law which should govern the composition of the exhordium? (X, i, 47–48)

The Greek poet's fiction anticipates all the possible practices of eloquence.[21] Literature thus comes before legal rhetoric; in fact, it lies at its very origin. If we accept what Quintilian has to say, then he has reversed the classical view that eloquence arose in judicial circles and was later transferred to literature. Rhetoric's origin in poetry means that literature is not merely pleasing, a diversion that accompanies the rhetor throughout his life (I, viii, 12), or even a handy supply of arguments whose authority comes from the prestige of the great poets (I, viii, 11); fiction is also the living source of rhetorical thought. Literature and rhetoric are twin sisters. Argumentation, and not argument, distinguishes them from one another. Each one employs identical means, and they differ only in their ends. Sophistry gives birth to them both, but literature's goal is desire, and rhetoric's is plausibility.

If rhetoric dominates the sciences, then they also depend in turn on literature. Quintilian (and medieval scholars after him) attaches the totality of knowledge to the powers of the signifier. Above all else, medieval *mathesis* is the knowledge of the signifier. For this reason, conflict between theology and the seven liberal arts is inevitable. The former is the divine science of the First Cause and not of words, whereas the latter are founded in rhetorical tradition and form the encyclopedia of human knowledge.

The Improper

Quintilian's ideas about language become an important issue with this claim that every discursive art originates in poetry. Particularly interesting is his doctrine of the proper. Usage, defined as *oratio Romana* (VIII, i, 2), or *latinitas,* Latinity, at the beginning of book VIII, is the foundation of propriety. It is "calling things by their right names" *[sua cuiusquerei appelatio]* (VIII, ii, 1). In antiquity, this meant both social convention and rhetorical adornment. "We should realize that without propriety ornament is impossible" (VIII, iii, 15).

Latinitas is first of all poetic and literary. Having taken Homer as his model, the Latin writer also presents himself as a master of the language. The child, the future rhetor, must practice "the art of speaking correctly and the interpretation of the poets" *[poetarum ennarationem]* (I, iv, 2). From its very start, linguistic learning includes the practice of explaining literary texts, the propaedeutic of fiction. This is because poets, or writers of any genre, and not the populace at large, are the revered founders of Latin (or Greek) usage: "Nor is it sufficient to have read the poets only; every kind of writer must be carefully studied, not merely for the subject matter, *but for the vocabulary; for words often acquire authority from their use by a particular author*" (I, iv, 4; emphasis added). In addition, the duality of language transforms all proper meaning bit by bit into figural meaning: "When we compare the language of our ancestors [Cicero] with our own, we find that practically everything we say nowadays is *figurative*" (IX, iii, 1; emphasis added). Finally, neither in book VIII nor elsewhere is there a positive definition of the propriety of language. The only exception is the tautological *sua cuiusquerei appelatio* that I have already mentioned. Like the definition of rhetoric, the definition of propriety in book VIII is negative. Propriety stands in opposition to the terminological vices shared, once more, by ethics and by rhetoric: obscurity, obscenity, ambiguity, impropriety.

Propriety can only occur in a utopian schema where the power of the signifier diminishes almost completely in relation to its signified. The less the signifier is an obstacle to meaning, the more proper it is, the more it "clings to the idea."

The doctrine of propriety in the *Institutio oratoria* clearly resembles the one found in Cicero. They both evoke a quasi-Nietzschean framework in which language is nothing but metaphor. Everything one can say is drawn from conventions that negate the apparent meaning, since they are strongly influenced by the rhetorical manipulations of the poets. The Latin masters of rhetoric, of course, had a doctrine of propriety. However, neither the notion nor the thing comes into play in it. Instead, the doctrine is dominated by *latinitas,* the network of social conventions produced within the language of the rhetors.

Therefore, rhetoric repels both the Other and meaning, revealing them as the unlimited demands of an imaginary that is always improper. At the same time, rhetoric is in permanent conflict with Christian discourse, since the latter, as we shall see, presupposes a propriety.

2
The Break: Tertullian

Moreover the law entered, that the offence might abound. But where sin abounded, grace did much more abound.

—Rom. 5:20

Tertullian represents a movement in the history of letters, second in importance only to the New Testament, that changes everything. The study of Cicero dominated Tertullian's intellectual formation, and from this master come his ideas on the rhetorical nature of thought and representation. Tertullian, however, rebels against these ideas and establishes an entirely new dogma, in which the Incarnation serves as the reference and signified of all fiction. His work sets the stage for a drama in and through which one must become separated from oneself. The Tertullian who once was a pagan rhetor changes into the Tertullian who strives to become a Christian rhetor. This will to break with the ancient world encompasses all aspects of pagan culture. The present study cannot discuss every aspect of Tertullian's work, for the rupture it represents attempts to make a homonymy of each and every thing that came before: religion, ethics, linguistics, rhetoric, sexuality, arts, and literature. One aspect of his thought, however, has been somewhat neglected by critics,[1] and setting aside other questions, I will limit myself to that. Tertullian proposes a new world of fiction (literary, but also pictorial and theatrical) that we are compelled to call Christian and that will have a decisive influence over centuries of writing and representation. Tertullian's corpus gives voice to the law of Christian representation, and as a consequence it clears the way for the literary exception in all its productivity.

THE PRE-TEXT

Tertullian is extremely attentive to discourse in all its forms. He devotes an entire treatise to one specific mode of reasoning that he employs again and again: the *praescriptio.* This master concept gathers together and formulates all the elements of the epistemological break that comes about in his work.[2] The word itself is not a neologism. Its polysemy has played a role for a long time in Latin discourse: In rhetoric, it is an objection to an argument; in philosophy, a rule, precept; in law, a precedent, exception;[3] in aesthetics and literature, a rule of art.[4]

Tertullian draws on and combines all these traditional meanings to give the word a new sense that contains his project's entire novelty.[5] The concept of *praescriptio* is incomprehensible if the word is defined by any of its previous usages. Instead, its meaning can only be found in Tertullian's writing, because it is now a homonym in relation to its antecedents.

Tertullian uses the word in its etymological sense, revealing a crucial dimension of its new meaning. *Prae-scriptio* means "what was previously written," and thus that which has the privilege of true anteriority. I propose to translate the term as "pre-text." Obviously, Tertullian is not speaking of the pagan tradition, whether literary, mythological, or philosophical. The word grounds everything in the tradition of the New Testament, insofar as it renews the Old Testament—the first writing known to humans, according to Tertullian.[6]

The pre-text produces a system of proof like no other. It is at once a testimony to a discursive truth and the trace of an event, of an empirical experience: "But, we promptly place against our corrupters the formal reply that there is one rule of truth, which proceeds from Christ and has been transmitted through His companions; and these conflicting interpreters will be found to be of somewhat later date than they."[7]

The ancient philosophers searched in vain for a way to bring together concept (of divine truth), experience (of the life of Christ), and writing into one event. Before the Gospels, these notions remained separate. The pre-text of the New Testament creates something new in the history of both religion and philosophy.

Nothing is beyond the reach of the pre-text:

1. In philosophy,[8] the general nature of the concept (God) is no longer eternal, its self-identity preserved in the Heaven of Ideas (Plato) or in the superlunar world (Aristotle). In a seeming contradiction, it is incarnated in the materiality of a specific human body; the concept becomes history and praxis: "Since, therefore, [the soul] has become flesh, the soul is a uniform solid body *[uniformis solidata];* it is also a wholly incomplex being, and an indivisible substance" *[et singularis tuta est et indiscreta substantia].*[9]

2. The Incarnation gives value to the human body, and also to all of *natura.* The Greek notion of the *chaosmos* is replaced by a concept of a world ordered by laws that, although mysterious, obey the divine will and so are rational.[10] Tertullian emphasizes that "[n]ature should, for us, be an object of reverence and not the occasion of blushes,"[11] and, again, "[n]o one denies—because everyone knows what nature of its own accord tells us—that God is the creator of the universe, and that the universe is good and has been made over to man by its Creator."[12]

3. This new meaning of *praescriptio* affects text and interpretation. "Text" in its very notion is now a *praescriptio,* for the New Testament becomes the written trace of a now-silent voice, a redoubling and treacherous sign of the sign (in Plato's words). The church fathers later drew consequences from Tertullian's formulation that he did not explicitly develop himself. The letter of the New Testament, and its spirit, are both Christ[13]—a metaphor for what is absolutely literal. The evangelical pre-text, both as a thought and, equally, as an empirical event, fuses history and eternity, practice and theory, body and soul, in one impossible configuration. Tertullian makes this claim with force and concision: "What is written cannot but have been" *[Non potest non fuisse quad scriptum est]* (*On the Flesh of Christ,* 3).

A completely unique relation between writing and reference now begins. In evangelical writing, the story of the thing is consubstantial with the thing itself. Here, we have an inconceivable identity whose manifest impossibility marks all medieval writing, no matter what its nature may be. The literature of the Middle Ages is continually challenged by a scriptural model that demands an account of both the event and the experience. This model, the testamental pre-text, is at the same time both a depository of experience and the experience itself, truth and the representation of truth. As a result, it gives to writing a dignity it did not have in pagan antiquity.

Tertullian begins the movement in Catholic theology that tries to make the pre-text into a matheme (a writing without remainder) and so to nail everything to the letter *X* of the Incarnation.[14] Theology ultimately fails in this project because the mystery of the God-man is a value that cannot be carried over or reduced in an equation. This equation must bring this *fides nominum,* "fidelity in name" (see below) into play to assure the consistency of its operation.

4. In rhetoric, the pre-text is just as pregnant with consequences. The oratory art is no longer attached to the imaginary of the *doxa* that it means to manipulate; rather, it is anchored to the one thing and to its truth. This *rhetorica christiana,* "Christian rhetoric," to use Jean-Claude Fredouille's expression,[15] is formulated in the *Apology:* "Who will dare to refute us, not by skill in eloquence, but by the same form with which we have established our proof: by means of truth?" (*Apology,* 46, 1).

When Tertullian anchors discourse to the reference and to the true, he is not refuting rhetoric. Instead, its usage becomes a homonym. It permits Tertullian to revive the entire rhetorical arsenal, including the sophistry of the rhetors and the formal arguments of the Gnostics.[16] The verbal arts are no longer at the service of a convincing *pseudos,* the imaginary. From this moment, rhetorical fiction offers a dogma whose context it provides and upon which it depends. "The truth verifies itself in fiction," and rhetorical fiction acquires an entirely new meaning.

5. The Incarnation also changes the way Tertullian, as a linguist, thinks about language. Tertullian has long been seen as a stylistic innovator (whether for better or worse), but this change also marks a radical break with the linguistics of previous rhetors. At the risk of an extreme schematism, I will reduce "pagan" linguistics (taught in schools throughout the Middle Ages) to the thought of Cicero and Quintilian. These are the thinkers whom Tertullian the ancient orator knows, and they represent what he combats.

As we have seen, the pagan rhetors defined "propriety" without reference to a thing. For them, the suitable is swept along in a series of diacritical distinctions; signifiers endlessly refer to other signifiers so that the thought being expressed (no matter how naturally or conventionally suitable it may be) always ends up as an analogy or a metaphor.

Tertullian's Gnostic adversaries remain faithful to this linguistic/rhetorical conception so that they can deny the Incarnation. They are obliged to submit the concept to metaphor, despite the textual evidence of the Gospels. Such a metaphorical reading of the Bible goes against its inspired propriety. It also threatens the very basis of language:

> All things will be in danger of being taken in a sense different from their own proper sense, and, whilst taken in that different sense, of losing their proper one, if they are called by a name which differs from their natural designation. Fidelity in name secures the safe appreciation of properties. *[Fides nominum est salus proprietarum.]* (*On the Flesh of Christ,* XIII, 2)[17]

Christian faith is equally a faith in the propriety of the language of the New Testament. This aporia of realism, of the thingness of language, is anchored in the Incarnation, which is held to be the absolutely true effect of a discourse. To clarify, I will appeal to Johannes Ereginus, a philosopher who came after Tertullian and who sums up perfectly what *On the Flesh of Christ* does when it defends propriety: "*He came unto his own* [John 1:11]; this means that God was incarnated in human nature" *[In propria ergo venit, hoc est in humana natura incarnatus est].*[18] The word *propria* as it appears in the Gospels must be understood in all of its potential meanings: linguistic, philosophical, and rhetorical. It grounds the suitability of the Incarnation for every field of thought. Propriety can no longer depend upon a particular language, or even upon *latinitas,* because the Incarnation must be made a synonym as such in all past and future languages. As a notion, it must become detached from all specific linguistic manifestations, from all particular languages. This is the paradox (or in theological terms, the mystery) of the empirical Incarnation.

PHANTASMS OF THE FLESH

On the Flesh of Christ is a polemic against the heresies of Marcion, Apelles, and Valentine. Despite their differences, these three hold a common dogma: Docetism (a word that comes from the Greek *dokein,* "to seem"). Simply stated, these Gnostics reject the Incarnation. According to them, human intelligence is inadequate to perceive the true nature of divinity, so Christ appeared in a fictional body. This explanation was a way of Hellenizing the novelty of the Christian message by reducing it to a variant of Greek mythology, but it is in direct contrast to the

New Testament's evident validation of its own pre-text. From a "Greek" point of view, the Incarnation is the supreme folly. The transcendent and eternal dignity of a god contradicts the notion of God truly incarnated in a body and thereby victim to all the degradations of the flesh. When a Greek god appears to men, his body is a simulacrum. By the same token, the Olympian gods are impassive, no matter what they may appear to undergo. To one holding this conception of the divine, what could be more repugnant than a divinity suffering the Passion in a real body?

Because the gods only intervene in earthly affairs through the medium of a false body, their impassivity contradicts the Incarnation in a variety of ways. First, there is the political scandal of God's death by crucifixion, a punishment reserved for slaves.[19] Then there is the social blunder of a God who works (Christ the carpenter); again, work, a life spent making things, is a servile function. Philosophical contemplation and the divine and eternal kingdom of ideas are the domain of the aristocracy. Third, time becomes linear: Christ's intervention in human affairs breaks what was thought of as a circle (the great year of the eternal return). Now and forevermore, there is a time before this event, and a time after it.[20] Finally, to Greek thinking, the union of body and spirit is ludicrous; it simultaneously elevates the dignity of matter and the body and degrades the realm of ideas.[21] Tertullian forcefully draws attention to the Marcionite hatred of the body that is revealed in their denial of the birth of Christ. In opposition to this hatred, there is the rhetoric of the suitable word;[22] for example:

> Come now, beginning from the nativity itself, declaim against the uncleanness of the generative elements within the womb, the filthy concretion of fluid and blood, of the growth of the flesh for nine months long out of that very mire. Describe the womb as it enlarges from day to day,—heavy, troublesome, restless even in sleep, changeful in its feelings of dislike and desire. Inveigh now likewise against the shame itself of a woman in travail, which, however, ought rather to be honoured in consideration of that peril, or to be held sacred in respect of (the mystery of) nature. (*On the Flesh of Christ,* IV)

By refusing the fundamental dogma of the Incarnation, Gnosticism tries above all to perpetuate pagan ideas about the world and its representation in knowledge. This is why, at the last, Tertullian sees no difference between those heretics who claim to be Christian and those who believe in mythology: "What difference is there between them, except it be that the heathen *[ethnici]* in not believing, do believe; while the heretics, in believing, do not believe?" (*On the Flesh of Christ,* XV, 4).[23]

Tertullian's target in *On the Flesh of Christ* is not just heresy but the entire structure of ancient thought.

The most important point for our purpose is the terminology that Tertullian uses when he condemns the Gnostics' phantasmal Christ. He repeatedly draws the reader's attention to moments in the heresies where a move to fiction turns the Incarnation away from realism: They dress Christ in simulated flesh (*carnem putativam; On the Flesh of Christ,* I, 4); the Marcionites fabricate a phantasmal birth (*configere phantasma;* I, 4) and a phantasm of flesh (III, 7); a childish imagination (V, 2) invented the Passion (*caro cum passionibus ficta;* V, 8). Put together, all these things are analogous to what Tertullian calls "the fables of nations" (*fabulas nationum;* IX, 2). This term refers to the different mythologies and literatures of the Mediterranean peoples. The Christian's task is to refute heresies, which always carry the signs of the mythology of a particular ethnic group (the Greeks, in this case) by proclaiming the transnational truth and reality of a paradoxical Incarnation.

But this is not all; Tertullian condemns a poetics of heresy from the outset. Gnostic discourse uses poetic license (*licentia heretica; On the Flesh of Christ,* I, 3), a notion that is the very mark of literature in Cicero and Quintilian.[24] Marcion, Appelles, and Valentine thereby empty Christ's life and Passion of all real content. If Christ's flesh was a costume, then his life was theater, even a deceitful comedy:

> Falsely did Paul "determine to know nothing amongst us but Jesus and Him crucified"; falsely has he impressed upon us that He was buried; falsely inculcated that He rose again. False, therefore, is our faith also. And all that we hope for from Christ will be a phantom. (*On the Flesh of Christ* V, 3)

Gnosis is thus not religion, ethics, theology, or philosophy. It is an empty aesthetic whose pseudofoundation is the literary discourse of false appearance—a toy for language jugglers:

> You ought rather to have brought Christ down, not from heaven, but from some troop of mountebanks *[circulatorio]*, not as God besides man,

> but simply as a man, a magician *[magus hominem]*; not as the High Priest of our salvation, but as the conjurer in a show *[spectaculi artificem]*; not as a raiser of the dead, but as the misleader of the living *[vivorum avocatorum]*. (*On the Flesh of Christ*, V, 10)

The heretic's Christ is a magician, a stage actor, a rhetor who produces a plausible discourse. His perverse workings are crystallized by Tertullian in one brilliant neologism, *avocator*. This one word demonstrates that Gnostic discourse has a profound identity with the oratory art. Furthermore, for the first time in the history of philosophy, phantasms can be defined in relation to an irreducible material basis: the body of the Incarnation. Tertullian has broken completely with every form of Platonism, a philosophy that uses the eternal idea as the yardstick to condemn appearance.

Cicero and Quintilian saw the very essence of language in the perpetual circular motion of the figured and figuration. The drama of rhetoric is thus played exclusively on the stage of language, the first form of all possible representations. With a blow that he hopes will go unanswered, Tertullian strikes this conception down even more violently than he does the Gnostic insistence on the costume of the flesh. The signifier must no longer refer to another signifier; instead, it must refer to a referent and to a letter that indicates propriety. Tertullian now can launch his attack against the Gnostic thesis, which makes flesh itself an illusion, a "psychic" flesh, a soul:

> The soul became flesh that the soul might become visible. Well, then, did the flesh likewise become soul that the flesh might be manifested? If the soul is flesh, it is no longer soul, but flesh. If the flesh is soul, it is no longer flesh, but soul. Where, then, there is flesh, and where there is soul, it has become both one and the other. Now if they are neither in particular, although they become both one and the other, it is, to say the least, very absurd *[perversissimum]*, that we should understand the soul when we name the flesh, and when we indicate the soul, explain ourselves as meaning the flesh. (*On the Flesh of Christ*, XIII, 1)

In heresy, the body of Christ is no more than a metaphor. The Christian must return to the *fides nominum* to restore the propriety of designations and referents. Otherwise, the flux of metaphor threatens to sweep language along, to enclose it in a radical nominalism in which "all things risk passing for others that they are not and losing that which they are."

"*RHETORICA CHRISTIANA*": HOMONYMY

Should we, then, throw overboard every element of pagan rhetorical thought—all literature, metaphor, ornamentation, figuration, and representation, all the theatrical aspects of language? Certainly not. Tertullian, aside from recommending the study of ancient authors, discusses the theatricality of language so that he can homonymize it.[25] In this way, he invents a sacred rhetoric, that is, one that is no longer fictional, but realist.

On Spectacles contains an explicit example of this rereading of pagan textuality:

> As for the origin [of spectacles]—which is mostly unknown and obscure for most of us—I had to do some extensive research, with no other resource than the arsenal of pagan literature *[ethnicalum litterarum].* Numerous authors have published collections on just this question. Here is their report on the origin of plays. (*On Spectacles* V, 1–2)

Homonymy does not destroy ancient words as words. It revalues them, working on both sides of the epistemological break at the same time. Tertullian, an antisophist by nature, uses sophistic arguments when they suit his ends. More surprisingly, he also grants to Miltiades, a Roman Christian, the title of "the church's Sophist" *(ecclesiarum sophista),* but in the nonpejorative, etymological sense of "wise" *(sophia).*[26]

In *On Spectacles,* Tertullian meditates on the actual nature of the tropes of cults and spectacles. There is no clearer example of the process of homonymy in the field of rhetoric, diction, and linguistics. Metaphorically, the tropes *(loci)* are also the commonplaces of rhetoric's arsenal. Their mercenary nature makes them neutral and virtual, pregnant with positive or negative meaning: "The *loci* themselves cannot stain us, only the acts that come from them" XV, 1).

Thus the inescapable conclusion: "[T]here is no prescript with regard to tropes" *[nulla est praescriptio de locis]* (VIII, 8). The topographical, or "topoigraphical" (rhetorical) commonplace is not in itself a pretext. Only the use that people—or the Holy Spirit, a force exterior to language and rhetoric—make of it allows one to determine whether the topoi are deployed for good or for evil. Just as the church built its temples on the same sites used by the pagan cults with no effect on the sacrament, the Christian writer can dig into the treasury of classical rhetorical topoi, so long as he reconsecrates them.

"*PLASTICA DEI*": THE COSMETICS OF THE CHRISTIAN BODY

Rhetoric's conversion to Christianity is nowhere more clear than in *On the Apparel of Women,*[27] a short treatise addressed to the faithful. One of the founding texts of medieval misogyny (woman, or more precisely, the vagina, is called "the Devil's gate" [*On the Apparel of Women,* I, 1, 2]),[28] its principal goal is to banish all the ornaments (clothing, makeup, jewelry, perfume) that serve feminine seduction and intensify masculine desire. Although the text is addressed specifically to women, neither Tertullian nor men in general are excluded from the demand for modesty. The sin of vanity afflicts everyone equally.[29]

For Tertullian, there is no doubt as to the origin of cosmetics: "[They come] from the devil, he who interpolates nature" (*On the Apparel of Women,* I, 1, 8).[30]

The fallen angel inspires the additions that corrupt the body that God has sanctified by creating it.

By conceiving of adornment in this way, *On the Apparel of Women* becomes a point-by-point counter-text to the pagan vision of ornament, for example, as it appears in Ovid's *The Art of Love.*[31] In his opening lines, the Roman poet declares that desire must be steered by artifice: "By art must love be guided." For Ovid, the natural body is always aesthetically defective; no divine intention can be seen in it, so art has to intervene. The body must be so skillfully covered that the artifice passes for the result of nature (II, 313), or chance (III, 155). The *cultus,* "adornment," exalted in III, 101 is thus a rhetoric of universal dissimulation: "Your looks are aided by dissembled art" (*The Art of Love,* III, 210).

As a consequence, *The Art of Love* is also a treatise on rhetoric and writing, revealing the spirit of the oratory art in minute detail. The success of the body's adornment does not depend on truth or sincerity. As Cicero's Anthony would have it (see chapter 1), it is measured by the ability to produce an embellishment that wins assent or enflames desire, which amounts to the same thing. The orator, the poet, and the woman in makeup all play the same game. They are judged by how well they yield to conventional wisdom and art—the models of their thought and their bodies: "Besides, treachery *[insidiae]* is alien to sacred bards, and *our* art too helps to shape our character" *[Et facit ad mores ars quoque nostra suos]* (*The Art of Love,* III, 539–40, emphasis added].

Ovid establishes the dominance of rhetoric and of adornment as successful illusion. *On the Apparel of Women* is the exact antipode of this submission of the body and writing to appearances. However, just as does his Latin forebear, Tertullian wants to do more than emphasize an ethical demand. A new art of fiction and of writing is forming itself here. In effect, "[w]hatever is born, that is the work of God. Obviously then, anything else that is added *[infigitur]* must be the work of the Devil" (*On the Apparel of Women,* II, 5, 4). Cosmetics is a fiction wrapped in scriptural terminology:

> For, surely, these women sin against God who anoint their faces with creams, stain their cheeks with rouge, or lengthen their eyebrows with antimony. Obviously they are not satisfied with the creative skill of God *[plastica Dei];* in their own person, without doubt, they censure and criticize the Maker of all things *[in ipsis redargunt et reprehendunt artificem omnium]*! Surely they are finding fault when they try to perfect and add to His work, taking these additions, of course, from a rival artist *[reprehendunt enim cum emendant, cum adiciunt, utique ab adversario artifice sumentes additamenta ista].* The rival artist is the Devil. (*On the Apparel of Women,* II, 5, 2–3)

Writing has everything to do with everything. On one side, there is the One Writer tracing the signs of the true on the pages of his creation; on the other, there is a rival power, an editor who interpolates and criticizes the primary manuscript. In the end, this rival power completely obliterates the original with the makeup of his perverse artifice. Such is Lucifer's ambition.

With this in mind, the chapter titles in the work (which, although they appear in the text, were made titles by later scholars) are clues to the rhetorical, poetic, and scriptural dimension of the prescription:[32] "Female toilet *[habitus]* has two possible purposes—dress and make-up *[ornatum]*" (*On the Apparel of Women* I, 4, 1).

One by one, the terms used in cosmetics spell out the perverse artifices of the oratory art and of rhetorical culture. *Habitus,* "dressing," also means for Cicero the "complexion, practically the tone of style."[33] The name assigned to Tertullian's treatise by the tradition refers to literally every element separate from the body and serving to embellish it: the objects placed upon it, such as luxurious cloth or jewels. One cannot overlook the general connotation of the term, however; the *cultus* is also "cult, religion," or even "culture, civilization." In rhetoric, on the other hand, it has the specialized sense of "cultivated style."[34] For Tertullian, *ornatus,* in its primary sense, is the things having to do with hairdressing and makeup, everything cosmetic applied directly to the body. Let us not forget that it also refers to the adornments of the oratory art, this charming, seductive, embellishing, seductive art that blends with the very essence of rhetoric and thought.

On the Apparel of Women is more than a simple denunciation of the feminine body and its adornment. It also attacks the pagan art of appearances along with the entire civilization conceived of as perverted by the false, by artifice, and by the obfuscation of nature.

This is not a demand to return to the nakedness of the natural state. Since the Fall and the cutting of the first fig leaves, this state has become profoundly negative.[35] It is obviously capable of inspiring God's creations, of diabolically turning them away from their divine destiny (marriage, procreation) and placing them in the service of an idolatry of the flesh:

> It is time for you to realize that you must not only shun the display of false and studied beauty *[confictae et elaboratae pulchritudinis suggestum],* but also remove all traces of natural grace by concealment and negligence, as equally dangerous to the glances of another's eye. For, although comeliness *[decor]* is not to be censured as being a bodily happiness, as an additional gift of the divine Sculptor *[divinae plasticae accessio],* as a kind of fair vestment of the soul, it must be feared because of the affront and violence on the part of those who pursue it. (*On the Apparel of Women* II, 2, 5–6)

Even though the Creator did bring natural beauty about, it still has almost the status of cosmetics and rhetoric. It is an *accessio,* a suspect addition or augmentation that improves not man's essence but the perverse use he can make of his appearance. After the Fall, beauty comes from culture and from the devil. A return to nature must not occur. Instead, there needs to be a way of appearing, a style, a cosmetics that works like pagan rhetoric but in a different spirit, to hide nature while revealing it. The purpose of ornamentation is not to supplement beauty but to bring spiritual virtue to light: "It is not enough for Christian modesty merely to be so, but to seem so, too" (*On the Apparel of Women* II, 13, 3).

This contradicts the rhetoric of persuasion. No longer is virtue to be produced as the plausible effect of the public use of language. The Christian ornament, as the exact inverse of sophistic and rhetorical uses of appearance, arises from interiority and ontology: "So great and abundant must be our modesty that it may flow out from the mind to the garb, and burst forth from the conscience to the outer appearance *[in superficiem]*, so that even from the outside it may examine, as it were, its own furniture—a furniture that is suited to retain the faith forever" (*On the Apparel of Women* II, 13, 3). As a consequence, the Christian cannot do without the surface, the ornament, rhetoric, style, and language. It is impossible to scorn ancient terms and traditional practices, but they can be respoken in a new, homonymous structure of thought in a way that shares nothing with its antecedents except sounds. This homonymy is the source of Tertullian's confidence in the most ornate rhetoric (the "African" or "Asian" style that tradition has attributed to him). Once language has been anchored in the Incarnation and in dogma, its metaphoric nature allows for a limitless flowering of figures and plural meanings. Repressed in the practice of the *bios*, Asianism resurfaces at the level of language.

Because the break with pagan rhetoric is not instantaneous, but takes place over generations, *On the Apparel of Women* can be read through the eyes of later scholars who drew from it. In his condemnation of adornment, Tertullian establishes a catalog of rhetorical tropes that medieval literature exploits, either for Christian or for other purposes. Here are some examples:

1. *The forbidding of jewelry* (I, 5, 1) reappears in other forms in such places as medieval lapidaries, the Saracen king's gemstone in *The Song of Roland*, and the intricate gold work of the Grail in Chrétien de Troyes' *Perceval*.

2. *The excessive care and coloring of hair* (II, 6, 1; II, 7, 1) can be associated a posteriori to the damsel combing her hair in *Perceval*, to Guinevere's enchanting comb in the *Chevalier de la Charrette*, and to Oisuese in the *Roman de la Rose*, whose principal occupation is her hair. These are eminently rhetorical figures in view of the metaphorical opposition that Geoffrey of Vinsauf draws in the *Poetria nova* between "hirsute" and "well-combed" discourse, showing his preference for the second.[36]

3. *The condemnation of mirrors* (I, 1, 3; II, 8, 2), which deceitfully

sanction the failure or success of adornment. To condemn mirrors is to reject a narcissism that uses the expedient of a man-made object to confirm its idolatry. In addition to this literal reading, the mirror also refers to a textual specularity, theorized by Geoffrey of Vinsauf and put into continual practice by medieval poets. Before these poets appear, Tertullian rejects the various forms of literary reflection as the devious temptations of idolatrous and diabolical pride. Here again, his goal is not to reject all linguistic specularity (he himself is a master). He refers to the blinding use of the imaginary in order to replace it with Saint Paul's perfect, clairvoyant vision. The ideal is to break through the appearance of discourse and arrive at the spirit that animates it. This spirit, since it underlies appearances, is not itself an appearance, and so comes to us through a nondistorting mirror: "For now we see through a glass, darkly; but then face to face" (1 Cor. 13:12). On the practical level, it is a matter of making the body the mirror of Christian virtues (of meanings).

4. *The injunction against precious fabric* (I, 1, 3) refers to the *vestitio,* the magnificent raiment that is the essence of rhetoric.[37] According to Geoffrey of Vinsauf, this is one of the metaphors that indicate poetic activity. For him, the writer is a weaver (Poetria nova, l. 60). As for the adulteration of natural fabrics by artificial coloring, the "fraudulent mixture of illegitimate color" *[adulterio colorum iniustorium]*" (*On the Apparel of Women,* I, 1, 8) also refers to the colors of rhetoric, to the *mixtura verborum,*[38] to the exact practice of writing described in *Renart Teinturier,* condemned in advance by *On the Apparel of Women,* since "that which God did not want, it is not permitted to produce" (I, 1, 3).

5. *Makeup* is condemned in terms that make it the analogy of all painting (to make oneself up, *expingere;* II, 1, 3). It is explicitly rhetorical, since it "calls upon the eyes" (I, 2, 1).

This list could go on indefinitely. Ornamental cosmetics is a magician's craft (*praestigias formae;* II, 8, 2), and as such refers to what Geoffrey of Vinsauf calls *Ars praestigiatrix.* It is also a drug, medication, or pharmaceutical (I, 2, 1; II, 5, 2; II, 13, 7), a theme that is equally well known to Plato (the *pharmakon*), Aristotle (*Rhetoric,* 1415 a 25), Quintilian (*Institutio oratoria,* IV, ii, 101), and Geoffrey of Vinsauf. The occurrences of drugs and medications in medieval romance as figures for writing are too numerous to mention. Tertullian condemns this literary pharmacopoeia before it arises, and he seeks to replace it with the "ointments and ornaments of the prophets and apostles" (*On the Apparel of Women,* II, 13, 7).

Tertullian wishes not to destroy rhetoric but to alter its character by linking it with an ethic, an aesthetic, and a philosophy that differ radically from the model of pagan oratory. Rhetoric must now be modeled on a conceptual *and* incarnate cause, and no longer in reference to the infinite variety of causes and the uncertainty of public opinion. The writing of the body, the signifier of desire, must bow to this one cause. Although Tertullian creates several key neologisms (*avocator, interpolator,* even *praescriptio*), he converts rhetoric rather than eradicating it. He produces a radical homonymy by repeating rhetoric's terms. Reigning over all his work is a shift of the concepts of rhetoric from experience to discourse. This double move takes place with an extreme finesse and skill despite its violence and radicality. The intermediary of a "source study" is inadequate to understand it. Such a study would overlook what is profoundly innovative in both Tertullian's thought and his practices by tying his work to previous efforts. It would give us a caricature of his project, showing it to be either a confirmation or a contradiction of previous positions.[39]

THE DEVIL AND FICTION

On Spectacles questions the theatrical aspect of pagan language in all its avatars, as it moves through the theater of mimes and histrions, the games of the forum, and horse races. On each of these stages, the gaze of the spectator comes together with the spectacle presented to it, in order to fulfill desire (*voluptates; On Spectacles,* I, 1). Since these same spectacles are forbidden to Christians, the scopic impulse must be changed and desire redirected, not toward the absence of spectacle but toward a Christian spectacle. Once again, Tertullian's treatise produces a homonymy, this time of theatrical terms. Aside from the "trivial" forms of the stage (mimes and histrions), *On Spectacles* takes aim at the whole of pagan fiction, condemning "classical" tragedy and comedy: "If we reject the learning of the world's literature as convicted of foolishness before God, we have a sufficiently clear rule also concerning those types of spectacles which, in profane literature, are classified as belonging to the comic or tragic stage" (XVII, 6).

Tertullian obviously wants at all costs to degrade all classical representation. The Christian may only study pagan culture and its theory *(doctrina)* if he sets all ethical considerations aside and uses his knowledge as an introduction to the literal reading of the Bible.

In its first move, the condemnation of classical representation takes up the hermeneutic critique of its pagan origin. Establishing that the games *(ludi)* of the forum all derive from cultic, pre-Christian institutions makes their idolatrous essence obvious: "But it is, after all, not the name *[causa vocabuli]* that matters; the real issue *[rei causa]* is idolatry" (*On Spectacles* V, 4).

Tertullian devoted an entire treatise to the notion of idolatry, "the principal crime of humankind, the gravest sin of the times, the only cause of condemnation."[40]

Because idolatry is passion for an image that directs itself only to the image, obscuring both its maker and what is represented, it has a relation to rhetoric. For example, chariot drivers are dressed in the "colors of idolatry" (*coloribus idolatriaei; On Spectacles,* IX, 5). Idolatry is also the ambition to make oneself up, to adorn oneself (*ambitio cultus et ornatus; De idolatria,* I, 4). These ambitions are not limited only to the dressing room. They are the process of the whole of pagan rhetoric.

Most important, idolatry is the place where humanity comes in contact with Lucifer:

> What, however, shall we call the chief and foremost manifestation by which the Devil and his pomp and his angels are recognized, if not idolatry? From this source, in a few words—because I will not dwell any longer on this subject—comes every unclean and evil spirit. (*On Spectacles,* XXIV, 2)

Satan is the active principle hidden simultaneously in the pomp of spectacles and of pagan cults:

> If we have shown that all of these things have been instituted for the Devil's sake, and furnished from the Devil's stores (for everything which is not God's or which displeases God is the Devil's), then this represents the pomp of the Devil which we renounce in the "seal" of faith. (*On Spectacles,* XXIV, 2)[41]

Lucifer is the high priest of the cult of idols, whether that cult worships in the temple, the arena, or the theater, whether idolatry appears in painting, sculpture, or mythology.[42] He assembles an artificial church, *ecclesia diaboli* (XXV, 50), a perverse institution that radically confronts God's church by mimicking it.

The cult of the demons is a cult of idols, of actors who play the roles of the gods on stage, of histrions, and so on, but also of mythological characters, pictorial representations, and statues. Each of these simulacra has as its model an original form of the idol: the statue of the pagan god. What is it? A nothing that deifies a dead man:

> We know that the names of dead men are nothing, even as their images are nothing. But we are not unaware of the identity of those who are at work behind those displayed names and images, who exult in the homage paid to them and pretend to be divine, namely, the evil spirits, the demons. (*On Spectacles,* X, 10)

At the moment of its consecration, the statue allows demons to dwell within it:

> "Not that an idol is anything," as the Apostle says, but because what they do, they do in honor of demons who take up their abode there at the consecration of the idols, whether of the dead, or, as they think, of gods. (*On Spectacles,* XIII, 2)

The majority of church fathers who come after Tertullian also see pagan religion as devil worship. This permits them to condemn all the cultural apparatus of the pagan world at once. Of course, Tertullian, who is trying to effect the Christian epistemological break, is distorting paganism for polemic ends. Neither the Greek nor the Roman religion held that the statues or the theater that portrayed the gods contained their essence. For a pagan spectator, such representations of gods, either in costume or in marble, were copies of copies. Each human form is already a copy of the Human Form that the gods put on when it pleases them to show themselves to men, and so neither the theater nor the statue can designate anything real in the true nature of the ancient god. The representations of mythology and of the cult are indications of the relation of the believer to the fiction. Mythology is very conscious of its explicit anthropomorphism. The patristic condemnation of Roman theater and religion transforms the very nature and spirit of pagan representation, which very simply did not have the realism that Christians attribute to it. The Christian homonymy of paganism depends on this realist reading of the sign and so inevitably calls it into existence.

In this view, Lucifer is an artist first of all, as well as the primary inspiration for all the seductive forms of fiction. The demon's intent is to rival divine nature and its creation by moving in the void of idolatrous representation. Lucifer is the rival angel, the bringer of the transgressive force (*vis aemula; On Spectacles,* II, 5) that adulterates the world in order to synthesize it for the ends of the "perverse administration" of the created (II, 11). One the one hand, there is God, the creator with integrity, and on the other, the corrupter, the interpolator: "The state of corruption differs vastly from that of innocence, because there is an enormous difference between the Creator and the perverter (*On Spectacles,* II, 7).[43]

Tertullian's neologism *interpolator* shows us that a homonymy is underway. Greek mythology's *daimon,* a beneficial intermediary, a protean being that lends its mutable body to the gods so they can become visible, becomes an evil spirit who falsely adds on to creation. Once again, this transformation takes place in reference to a double scriptural metaphor. The true writer, God, writes his will into the cosmos, while the "power of the rival and interpolator angel" (II, 12) adds on to and adulterates the primary text. Every act that claims to be creative (the literature of the period, spectacles, sculpture, and painting) is excluded rigorously from Christianity. Tertullian condemns all art simply because it comes from Lucifer. A posteriori, one whole aspect of medieval writing, especially nonedifying (that is, nontheological) writing, is cast into the ranks of evil. Tertullian's discussion will later be used to condemn many other cultural objects, such as the medieval manuscript, whose authentic and original author has always disappeared. Also condemned are the constant interpolations of medieval copyists and their additions and amplifications (to such a degree that it is not until the nineteenth century that the primary text appears, and then only as another fiction). Finally, and foremost, this condemnation also rules out any ambition, explicit or implicit, to use poetry to rival the incarnate Word.

In all manifestations, art is a perverse idolatry, according to Tertullian's dogma of Christian discourse. As a result, medieval art, even before it exists, becomes a vast refuge for diabolic negativity at the very moment it no longer mimics the letter of creation and Incarnation. Christian doctrine casts the shadow of art, bringing about its transgressions in order to repress it. For this reason, the church fathers conceived of art as either repeating or contesting the canon. Art's negativity is not local, folkloric, or particular; rather, it is conceptual and universal. All creation is at risk, since "Satan and his angels have filled the whole world" (*On Spectacles,* VIII, 9).

Tertullian's work has an unintended consequence. If he severely restrains the autonomy of the writer, he unwittingly at the same time, offers the temptation of a diabolic imitation, of a perverse *artifex,* ("artist"). Medieval writing, rather than serving the church, casts itself in the mold of Gnostic Docetism and the Cathar heresy. There is an endless play of the temptation of pride as it is presented in *On Spectacles,* to the point of transforming God himself into an artist, albeit one who produces "original" images.

The homonymy of the word *plasma* and its cognates is at the core of this diabolic concept of art. To my knowledge, the word first appears in the Western tradition in Gorgias's *Elegy to Helen.*[44] In this first usage, its meaning is positive: a human word that creates the world as a simulacrum. This is exactly the meaning that Martianus Capella will later give to it (see chapter 4). In sophistry's *plasma,* it is man who creates the world, and whether that world is fictional or not is of little importance, so long as it is convincing. On the contrary, the very first Christian writers homonymize *plasma* into the sole privilege of the only Creator *(plastica Dei).* For Prudence, *plasma* is the man made of clay (*Cathimmerinoni* 7, 184). *Plasmatio* for Saint Jerome (*Epistulae* 22, 38) designates divine creation. And for Tertullian (*Adversus Judaeos,* 2), the *plasmator* is God.

CHRISTIAN REPRESENTATION

Tertullian knew that representation and its pleasures are indispensable for us, just as it is impossible for a Christian to dispense with rhetoric. Near the end of *On Spectacles,* Tertullian proposes a new form of representation meant to bring delight specifically to Christians. The text substitutes, point by point, Christian spectacle for pagan pleasures, those "drippings of honey from a poisoned cake" (XXVII, 5), replacing them with images drawn entirely from the Bible and from evangelical morality: "To trample underfoot the gods of the heathen, to drive out demons, to effect cures, to seek revelations, to live unto God—these are the spectacles of the Christians, holy, everlasting, and free of charge" (XXIX, 3).

The Christian spectacle is proposed in terms that damage unbelievers, and probably the apologete's flock as well. The spectacles of the circus, as we know, held an important place in the life of ancient Rome, equal to that of the bread. The people spent two hundred days a year there. Yet no matter what its form, the exterior, diabolic spectacle must be replaced with a vision that is both interior and exterior. The "world's contests" will replace the games of the forum; the liturgy of the church, the pagan cults; the blood of Christ and his martyrs, the blood of gladiators; the combat of virtues and vices, the fistfights of the arenas. The theater will now be that of the resurrection of the dead, and its finale will be the Last Judgment, when the artists who make idols are eternally damned to offer to the Christian gaze the contortions of their bodies writhing in the flames of hell:

> Whom else shall I behold? Those wise philosophers blushing before their followers as they burn together, the followers to whom they taught that the world is no concern of God's, whom they assured that either they had no souls at all or that what souls they had would never return to their former bodies? The poets also, trembling, not before the judgment seat of Rhadamanthus or of Minos, but of Christ whom they did not expect to meet. Then will the tragic actors be worth hearing, more vocal in their own catastrophe; then the comic actors will be worth watching, much lither of limb in the fire. (*On Spectacles,* XXX, 4–5)

The form of representation proposed by Tertullian has an entirely new status. No longer will physical images address themselves to the scopic impulse. Instead of a show of the flesh, there is now one of the spirit. However, this does not imply a move from physicality to phantasm. Christian representation is at once real (the passions of Christ and of the martyrs), symbolic (the cult), and eschatological (the Last Judgment). It links the image to the body and to the spirit in an unbreakable union: "What praetor or consul or quaestor or priest with all his munificence will ever bestow on you the favor of beholding and exulting in such sights? Yet such scenes are in a measure already ours by faith in the vision of the spirit" (*On Spectacles,* XXX, 7).

Tertullian's initial suppression of the Asiatic ornamentation of life ultimately works in the opposite direction. First returning in his ornate style, it then becomes real with the baroque spectacle of the end of time. Apocalyptic writing points toward a future Incarnation. In the same move, spiritual imagination no longer has anything to do with the perverse vacuity of the idols when dogma creates a homonymy of the spectacle and of literature, just as it did with the tropes of the cult and of rhetoric. These homonyms occur at the risk of also producing a paradoxical homonymy of the thingism of the biblical pre-text.[45] Although Tertullian obstinately drives the literary exception back onto the law of Christian representation, his ultimate model of fiction carries its own impossibility within it. Just as Saint Augustine will demonstrate, literature cannot bend to fit this model. Tertullian is a creator of language, what Roland Barthes calls a logothete, and his formulation of a strict law of representation produces the most breathtaking Asianism. This is a supplementary proof, if one were necessary, that dogmatism does not necessarily lead to sterility; rather, it often ends up in the singularity of the literary exception. The freedom of Tertullian's writing comes not from the destruction of a dogma but from the delineation of one. Returning continually to the same place, dogma provokes the multiplication of singularities. Tertullian's radical homonymy gives birth to words that escape his model and flirt with an *interpolator* that was previously unknown.

3
Fornication: Saint Augustine

Because he took up the struggle against rhetorical teachings on the one hand and Docetism on the other, Saint Augustine can be seen as expanding on and refining Tertullian's thought (although the saint was not otherwise fond of his forebear). His works combine philosophical and linguistic reflection with a meditation on the nature of fiction. These two are completely parallel, but to show this, we have to overlook two of Augustine's fundamental innovations.

First, Augustine links the Christian subject not only to religious doctrine but also to the writing of autobiography. His *Confessions* are written entirely within the logic of the Christian epistemological break, yet they also open new territory by combining a particular, unique *bios* with the example of the Christian who is always above and beyond his life. The Incarnation is the model that the *Confessions* take at the beginning in posing the questions "Quis ego? Qualis ego?" [I who? Which I?]. Like the Incarnation, such questions represent a discursive individuation of the subject. The response, like its model, is also the story of a life. Augustine, as an autobiographer, surpasses pagan fiction, unlike Tertullian, who reveals himself only rarely.

Augustine's second innovation derives from his conception of language. Tertullian, as we have seen, holds to the *fides nominum,* all the while risking an aporia that opens him up to Docetism. Autobiography, in contrast, is in crucial and essential contact with the fictional essence of language, and so Augustine's very writing faces a fundamental problem. The basic project of the *Confessions,* then, is to frame an autobiographical theory of Christian and pagan fictions and to lay out the means to distinguish between them.

The fictional essence of language is a continual diabolic threat to the *Confessions;* Augustine perpetually encounters this threat, since his entire project takes place in reference to it. A logic of references (to the *bios* and the Incarnation) is utterly necessary here, as is a continual exorcism. To combat the forces of Lucifer and of the literary exception, the *Confessions* require both the law of the model and the law of proscription. This study's goal is not to make Augustine into an ambivalent historical source for the medieval practice of writing fiction. The structures of the two are so obviously analogous, however, that it would be a mistake not to discuss the issue. There is a similarity between Docetism and the literature of the Middle Ages. This similarity also carries over to certain "modern" critical theories that are anticipated in medieval fiction. This is to say that often the writers of the Middle Ages oppose Augustine and the church and take Lucifer's side.

TRUTH: ITS TROPE AND SYSTEM

The physicality of the Incarnation assures that all Christian discourse takes place with only one trope and within one system. Far from reducing meaning to a unity, this trope and system produce an infinity of meanings.

As a consequence, there is one task that no discourse, no writing can accomplish in the *Confessions*—to prove: "I, too, O Lord, make my confession aloud in the hearing of men. For although I cannot prove to them that my confessions are true, at least I shall be believed by those whose ears are opened to me by charity" (X, 3).[1] The text explicitly raises the question of its own legitimacy. To answer it requires a rereading of Genesis, which Augustine perceives as the genesis of all writing. Thus, the "addition" to the *Confessions* of the last three books is structurally justified, although in the secondary literature, they are often considered to be an appendix.[2] They play a central role in the coherence of the Augustinian project, and after the fact, they are completely indispensable in legitimizing his project.

The introduction to book XI shows the formal coherence of these last three books. It begins, as do the others, in the standard register of the *confessio,* in all three meanings of the word (admission of sins, praise of divine providence, and witness of faith meant for the Christian community): "I have long been burning with desire to contemplate your law and to confess to you both what I know of it and where my knowledge fails" *[confiteri scientam et ignorantiam meam]* (XI, 2).

One literary genre encompasses both the first ten books of the work and the last three. Concluding with a discussion of Genesis causes the story of the individual conversion to open onto a general science, one that also legitimizes all possible writing. Augustine's individual story requires this reading of Genesis in order to achieve a generality that gives authority to the *Confessions* themselves. In effect, the twelfth book sets out the actual paradigm of the writer: Moses, the scribe of the Tablets of the Law and the inspired author (for Augustine) of Holy Scripture. He functions as the model for every church father and, furthermore, as the canon for all writing to come. The nature of his example is such that Augustine identifies with him from the first, through the indirect means of a hypothesis:

> If I had been Moses and you had made it my task to write the book of Genesis, I should have wished you to give me back such skill in writing and such power in framing words *[eloquenti facultatem texendi sermonis modum],* that not even those who as yet cannot understand how God creates should reject my words as beyond their comprehension. (XII, 26)

The Mosaic style, his rhetoric's register, is the utopian foundation of the *Confessions,* the starting point and joyful destination where rhetoric and writing change into truth. But as with the *Confessions,* with Genesis an important question remains open. How can one be certain that Moses spoke the truth? At first, the interpreter would like to be able to question the author of Genesis directly:

> Moses wrote these words. He wrote them and passed on into your presence, leaving this world where you spoke to him. He is no longer here and I cannot see him face to face. But if he were here, I would lay hold of him and in your name I would beg and beseech him to explain those words to me. (XI, 3)

Yet even if it were to occur, this impossible dialogue still could not authenticate the biblical text for the simple reason that, as Augustine himself states, the truth of a text can never be reduced to the intention of its signatory (see chapter 6). The truth of the text can surpass its writer, particularly if he has been inspired by the Holy Spirit. In this case, reference to a personal opinion is useless:

> How can it harm me if I understand the writer's meaning in a different sense from that in which another understands it? All of us who read his words do our best to discover and understand what he had in mind, and since we believe that he wrote the truth, we are not so rash as to suppose that he wrote anything which we know or think to be false. (XII, 18)

Thus, Moses' writing speaks *alongside* him. It dismisses the man and renders all recourse to an authorial intention unnecessary and impertinent: "If I am asked which of these opinions was held by Moses your servant, [I] admit that I do not know. If I did not confess this to you, O Lord, these words that I write would not be my confessions" (XII, 30).

The failure to find the writer in the text establishes the pertinence of a particular reading. This only seems paradoxical, however. Once again, it affirms the necessary impenetrability of divinely inspired writing, since the intention of the one who wrote it plays no part.

In other words: The Bible's multivalent meanings show that it has something unknowable in its margins, the actual unconscious meaning of the exegete: "As he wrote those words, he was aware of all they implied. He was aware of every truth we can deduce from them and of others besides that we cannot, or cannot yet, find in them" (XII, 31).

The *Confessions,* like their model, are also an inexhaustible reservoir of meaning, since this meaning cannot be completely formulated. This occurs because the polysemy of the interpretation of biblical texts is immediately applicable to Augustine's writing. Weighing his work on the scales of a Genesis, Augustine uses a hypothesis to distinguish his own text from the Old Testament and its *auctoritas* ("authority"):

> For my part I declare resolutely and with all my heart that if I were called upon to write a book which was to be vested with the highest authority, I should prefer to write it in such a way that a reader could find re-echoed in my words whatever truths he was able to apprehend. I would rather write in this way than impose a single true meaning so exclusively that it would exclude all others, even though they contained no falsehood that could give me offence. (XII, 31)

The meanings of a writing depend on how things *(rebus)* are perceived by the reader, and not on the univocal intention of the author. The *Confessions* thus explicitly hand themselves over to the (qualified) freedom of interpreters: "And now, O Lord, I make my confession in this book *[in litteris]*. Let any man read it who will. Let him understand it as he will" (IX, 12). Such a statement resonates with contemporary criticism. However, Augustine could not anticipate the modernity of both a writing and a reading that are polysemic and disseminating. In contrast, immediately after the *Confessions* propose the absence of an authorial and interpretive guarantee of meaning, they undergo a series of procedures whose goal is to limit the uncertainty and ambiguity that weigh upon the text.

These procedures begin by transforming subjective opinion into general truth. With the elevation of authorial opinion to truth, the speaker is depersonalized and becomes simply the spokesman for a statement that belongs to everyone in its scope and pertinence. Its author, for all purposes, becomes superfluous: "And for the very reason that they are true, these opinions are not their own property" (XII, 25).

Second, the writer must disappear so that the truth of his statements can be heard. This is not a disappearance in elocution alone (such as we find in Mallarmé); it is a real one as well. Moses' death and that of the apostles and martyrs of the faith, are a necessary condition for their authority. Writing only rises to the generality of truth through the death of its author: "Those men are dead, and by their death this solid shield, the authority of your words delivered to us through them, is raised on high to shelter all that lies beneath it. While they lived on earth, it was not raised so high, nor spread so wide" (*Confessions,* XIII, 15).

The same can be said for the *Confessions.* A biographical reading is only partially adequate at best, since the life of the meaning only becomes free with the disappearance of the writer. What we have here is auto-thanato-graphy, not auto-bio-graphy, and so the legitimacy of the *Confessions* has nothing to do with the disappearing speaker of modern poetics. Martyrology, in its etymological sense, contains death's imprint. It is a positive sign and a retrospective proof of the author's life, just as Christ's death on the cross proves his Incarnation. The author's disappearance assures the return of his speech, through irrefutable testimony to his incarnation.

In the same way that the speaker vanishes in his truthful speech, the truth assumes the paradoxical effacement of national languages. None of the tongues of the diminishing Roman Empire is capable of assimilating the universal language in which speech declares itself. Yet one by one, the truth can take on the form of each language. If the truth can only become audible through the double individuation of a particular language and a particular person, it is essentially inside/outside of all enunciation. It is an inter-diction:

> But how should I know whether what [Moses] said was true? If I knew this too, it could not be from him that I got such knowledge. But deep inside me, in my most intimate thought, Truth, which is neither Hebrew nor Greek nor Latin nor any foreign speech, would speak to me, though not in syllables formed by lips and tongue. It would whisper "He speaks the Truth." (XI, 3)

Augustine reaffirms Christianity's universal vocation as it is defined in Acts 10 and 11, when he once more detaches evangelical truth from Roman/Latin culture. Truth's transglossia is made historically necessary in the collapse of *latinitas,* and Augustine provides a concrete example of the effects of this collapse in Africa. More important (and several centuries ahead of his time), he combines religious and historical factors to elevate popular languages to languages of thought and truth. Of course, this relation is totally foreign to Cicero's rhetorical conception of thought.

Even though it is universal, Christian truth is addressed not to all but only to those who admit its possibility: "This is what I wish my true brothers to feel in their hearts. I do not speak of strangers or of *alien foes, who make treacherous promises, and lift their hands in perjury*" (X, 4; emphasis added).

Speech and writing are merely traces of a silent transcendence that contains the truth and its interpretations. They are an interiority that must try to fit itself to an exterior discourse. The source of speech and writing is an inexpressible cry:

> And I make my confession, not in words and sounds made by the tongue alone, but with the voice of my soul and in my thoughts which cry aloud to you. Your ear can hear them. For when I am sinful, if I am displeased with myself, this is a confession that I make to you; and when I am good, if I do not claim the merit for myself, this too is a confession. For you, O Lord, give your benedictions to the just, but first you make a

just man of the sinner. And so my confession is made silently in your sight, my God, and aloud as well, because even though my tongue utters no sound, my heart cries to you. (X, 2)

Finally, because God is omniscient, the *Confessions* are entirely superfluous. Writing, making public, only has meaning and necessity when humans address other humans: "I need not tell all this to you, my God, but in your presence I tell it to my own kind, to those other men, however few, who may perhaps pick up this book" (II, 3).

The whole problem is thus one of transmitting what Augustine calls the "Inner Master" or the "ear of the heart"[3] when he is referring, respectively, to the source of speech or to its interpreter. There is a blank, a silence, and a nonarticulation that must be put into a language, but this action can do nothing but destroy them. How can writing (literature), doomed to be fictional, account for and legitimize meaning?

GENEALOGIES OF LANGUAGE

The *Confessions* conceal the genesis of a particular human being in such a way that it cannot be restored. The *infans,* "who is mute," retains no trace of the past that nevertheless formed him (language, in Augustine, is always combined with the possibility of memory): "I do not remember that early part of my life, O Lord" (I, 7). Death has overtaken the very beginnings of life: "My infancy is long since dead, yet I am still alive" (I, 6).

The identity of the subject does not come about through its human birth. Rather, the child is speechless and abandoned on the edge of the chasm of its open mouth. Birth is continuously deferred in a *naescio,* "I do not know," and a *non memini,* "I do not remember"—a purposeful repetition of the hermeneutic doubt about Moses' intention:

> Answer my prayer and tell me whether my infancy followed upon some other stage of life that died before it. Was it the stage of life that I spent in my mother's womb? . . . But what came before that, O God my delight? Was I anywhere? Was I anybody? These are questions I must put to you, for I have no one else to answer them. Neither my father nor my mother could tell me, nor could I find out from the experience of other people or from my own memory. (I, 6)

In the metaphorical equation of divine cause/providence[4] with mother's milk, human birth disappears completely. Milk thus becomes a "divine" flux of meaning:

> So it was that I was given the comforts of woman's milk. But neither my mother nor my nurses filled their breasts of their own accord, for it was you who used them, as your law prescribes, to give me infant's food and a share of the riches which you distribute even among the very humblest of all created things. (I, 6)

The flow of milk erases the mother who produces it. In her place is an affirmation of the primary Cause. Because this Cause is concealed in mystery, it cannot account for the childhood of the subject. His birth is forever inaccessible until later, when maternal discourse fills in this gap by telling the adolescent of the forgotten time of the *infantia,* "infancy": "I do not remember that early part of my life, O Lord, but I believe what other people have told me about it and from watching other babies I can conclude that I also lived as they do" (I, 7). The mother and the nurses that act as her substitutes play a determining role in knowledge of one's childhood: "But you have allowed men to discover these things about themselves by watching other babies, and also to learn much from what women have to tell" (I, 6).

However, neither the mediation of maternal speech nor adult observations can make a human subject's own birth fully knowable. Infancy separates the subject from itself and subjugates it to another's story, and thus to language. Since birth is contaminated by a language that cannot speak it, and since direct observation is impossible, birth cannot serve as a figure for the absolute beginning.

In the substitute beginning are thus the mother and her word. This primacy only lasts a brief time because acculturation, an "institutionalized violence,"[5] soon brings about a fundamental shift. From the gynocratic kingdom that gives speech, Augustine passes to a phallocentric territory dominated by his father, who is then replaced by schoolteachers. This movement coincides precisely with the move from maternal speech to paternal writing. The writing of the text of the *Confessions* only becomes possible in a succession of breaks from an original birth, breaks that Augustine conceives of as repetitions of the Fall and of original sin.[6]

Entry into the schools both implies a sexualization of the speech/writing dichotomy and, through the effacement of the mother, establishes a more profound concealment: that of the Christian faith by pagan unbelief, of which Monica and Patricius are, respectively, emblematic. Because of its tainted paternal origin, writing as such is devilish.[7] Thus, Monica tries with all her might to remove the child from his father and from the principles of unbelief and division that he symbolizes, in order to place the child under the authority of the spiritual Father: "She did all she could to see that you, my God, should be a Father to me rather than he. In this you helped her to turn the scales against her husband, whom she always obeyed because by obeying him she obeyed your law" (I, 11).

The mother is caught in an inescapable double bind. When the husband does not believe, the subordination of wife to husband is in radical opposition to the imperative of faith. The son's acculturation thus takes place inside an irreconcilable division that fractures the maternal language/speech of faith and the paternal discourse/writing of unbelief.

The division also produces a double sexual ethic. Monica is obliged to be continent. Figuratively, this is a castration that unites spiritually with the law of the Other in a secret that excludes the father: "I well remember what her wishes were and how she most earnestly warned me not to commit fornication and above all not to seduce any man's wife" (II, 3).

For the moment, Augustine holds this "womanly advice" in contempt, but later, when he stops writing of Monica's body and begins to speak of her soul, he will recognize its worth. This puts him in accord with Saint Paul's opposition of letter and spirit. Monica, in effect, is "feminine in dress only, but masculine in spirit" (IX, 4).

Contradicting his wife's wishes, Patricius (who is well named) commands that the "brambles of the passions" sprout on his son's head, and so he represents the superego's imperative for pleasure. For the father, the first signs of Augustine's puberty mean the birth of heirs. However, it is Patricius who is to reap the rewards of his demand, without assimilating it to the will of divine providence:

> One day at the public baths he saw the signs of active virility coming to life in me and this was enough to make him relish the thought of having grandchildren. He was happy to tell my mother about it, for his happiness was due to the intoxication which causes the world to forget you, its Creator, and to love the things you have created instead of loving you, because the world is drunk with the invisible wine of its own perverted, earthbound will. (II, 3)

However, the contradictory wishes of mother and father unite in one goal, the "hope of letters" *(spes litterarum):*

> Both my parents were unduly eager for me to learn, my father because he gave next to no thought to you and only shallow thought to me, and my mother because she thought the usual course of study would certainly not hinder me, but would even help me, in my approach to you. (II, 3)

Education is fundamentally ambiguous. On the one (paternal) hand, it is the path to power and honor, an emblem of unpardonable vanity, and on the other (maternal) hand, it is the path to a correct reading of the Bible (a conversion). Unknown to Monica, education is the only means the Christian apologete has at his disposal for persuading the doubtful.

The problem is that the way of scholars is also "the river of Hell" (*flumen tartareum;* I, xvi, 26). The mother's command is superseded by that of the diabolical and unbelieving father. The schoolteachers are all sophists, and so they only care about the form of discourse and its power of persuasion, not its basis in truth (and Augustine's example, the phrase "human being," is an ideal illustration):[8] "A man who has learnt the traditional rules of pronunciation, or teaches them to others, gives greater scandal if he breaks them by dropping the aitch from 'human being' than if he breaks your rules and hates another human, his fellow man" (I, 18).

The essence of the controlling model is demonic, a seductive and prevaricating angel *(transgressor),* linked forever to a certain type of elevated style:

> I was expected to model myself upon men who were disconcerted by the rebukes they received if they used outlandish words or strange idioms to tell of some quite harmless thing they might have done, but reveled in the applause they earned for the finest flow of well-ordered and nicely balanced phrases *[copiose ornateque]* with which they described their own acts of indecency. (I, 18)

Augustine was at first a rhetor, one of "those who traffic in literature" (I, 13). He was an exact image of Plato's sophist, who auctions off an art of seductive speech, and not an art of thinking. Such an art gives the lie to its teacher. Because it is perverse, the process of ancient education as a whole is repudiated as a Luciferian error: "It is true that curtains are hung over the entrances to the schools where literature is taught, but they are not so much symbols in honour of mystery as veils concealing error" (I, 13).

So the very writing of the *Confessions,* insofar as it was taught to Augustine in a scholastic "river of Hell," is stamped with Lucifer's seal.[9] In order to distinguish the *Confessions* own rhetorical nature from the form of pagan discourse, they must repeatedly draw attention to rhetoric's inherent satanism. Augustine's principal tactic is the appeal to another education, the Other's education, radically opposed to what one learns in school: "Obviously the knowledge of letters is not more deeply engraved in us than the law of conscience against doing to another what one would not bear if done to oneself" (I, 18).[10]

The second, simultaneous move takes place on a completely different level. The *Confessions* again pull away from pagan discourse when they reveal two opposite textual destinies for the mother and the father. Monica becomes a pure signifier, her death making her name deathless. In a way, the *Confessions* are her headstone, her maternal tomb. At the end of the ninth book, there is a prayer for the dead mother that is also an appeal to the faithful to join in. Her memory is kept alive in literature: "So it shall be that the last request that my mother made to me shall be granted in the prayers of the many who read my confessions more than in mine alone" (IX, 13).

Patricius meets an entirely different fate. The funeral rite that embalms the maternal name stands in stark contrast to an incidental passage whose brevity kills Patricius off more surely than would a long condemnation of his faults (III, 4). The text separates itself from the paternal curse by neglecting the father and instead raising a monument to the mother. This represents another move meant to tear the book from the Satanic grip of rhetoric, because the two share such similar methods. The *Confessions* establish a homonymy through the use of rhetorical ornament, changing the ornament of letters into truth's tool. The maternal body, the spirit of faith representing the rise of a new culture, is entombed beneath the *Confessions.* So the father necessarily returns, but this time as a phantom with no body, like a Ciceronian figure, for example, or any other rhetorical trope. The name of the father is the very locus for this homonymy. The function of the *Confessions*' verbal cenotaph is to exorcise the diabolical ghost of ancient culture that continually arises within its pages.

Adeodatus (meaning "God-given"), Augustine's illegitimate son, is also fated to play out this Oedipal scene.[11] There is every indication that he represents, through a play on words (*liber,* in the Latin original, means "book," but also "child"), the text itself. His intellectual gifts permit him to be his father's interlocutor in Augustine's *De magistro,* and his premature death (and Augustine thanks God for punishing his own sins so justly) makes the *Confessions* a substitution and redemption for this son of sin.

BLANK LANGUAGE AND ECSTASY

Many scholars have written very detailed and competent critiques of the several treatises that Augustine devoted to the question of language.[12] We could leave these treatises aside were it not for the fact that the *Confessions* also propose a linguistic theory. In the *Confessions,* the question of language is linked to the history of the subject, which is to say, to the destiny of the text itself.[13]

One metaphor returns again and again under Augustine's pen as a figure for words: the vase. The signifier is a container. It is pure form, pure virtuality, and thus equivocally either good or bad according to the intent of the speaker. As Augustine writes on the subject of grammarians, "I have nothing against the words themselves. They are like choice and costly glasses, but they contain the wine of error which had already gone to the heads of the teachers who poured it out for us to drink" (I, 16). Or, on the subject of Faustus, the Manichaean orator, "I had learned that wisdom and folly are like different kinds of food. Some are wholesome and others are not, but both can be served equally well on the finest china dish or the meanest earthenware. In just the same way, wisdom and folly can be clothed alike in plain words or the finest flowers of speech" (V, 6).

The signifier has a mercenary quality. It remains neutral, somewhere between good and evil, but all possibility of perversity comes from it. Everything depends upon the speaker's motivation. He can arbitrarily choose to use language for good or for evil, and he bends the rhetorical and stylistic forms to his purpose. Thus, language is always embodied in a particular discourse, the more so because the vase metaphor relates equally to the individual as a signifier. A biblical allusion (2 Tim. 2:21) provides the analogy: "They saw his possessions taken from him and cleansed, so that he was *proved to be the object of his Lord's regard, hallowed, and serviceable, and fit for all honorable employment* (*Confessions,* VIII, 4).[14]

The sign's arbitrary nature (in ancient linguistics, signs were held to name *ad placitum,* "at pleasure"), language's ethical indifference, means that man must exercise his free will, thus making the development of an ethic of discourse all the more necessary.

A latent, consubstantial lack marks language, which any ethic must take into account. Language perpetually disappears, and this vanishing is a necessary condition for any discourse: "Our speech follows the same rule, using sounds to signify a meaning. For a sentence is not complete unless each word, once its syllables have been pronounced, gives way to make room for the next" (*Confessions,* IV, 10).

Symmetrically, intellection only occurs in a never-ending succession of articulated syllables. "It is one of these same bodily senses that enables you to hear the words I speak, but you do not want the syllables to sound forever in my mouth: you want them to fly from my tongue and give place to others, so that you may hear the whole of what I have to say" (*Confessions,* IV, 11).

There would be nothing but an unmediated cacophony if one no longer respected the alteration of sound and silence. A statement is never grasped as a whole; rather, it must be perceived through the vanishing of its individual elements. Language is not only the desire for a unity that never comes, but by reason of its necessary imperfection, it is also grafted onto the fleeting, the transitory. Ultimately, language is an image of death, under the rule of the contingency that strikes all created things. That it is impossible to seize its totality is emphasized in the analogy between language and people. Augustine makes this remark about memory: "It is a faculty of my soul. Although it is a part of my nature, *I cannot understand all that I am*" (*Confessions,* X, 8; emphasis added).[15]

The mercenary and double nature of the signifier turns discourse into the greatest form and practice of sin: "The human tongue is a furnace in which the temper of our souls is daily tried" *[Cotidiana fornax nostra est humana lingua]* (*Confessions,* X, 36).

Incapable of grasping another of God's names—totality/truth—human language is doomed to the curse of fragmentation and difference. A profound contradiction overwhelms it: Although it suffers aphasia on the subject of God, language is simultaneously the indispensable but incomplete instrument of communication, of praise, and of prayer: "You are my God, my Life, my holy Delight, but is this enough to say of you? Can any man say enough when he speaks of you? Yet woe betide those who are silent about you!" (*Confessions,* I, 4).

However, there is an inhuman language. Augustine describes it during a dialogue with Monica when he discusses Ostia's ecstasy. It is significant that the "language of truth" comes forward in an exchange with the mother, and thus places her in contrast with the sophistic discourse of the rhetors and of the father:

> Suppose, we said, that the tumult of man's flesh were to cease and . . . his dreams and the visions of his imagination spoke no more, and that every tongue and every sign, and all that is transient grew silent. . . . Suppose, we said, that after giving us this message and bidding us listen to those who made them, they fell silent and he alone should speak to us, not through them but through his own voice, so that we should hear him speaking, not by any tongue of the flesh or by an angel's voice, not in the sound of thunder or in some veiled parable, but in his own voice, the voice of the one whom we love in all these created things; suppose we heard him himself, with none of these things between ourselves and him. (*Confessions,* IX, 10)

Divine language is opposed to human language in each of its characteristics. Being without history (having no crime or desire), it goes inhumanly beyond the signifier, beyond difference, and beyond the sign. It is the language without language, because a timeless, eternal language could only be a silent one. Augustine emphasizes that because human time is continuous, it is incompatible with the eternal language. If it were to occur in reality, not only would we be in the "glory of the Lord," but also, the end of time would be known to us: "But when is this to be? Is it to be when we all rise again, but not all of us will undergo the change?" (*Confessions,* IX, 10).

The *Confessions* endlessly write toward this utopic, signless language and are thus self-contradictory. Although they can never achieve the goal of divine speech, the *Confessions* describe it as it is unveiled in the mystery of the Incarnation:

> It is in this way, then, that you mean us to understand your Word, who is God with you, God with God, your Word uttered eternally in whom all things are uttered eternally. For your word is not speech in which each part comes to an end when it has been spoken, giving place to the

> next, so that finally the whole may be uttered. In your word all is uttered at one and the same time, yet eternally. If it were not so, your Word would be subject to time and change, and therefore would be neither truly eternal nor truly immortal. (XI, 7)

The inarticulate language is also a paradigm for what the angels hear when they listen to God. They are the metaphorical book where the divine truth writes itself, a text without temporality, where everything can be read simultaneously:

> For they gaze upon your face and there, without the aid of syllables inscribed in time, they read what your eternal will decrees. They read your will, they choose it to be theirs: they cherish it. . . . The book they read shall not be closed. For them the scroll shall not be furled. For you yourself are their book and you forever are. (XIII, 15)

Theography (this term is only an inadequate metaphor) and the angelic hermeneutic are totalizing figures for the system of truth that redeems the curse of human language, this anthropography that undergoes a mortal difference. Angelotheolalia, by its eternity, also gives meaning to the succession of historical time. So the opposition between theo- and anthropography is a metaphor for the opposition between eternity and time:

> Time derives its length only from a great number of movements constantly following one another into the past, because they cannot all continue at once. But in eternity nothing moves into the past: all is present. Time, on the other hand, is never present all at once. The past is always driven on by the future, the future always follows on the heels of the past, and both the past and the future have their beginning and their end in the eternal present. (XI, 11)

The last three books of the *Confessions* retroactively establish divine writing as the Mosaic model and also as the model for the whole of the text, and so the text can only be saved by a theography/angelolalia that it cannot attain. Augustine's entire project is trapped in the tension between the rhetorical "river of Hell" and the pure absence of the signifier.

THE PLACE OF FICTION

In the *Confessions,* fiction is always a seduction of the senses, and there is nothing more fictional for Augustine than the woman as he sees her through his own narcissism. There is no way to separate fiction from eroticism, from a mirror image of the impasses of desire. Because the imagination produces both woman and literature, they are a sign for the sins of the spirit, a more serious "fornication" than anything the flesh may do. The theater of the histrions lived on, despite Tertullian's tirades against it. *On Spectacles* had no effect on its age, and so we must listen for its resonance in the texts that echo it (in the *Confessions,* for example) and not in history.

Augustine's critique differs from Tertullian's because it is Augustine himself, the autobiographical subject, who is implicated in sin, and not "the Christian." The two authors correspond when they accuse the theater of inverting the world of real suffering and delight, replacing it with a fictional representation that gives pleasure to the spectator. It is folly to identify the spectator and the spectacle, according to Augustine:

> I was much attracted by the theatre, because the plays reflected my own unhappy plight and were tinder to my fire. Why is it that men enjoy feeling sad at the sight of tragedy and suffering on the stage, although they would be most unhappy if they had to endure the same fate themselves? Yet they watch the plays because they hope to be made to feel sad, and the feeling of sorrow is what they enjoy. What miserable delirium *[insania]* this is! (III, 2)

Furthermore, the theater seduces the spectator, causing him to enjoy the sign produced by the thing, and not the thing itself: "In those days I used to share the joy *[congaudebam]* of stage lovers and their sinful pleasure *[fruebantur]* in each other even though it was all done in make-believe *[imaginaria]* for the sake of entertainment" (III, 2). Augustine's difficulty is that his vocabulary matches that of the spectacle, and so he must homonymize its terms. He speaks of the *gaudium* (the joy of the happy Christian life) and of the *frui* (the delight in God, *fruitio Dei*), and these terms are essential elements of his theology with regard to the relation of man to God.[16] These homonyms must in no way be tainted with ambiguity, in spite of the identity that threatens the signifiers. There is not even one step from theater's mimicries to those of literature. Augustine takes a written play as his paradigm for all literature: *The Eunuch* by Terence, the "infernal torrent" that he read in grammar school. The text is the object of a very complex staging:

> But for a certain passage in Terence, we should never have heard of words like "shower," "golden," "lap," "deception," "sky," and the other words

> which occur in the same scene. Terence brings onto the stage a dissolute youth who excuses his own fornication by pointing to the example of Jupiter. He looks at a picture painted on the wall, which "shows how Jupiter is said to have deceived the girl Danae by raining a golden shower into her lap." These are the words with which he incites himself to lechery, as though he had heavenly authority for it. (*Confessions,* I, 16)

The first attack is launched against the rhetors, those who are faithful to Cicero's doctrine. In opposition to Augustine's "Christian" (referential, thingist) linguistics, they maintain that meaning only comes from a poetic fiction, at the expense of common usage. To criticize them, Augustine condemns the essence of fiction, which is four steps removed from Platonic Truth.[17] Four steps, because not only does the play mimic physical things (which are copies of the Platonic Ideas, and they, in turn, mimic the Good), but the stage backdrop depicts the action of the play, placing the entire work in a double *mise en abyme.* However, Augustine's discussion of the play leaves out one important detail. The *Confessions* nowhere mention the trick that the play's main character, Charea, employs to be able to enjoy the favors of the courtesan Thais: He pretends to be a eunuch so that he can enter the harem where she lives. This omission points to the fundamental distinction between the (twice) fictional emasculation staged by Terence and the symbolic castration of the continent Christian (I will come back to this). These notions are too similar not to undergo a homonymy that separates the fictional from the real.

Finally, following a line of reasoning that Augustine will expand on in *The City of God,* the polemic culminates by re-intensifying its debate with Greco-Roman religion. The entire anthropomorphism of the pagan pantheon is put back into play through Terence. A mural painted by the hand of man in a play written by the hand of man, a simulacrum of a simulacrum, displays the false image of an idol whose immorality and origin alone are sufficient to discredit it. And yet, far from being discredited, this lying image incites Charea to imitate and repeat the fornication it depicts. Furthermore, because this simulacrum stirs Charea's desire, it is also an effective paradigm for the spectator who identifies with the actor. The image is thus a radical antithesis to the Christ of the Incarnation; it is an evil trap that presents a bodiless god and asks us to believe in it. Homer is the name that governs literature as a whole in the

Confessions. He is the synecdoche for all mythological fiction. Whereas Quintilian assigns Homer a positive role (see chapter 1), Augustine forces him to undergo the homonymy of Christian values. Homer is now the negative paradigm of the pagan fiction that gives itself the authority and the privilege of creating idols/simulacra that incite one to fornication:

> Can any schoolmaster in his gown listen unperturbed to a man who challenges him on his own ground and says, "Homer invented these stories and attributed human sins to the gods? He would have done better to provide men with examples of divine goodness." It would certainly be nearer the truth to say that Homer certainly invented the tales but peopled them with wicked human characters in the guise of gods. (I, 16)

As Tertullian was careful to point out, fiction and mythology are fundamentally linked. Religious literature is a wheel that turns to become the religion of literature, of aesthetics, and of Eros. Lucifer, the power of ornament, is the goal hidden behind the impure pagan rite. He does not exist in himself; he exists only when he slips into each of the idols created by the "fable of nations." Whether the literary simulacrum is theatrical or textual, its structure has a direct and real effect upon the subject. Augustine becomes aware of this in grammar/sophistry school when he reads the *Aeneid,* the canonical text of *latinitas:*

> What can be more pitiful than an unhappy wretch unaware of his own sorry state, bewailing the fate of Dido, who died for love of Aeneas, yet shedding no tears for himself as he dies for want of loving you? O God . . . I did not love you. . . . I embraced another. . . . to love this world is to break troth with you. . . . I did not weep over this, but instead I wept for Dido, who surrendered her life to the sword. (*Confessions,* I, 13)

The young Augustine cries not for his narcissistic image, reflected in Dido's suicide, but for the death of a simulacrum. It is also important to note that he feels pathos over a suicide, an act condemned by the church. As soon as the words "death" and "suicide" appear in a literary text, they, like all textual citations, should be enclosed in quotation marks to indicate their fictional status. Christian homonymy continually tries to do this to literary fiction to indicate clearly its perverse status—an operation that literature always resists. Most important, Augustine cries for the death of a sign, for a product made by human imagination, and not for a divine creation. This sign, it is also important to note, stands for a woman and her desire. The reader and the sign are no longer sexually differentiated, because the reader identifies with the literary character. This identification violates the order ordained by God.

Fiction dies the moment the reader makes an idol of it, a demonic empty figure pointing to absence and nonbeing. The reader/sinner is tricked by his teachers into "fornicating" when he shapes the sign into a figure of desire. Because identification with the sign is a false presence, the reader, by removing the quotation marks from the sign, also erases absence. This action simultaneously conceals the actual literary nature of fiction and its awareness of its own identity.

Augustine, having condemned both theater and identificatory reading (and literary fiction along with them), has also radically broken with Aristotle's doctrine of catharsis and the pathetic.[18] Fiction no longer purifies the passions; it is moral pollution because it is idolatry. However, as in Tertullian's thinking, this is not to reject ancient literature completely: "Verses and poems can provide real food for thought, but although I used to recite verse about Medea's flight through the air, I never maintained that they were true *[non asserebam];* and I never believed the poems which I heard others recite" (*Confessions,* III, 6).

Literature is no longer a danger when it admits its limits and becomes distinct from a plausible rhetoric pretending to the truth. The study of great literature lays the ground for reading the Bible and understanding its use of fiction (parables, prophecies, allegories, and the like). However, the Gospels' use of fiction makes a complete homonym of the very notion of fiction. Even if pagan fiction is always a lie, whether explicitly or not, the same cannot be the case for biblical fiction. (*Confessions,* II, 51); and elsewhere: "All parables and figures for signifying anything which are not to be taken literally, but in which one thing must be understood for another, will be called lies. A deplorable consequence!"[19]

Christian fiction necessarily relies on the distinction between true meaning (guaranteed by the Incarnation) and figurative meaning (guaranteed by the Holy Spirit). The Bible's use of rhetoric thus rescues rhetoric's entire arsenal of figures and the use of metaphor in particular:

> He who thinks this can bring this charge against all figurative expressions, be they ever so many. In this way, what is named a metaphor, that is, the so-called transfer of some word from its own object to an object

> not its own, could be called a lie. [There follows a list of biblical metaphors.] They should be judged as prophetic expressions and actions put for the understanding of those things which are true.[20]

And so we can now distinguish between truthful (Christian) fiction and the pagan literature of lies:

> What I call the fabulous kind of falsehood is the kind which is committed by those who tell fables. The difference between deceivers and fabulists is this: every deceiver wants to deceive, but not everyone who tells a fable has the desire to deceive.[21]

The Christian dogma of fiction finds its positive definition in this homonymy. Augustine thus allows one to use fiction, and its handmaid rhetoric, but at the cost of an enormous restriction: Fiction can be no more than the trace of evangelical truth and must continually point to it. Yet this restriction in no way nails metaphors to a fixed meaning. Anchoring tropes to theology's Object gives them new authority as the structure of thought. Having condemned rhetoric's endless use of metaphor, patristic thought revives it in the very heart of its system. Now the Incarnation plays the double role of legitimizing meaning and giving it the freedom of plurality.

THE "IMMENSE FABLE"

Augustine, discussing the story of Medea in flight, points out its implausibility and thus reduces it to a harmless fiction. Later, the *Confessions* take on Manichaeism, a more fearsome discourse because it seeks to create belief, and not delight:

> Surely the fables of the poets and the penmen are better than the traps which those impostors set! There is certainly more to be gained from verses and poems and tales like the flight of Medea than from their stories of the five elements disguised in various ways because of the five dens of darkness. These things simply do not exist and they are death to those who believe in them. (III, 6)

The religion founded by Manes had reached its high point by the end of the fourth century. Its territory spread from Africa to Turkestan, and it seemed to be on the verge of becoming the universal religion. This was its declared ambition, according to its founder:

> The writings, wisdom, visions, parables, and psalms of all previous churches are in all ways united in the Church of Wisdom that I have revealed to you. Just as a river joins with another river and forms a powerful current, so I have added old books to my writings. Great wisdom has been made from them, such as has never been known in preceding generations.[22]

Although Zoroastrianism lies at its core, Manichaeism's principal trait is its ability to assimilate widely varied systems of thought. It draws on certain Buddhist principles from the East, and from the West, it denies all specificity to Christianity by including it among the "wisdoms." Christians claim to have broken away from all ancient traditions, but Manichaeism nevertheless integrates Christianity into a system drawing on the diverse languages, doctrines, and religions of the known world. Even more menacing is Manichaeism's direct rivalry with the Roman church's centralizing and universal vocation. Augustine, by his own admission, was a Manichaean for nine years (around 373–383). His writing thus has a double goal: on a general level, to fight the expansion of Manichaeism; on a personal level, which naturally resonates everywhere throughout an autobiography, to demonstrate that he has broken with himself and his past heresy. The *Confessions* (circa 397–401) appear to have been written in the middle of Augustine's major anti-Manichaean period (circa 388–404), when tract after tract against this heresy flowed from his pen,[23] and of course there are resonances between the *Confessions* and these tracts. By exposing the sect's doctrinal "errors," Augustine is also cleansing himself of his Manichaean stain. His autobiography therefore stands as a monument to, and proof of, this break.

For our purposes here, it matters little that this refutation is undeniably partial and polemic. We are only interested in its structural function in the scriptural economy of the text. By clarifying this function, we will also bring into relief the logic that condemns literary fiction as heresy.

1. When discussing the authority of his own words, Manes claims to be the Holy Spirit made flesh, reducing Christ to a prophet of the new Messiah: "[He led] his followers to believe that they were following no ordinary man, but your Holy Spirit" (*Confessions,* V, 5). Because Manes is the Holy Spirit, everything he writes is also a divine revelation. Among all of the wisdoms, Manes is the only leader to reach such a level of pretension. As we have seen, however, this sort of legitimation is the very

sign of an apocrypha for Augustine. The circular system, or the "signature," of a text does not give it its authority; truth is not guaranteed by its speaker, or vice versa. Authority comes, instead, from the text's exterior in its relation to revelation.[24]

2. The Incarnation's status is once again placed in question. If Manes is the Paraclete incarnate, it necessarily follows that the body of Christ is fictional, in accord with the Docetism that Tertullian fought. And again, the entire doctrine of the Incarnation itself must be declared a fiction. For Augustine, on the other hand, the mediation of Christ incarnate between humans and God is obviously indispensable:

> But there is a true Mediator, whom in your secret mercy you have shown to men. You sent him so that by his example they too might learn humility. He is the Mediator between God and men, Jesus Christ, who is a man, and he appeared on earth between men, who are sinful and mortal, and God, who is immortal and just. Like men, he was mortal: like God, he was just. (X, 43)

Any other mediator is a demon: "It was no mediator that they found. It was the devil, passing for an angel of light, and it was a potent lure for their proud flesh that he was not a creature of flesh and blood" (X, 42).[25] As is the case in every Gnostic religion, the Manichaean mediator is disincarnate, emptied of all concrete empirical value.

3. Just as the Marcionites did, the Manichaeans undertake to modify the New Testament where it does not support their beliefs. According to them, the authors of the Gospels did not sign their works and so did not "authenticate" them. Furthermore, they hold that later authors rewrote the Gospels to bring them into accord with Judaism: "They claimed that the books of the New Testament had been tampered with by unnamed persons who wished to impose the Jewish law upon the Christian faith" (*Confessions,* V, 11). For the Gnostics, it is only a small step from this claim to the claim that the Bible is matter to be shaped both in its reading and in its writing: "They could produce no uncorrupted copies" (V, 11).

At the same time, the Gnostics desanctify the Gospels and make them irrational: They now have the status of literary myth. If the revealed text is not protected from transformation, then this practice becomes an a fortiori permission to modify all texts, whatever their status. We know the medievals took great delight in altering literary texts, often to such a degree that it is impossible to authenticate this or that version of a romance, a poem, or a play. At least until Guillaume de Machaut, it was common medieval practice to continue, expand, abbreviate, rewrite in prose, produce concurrent versions, and refer to fictional authors. Fiction did not enjoy the authority and the sacred status accorded to the Bible. As a natural result, literary practice seemed to be placed under the umbrella concept of the heretical text. Inversely, the modern obsession to authenticate the original and signed text is one of the surest indications of a sanctification of literature.

4. The *Confessions* portray the Manichaeans proposing an erroneous system of reading *en abyme:*

> But if some sanctified member of the sect were to eat the fig . . . he would digest it and breathe it out again in the form of angels or even as particles of God, retching them up as he groaned in prayer. These particles of the true and supreme God were supposed to be imprisoned in the fruit and could only be released by means of the stomach and the teeth of one of the elect. (III, 10)

The Manichaean saint frees the spiritual essence from its matter. (According to the doctrine's dualism, matter is stamped with the seal of diabolical creation.) He understands his world as digestion and the production of fecal matter, which means that his materialism is fashioned by his phantasms.

Obviously, this imaginary materialism is not limited to figs. Manichaeism, as with all gnoses, arises in myth. It is a theosophy or a cosmogony before becoming a philosophy or a rational science.[26] This false science is thought to give credence, in a circular system of proof, to the interior germ of the doctrine, which in turn allows one to explain the world. Augustine broke with the sect over just such fallacious arguments. When he presses Faustus, the prestigious Manichaean, to clarify the incoherencies in the cosmogony, Faustus is forced to admit his ignorance. Manichaean cosmology is upset by the more exact astronomy that Augustine now possesses, that of the Roman astrologers. Now those who call the Gospels fables are in their turn accused of storytelling:

> The Manichean books are full of the most tedious fictions about the sky and the stars, the sun and the moon. I had badly wanted Faustus to compare these with the mathematical calculations which I had studied in other books, so that I might judge whether the Manichean theories

were more likely to be true or, at least, equally probable, but now I began to realize that he could not give me a detailed explanation. (V, 7)

Manichaean doctrine is integrally associated with a fantastic cosmology, and to doubt that cosmology causes the central dogma to collapse. The question of epistemology is an important factor in Augustine's disaffection with the Manichaeans: "So it was that, unwittingly and without intent, Faustus who had been a deadly snare to many now began to release me from the trap in which I had been caught" (V, 7).

THE ETHOS OF LANGUAGE

The *Confessions* present the Manichaeans as the final and the most dangerous manifestation of the sophists, grammarians, and rhetors who taught Augustine. The Manichaeans practiced the Asiatic aesthetic of copious rhetorical ornamentation,[27] and literary fiction in the pejorative sense was their principal concern (Augustine calls these *figmenta inania,* III, 6; *longis fabulis,* VI, 3; *phantasmata falsa,* III, 6 and III, 7). This activity is the seal of their folly (*dementia,* V, 5), of their delirium (V, 4), and of their senseless pride (*vesana superbia,* V, 5). Augustine assembles the evidence for his prosecution by showing that heresy has an ethical position toward language and its use:

> I fell in with a set of sensualists, men with glib tongues who ranted and raved and had the snares of the devil in their mouths. They baited the traps by confusing the syllables of the names of God the Father, God the Son Our Lord Jesus Christ, and God the Holy Ghost, the Paraclete, who comforts us. These names were always on the tips of their tongues, but only as sounds which they mouthed aloud, for in their hearts they had no inkling of the truth. (III, 6)

The Manichaeans are the worthy heirs of the Sophists and of Roman rhetoric. They hold that the pure signifier is the locus of meaning, in opposition to the Christian theory of language that continually tries to link the signifier to the truth of the thing, which grants the Christian the authority to spin as many metaphors as he wishes.

For Augustine, Manichaeism is a diabolical trap that leads directly to profanation and death. He wants to escape its "muteness," to untie the knot, to come unstuck from the glue, to stop the confused proliferation of signifiers. He must then formulate, all at once, a logic, an economy, an ethic, and the practice of the break (of homonymy). The whole problem is that the *Confessions* are not sufficient to the task because they are overwhelmed by all the impasses of language, depending, as they do, on rhetoric and the mortal nature of the signifier. Something Manichaean lies at the heart of any written theory or philosophy. Augustine himself makes the reader aware of this. In writing of his commentary on the Psalms, he knows that his reading is capable of being diverted from its meaning by the Manichaeans: "They would not have understood how this cry came from my inmost heart, when I was alone in your presence" (IX, 4).

The text must be assured of the authority of the blank language and of the listening of the heart, and so it appeals to the silent interiority/exteriority that is the trace of the Other. On the other hand, the signifier requires a practice and an experience (an incarnation) that authorizes it and legitimates it. The *Confessions,* being a text, cannot form the basis for a logic of rupture by themselves. They are in constant danger of equivocation with what they mean to overcome. There are two crucial examples, one regarding Augustine's mother, and the other, Manichaeism.

MONICA DREAMS

> She dreamed that she was standing on a wooden ruler,[28] and coming towards her in a halo of splendour she saw a young man who smiled at her in joy, although she herself was sad and quite consumed with grief. He asked her the reason for her sorrow and her daily tears, not because he did not know, but because he had something to tell her, for this is what happens in visions. When she replied that her tears were for the soul I had lost, he told her to take heart for, if she looked carefully, she would see that where she was, there also was I. And when she looked, she saw me standing beside her on the same rule. (III, 11)

Artimidorus of Daldis founded the ancient science of oneirology, the study of dreams. His system begins with the distinction of two categories of dreams. There are dreams inspired by the dreamer's past *(insomnia)* and those that predict his future *(visa).* Monica knows how to distinguish between dreams that are indicative of her own desire and those that are sent to her by God. What distinguishes *insomnia* from *visa* is, importantly, outside language and a fortiori outside the text. Monica's ability arises from a voiceless experience: "She always said that by some sense, which she could not describe in words, she was able to distinguish between your revelations and her own natural dreams" (VI, 13). Because of its indescribable perfume, the dream in book III is no doubt one of these true revelations, the divine response to human anguish, a response that Augustine will elsewhere call *visiones et responsae tua* (V, 9). The text explicitly calls this dream a *visum* (III, 9).

The dream is a place where the Other speaks. It is here that Monica learns what is previously unknown to her. The angel (the luminous young man) conveys an unconscious wisdom, and accordingly he causes the dreamer to observe things that she has not seen. We seem to be very close to Freud. The formula *"Ubi esset illa, ubi esset et me"* [Where she was, I was too] appears to be a precursor of *"Wo es war, soll ich werden"* [Where the id was, the subject will become]. The analogy between these two is limited by the fact that for Augustine, the unconscious reveals not a desire for death but the divine will. "God is unconscious,"[29] progressively, if incompletely, unveiled in the conversion.

The following day, mother and son interpret the dream. Whereas Augustine wants to twist it around so that its meaning is favorable to him (so that Monica will join him in Manichaeism), it is Monica who provides the key to the dream: Her son will repudiate his error and rejoin her faith. The dream thus structures the son's itinerary of conversion. This is not a purely spiritual journey; the dream is also a road map for Augustine's biography. Augustine leaves his mother to go teach pagan rhetoric first in Rome, then in Milan. In 388, he returns to Tagaste, city of his birth, to live a monastic life. He begins his activity as the bishop of nearby Hippo in 395. His life is a combination of a spiritual and a geographic grand tour in which he is separated from Monica and returns to her. She is both his starting point and his final destination.[30] The map described by the mother's dream is realized through the act of conversion, so that without the act, the dream would be an empty sign, an *insomnium* coming from a fantasy of the son who formerly interpreted the dream.

The day after his conversion, Augustine recalls the pregnancy of the maternal dream. "You converted me to yourself, so that I no longer desired a wife or placed any hope in this world but stood firmly upon the rule of faith, where you had shown me to her in a dream so many years before" (VIII, 12). The maternal dream is the origin of both Augustine's textual activity and his Christian practice. Divine law reveals itself in dreams; the law is the dream. Now we are faced with a double question: What is dreaming, if the rule of the Real (God) shows itself in a dream? What is it to wake up, if returning to the Real (and as a consequence to oneself) is to live out Monica's dream?

The *Confessions* interpret the Manichaean period, the peak of all textual fictions (sexuality, theater, rhetoric, literature) as a long, horrific nightmare (*phantasmatibus illis meis,* III, 1). In parallel, heretical doctrine is also dream food because its cosmo-theology is false. Continuing the metaphor, this doctrine cannot nourish the spirit of its adherent because he is in the grip of fantasies. The homonymy of *visum* and *insomnium* can only occur through an appeal to a logical criterion of reality (the representation of the cosmos). In fact, the heretic is he who refuses to wake up. He wants to continue his dream of a fabulous mythology at all costs:

> The food we dream of is very like the food we eat when we are awake, but it does not nourish because it is only a dream. Yet the things they [Manichaeans] gave me to eat were not in the least like you, as I now know since you have spoken to me. They were dream-substances, mock realities, far less true than the real things which we see with the sight of our eyes in the sky or on earth. (III, 6)

Augustine's first reading of the neo-Platonists causes a jarring alarm to go off in his soul. His first intellectual steps toward conversion are also an encounter with the Real. The true text distinguishes itself from literary fictions through its effect: not one of phantasms of identification, but one of a return to the Real. The Manichaean folly literally goes to sleep, forgets itself, and is lost, while reason wakes up. In opposition to the heretics, who conceive of divinity as material, Augustine grasps the neo-Platonic truth of spiritual substance: "And I became drowsy and slept away my madness. I awoke in you and saw that you were infinite, but not in the way I had supposed. This I saw, but it was not with the sight of the flesh that I saw it" (VII, 14).

The next step, actual conversion (made concrete through the sacrament of baptism), is also described as a difficult waking from sleep:

> I bore the burden of the world as contentedly as one sometimes bears a heavy load of sleep. My thoughts, as I meditated upon you, were like the efforts of a man who tries to awake but cannot and sinks back into the

depths of slumber. No one wants to sleep forever, for everyone rightly agrees that it is better to be awake. (VIII, 5)

The conversion plays out the maternal dream of the *regula,* but not through a simple repetition. The circuit that Augustine travels in his conversion goes through a worldly experience outside the text. He has clearly demonstrated that desire and the text are aspects of heresy and that heresy is a phantasm and a dream. It then follows that any homonymy between this sort of dream and the dream of a divine law requires a passage through the empirical world.

ECONOMY AND LOGIC OF THE BREAK

The need to act out Monica's Christian vision through empirical practice intensifies at the moment of the ascetic conversion. Augustine must *really* cut the biography in two. To return to the *regula* is to abstain both from sexuality and from the rhetors' literary and poetic ambition. Augustine must pull up the very roots that carnal and spiritual fornication put down during adolescence: "The narrow means of my family obliged me to leave school and live idly at home with my parents. The brambles of lust grew high above my head and there was no one to root them out" (II, 3). The spiritual break is a symbolic castration, as Augustine writes after his conversion: "The voice of Truth had told me that there are some who have *made themselves eunuchs for the love of the kingdom of heaven.* But he also said, Let only those *take this in whose hearts are large enough for it*" (*Confessions,* VIII, 1).

This passage operates on two parallel levels. On the first, the Christian is called to abstinence rather than to a real emasculation. This abstinence, however, is a symbolic break from the world, a break that mirrors the separation between the figurative and literal meanings of the Gospels. What is at stake in this demand is nothing less than the unity of the subject: "Truly it is by continence that we are made as one and regain that unity of self which we lost by falling apart in the search for a variety of pleasures" (*Confessions,* X, 29).

This unity can only remain utopic. The subject cannot bind together the elements torn apart in the schism that produces him, except at the final moment when the dead are resurrected. Simply put, unity cannot be had in human time. Just as Ostia's blank ecstasy, even though impossible, is the only way a fragmented human language can be made whole, so the human subject cannot do more than hope for reconciliation with himself. The body resists conversion, as the *Confessions* make clear with faultless analytical certainty. The ascetic does not have control over his obstinate and unconscious memories. His waking will cannot suppress the return of past pleasures in phantasms and representations. On its own, the body remembers each perverse pleasure attached to images and to rhetoric. The Real of the Incarnation has to be radically distinguished from an *incorporation,* the images of memory:

> But in my memory, of which I have said much, the images of things imprinted upon it by my former habits still linger on. When I am awake they obtrude themselves upon me, though with little strength. But when I dream, they not only give me pleasure, but are very much like acquiescence in the act. The power which these illusory images have over my soul and my body is so great that what is no more than a vision can influence me in sleep in a way that the reality cannot do when I am awake. (X, 30)

The *Confessions* assert that the subject is divided by the existence of unconscious desire. No matter in what it consists, this division produces an obscure area in the subject that conversion cannot eliminate:

> It is deplorable that within me is such a dark night *[plangandae tenebrae]* that hides my true nature from me such that when my spirit questions itself on its own movement, it does not dare have too much confidence in itself. For that which is hiding within it remains a mystery if experience does not reveal it. (X, 32)

From this comes the superb formula of the *Confessions:* "There is such a difference between myself and myself *[tantum interest inter me ipsum et me ipsum]* between that moment when I fall asleep, and when I wake up again" (X, 30). Here sleep stands for all the phantasms of fiction. It clings to the very essence of human representation and language, and so sleep can never be fully dismissed in the daylight of faith and enlightened consciousness. This is why the desire for unity with the mother, with faith, and with oneself (for it is all one) develops with complete rigor from Monica's dream. In human time, the subject can never claim to be entirely awake unless he should recognize his inadequate hold on the Real. The dream as *insomnium,* as the phantasm of desire, which appears as literature, fiction, and Manichaeism, threatens the subject at every step. The Christian break brings about a deferral that is forced to repeat itself. One cannot dismiss the past, time, representation, the body, or the unconscious. For this reason, rhetorical fiction cannot be fully repudiated. Even though the text strains with all its might to do just that, it can never achieve its goal. It is impossible to wake up from all dreaming, renew all words, and in a final absolute homonymy dismiss all ambiguity.

PROSOPOPOEIA

The schools of rhetoric in late antiquity frequently assigned exercises in paraphrasing. In order to improve upon a text, whether verse or prose, one need only rewrite it in prose. Quintilian made such paraphrasing a literary genre in its own right, and his work lies at the origin of the prose transcriptions that emerge in the thirteenth century.[31] As a schoolboy, Augustine was not exempt from these exercises: "I had to recite the speech of Juno, who was pained and angry because she could not prevent Aeneas from sailing into Italy" (*Confessions,* I, 17). This apparently anodyne practice comes in for a severe condemnation. "I had been told that Juno had never really spoken the words, but we were compelled to make believe and follow the flight of the poet's fancy by repeating in prose what had been said in verse" (I, 17).

In paraphrase, the teacher perversely forces the student to lie. The highest form of this exercise is to rewrite Virgil, which is to say, pagan fictions, both religious and literary. Such paraphrase represents simulacra—that is, the ancient divinities, made by humans—and causes them to speak. For this reason, we can rebaptize it. It is a prosopopoeia that gives speech to a double void: first, that of the pagan past (whose death gives no authority to the lines, which is the exact contrary of the martyrs), and second, that of a nonexistent divinity.

This perverse straying into fiction is repeated later in the text, where it takes on erotic connotations (still in accord with fiction, as we have established more than once). Augustine presents, through a prosopopoeia, the voices of his past pleasures—the ones that keep him indefinitely from converting himself:

> I was held back by mere trifles, the most paltry inanities, all my old attachments. They plucked at my garment of flesh and whispered, "Are you going to dismiss us? From this moment we shall never be with you

> again, for ever and ever. From this moment you will never again be allowed to do this thing or that, for evermore." (VIII, 11)[32]

Prosopopoeia is one of the forms of fornication attached to fiction. It must be distinguished from the voice of the interior master and also from the voice of the angel who provoked the conversion in the garden in Milan, that voice from a nearby house, or from a divine source, that told him to take up the book and read (VIII, 12). This is a crucial moment in the autobiography, on a purely textual level, a prosopopoeia framed by writing and rewriting.[33] But this distinction, as we know well enough now, cannot be made within the *Confessions* because they take place in the diacritical space of words and language. Authenticity depends on language's Other (the thing, the Real, the Incarnation, the event). The entire autobiography calls for a double reading, caught inside the real event but always disappearing in its presentation and its necessary move to metaphor in a rhetoric of writing.

4

Knowledge and Lacunae: Martianus Capella

All we know of Martianus Capella, the author of *The Marriage of Mercury and Philology,* is what this one text wants to teach us, but we must consider the evidence with caution, for it is an integral part of the literary fiction. Critical conjecture places Martianus in Carthage sometime between A.D. 410 and 439, which makes him Saint Augustine's contemporary, give or take a generation. However, whereas Augustine was a Christian, Martianus's work represents one of the last coherent treatises on the structure of pagan knowledge.

The medieval schools elevated the *Marriage,* along with Isidore of Seville's encyclopedia, to the status of a pillar of culture and of pedagogy. Its anti-Christian thesis represents one element of the schizophrenic structure that everywhere haunts medieval culture, so it can be considered in its own right as the very "source" of the resistance to homonymy in the literature of the Middle Ages. It thus plays a crucial role in my project.

To interpret the *Marriage* presupposes paying a great deal of attention to its allegorical framework. Allegory, which is obviously at work in the first two chapters, relating the courtship and marriage of Mercury (communication, rhetoric) and Philology (knowledge), is not limited to this section of the book; rather, it extends throughout the entire encyclopedia. The text sets before itself a double mirror in which it is to be read.

Its reflections bounce between the fiction of a doctrine and the doctrine of fiction (allegorical framework) that establishes it. In this play of reflections, doctrinal statements bring the allegory into focus, and this allegory in its turn shapes knowledge. Located in this play are the indications of a desire to write; it is these indications that we will try to decipher.

STRATEGIES OF ENUNCIATION

From the very beginning of the text, Satire, as an allegorical figure, claims responsibility for the fiction. She is the muse who inspires the book, and she is also an indication of its genre. Satire (etymologically, a stew) tosses together passages from poetry and prose along with passages of diverse meanings in one signifying pot.[1] From the first page, Martianus uses a cryptic and equivocal language that designates two signifieds in the one name of his muse. As he writes to his son, who, in another mirror effect, bears the same name as his father, "I shall unfold to you a story which Satire invented in the long winter night and taught me by the dimming lamplight" (2).[2]

Under the general heading of "story" or tale or fiction, Satire dictates a model text to the author, her faithful, subservient spokesman and scribe. At the end of the text, Martianus repeats the muse's opening speech and describes its influence. Thus, the writer's apparent lack of responsibility frames the text: "Our garrulous Satire has heaped learned doctrines upon unlearned, and crammed sacred matters into secular; she has commingled gods and the Muses, and has had uncouth figures prating in a rustic fiction *[plasma]* about the encyclopedic arts" (998).

Satire produces and signs her doctrinal fiction as a *plasma* that has nothing at all to do with a Christian creation of the world. She mixes publishable knowledge with the unspeakable secrets of an initiate. She also repeatedly blames her stenographer for any defects in the compendium, reproaching him for the triviality of the work, calling it a collection of worthless nuts *[nuges]*, and comparing his mind to that of an old woman (997–1000). Moreover, the scribe presents himself as a *puer senex:* the child with the wisdom of the elderly, or the childish wise man—it is all the same. Like a sleeping priest, he contrasts with his homonymous son, who is emblematic of the serious (2).

The irony is obvious. Why should Satire choose a scribe of such limited talents to record her words?

These self-deprecatory lines, playing on the trope of affected modesty, are not anecdotal. They introduce us to the second great principle that guides our reading of the *Marriage:* the inherent irony of a discourse with a double foundation.

Let us return to the first axiom of our reading (that of the reflexive game between doctrine and allegory) to find the theory of irony in the fifth book, whose topic is rhetoric: "Irony is a pretense, commonly used by Cicero, and a striking figure, in which we say one thing and mean another" (523).

Satire whispers a model text, but one that is peppered with irony (the equivocation of meaning that in rhetoric, contains the subcategories allegory and metaphor). The treatise as a whole, then, must be read in a series of splits and reversals, as fable *and* as doctrinal exposé. Underneath allegory and mythological fable lies the seriousness of a knowledge (most likely that of an initiate) that we must decipher. In the very texture of the driest doctrinal abstractions, copies and paraphrasings, one must suspect a different meaning that obviates them, a hidden smile, even the echo of a burst of laughter. Because of this duplicity, the *Marriage* as a whole is a cryptogram, and for reasons that we can only begin to guess. Could it be a book of concealed pagan propaganda written at the very moment the Roman Empire is undergoing massive Christianization? Did Martianus address his work to a small circle of initiates who alone could grasp its secret scope as an introduction to the hermetic mysteries? A response is impossible, and besides, there is almost no need for a phylogenic explanation when ironic inversion and its reflexivity lead us to the heart of the principle of writing that governs the *Marriage.*[3]

A reflexive and ironic reversal holds sway over Martianus's masterful speech, and to such an extent that a mirror constantly sets a *reversed* caricature (an imaginary) before our gaze. At the beginning of book VIII, on astronomy, the muse heaps abuse on Martianus for having described Silenus's drunkenness, when he collapsed in a belching heap in front of the gods, provoking the Homeric laughter of the Elysians:

> While this animated mirth was at its height, Satire, who always considered it her responsibility to edify and reprove my thoughts, said, "You, Felix, or Capella, or whoever you are, with a sense to match the beast's whose name you bear [Capella, "she-goat"], are you going out of your mind with the intrusion of this unseemly jesting? You must realize that

> you have brought raucous laughter into a heavenly assembly and that it is a reprobate act in the eyes of the gods, and of Pallas in particular, to represent someone prating nonsense like a madman." (806)

Martianus appears to be in control of the space of divine representation, despite (or because of) his cognomen, which places his work in the sphere of bestial, capricious, feminized desire. The gods' laughter flies in the face of their impassive nature. Satire, opposed to the play of fiction, tries to drive this mastery out for the sake of the seriousness of science: "You would rather fashion cheap and silly fictions than listen to a girl discoursing on the stars" (808).

However, through this claim to be responsible for writing the scene with Silenus, Martianus for the first time demonstrates his creative independence from his muse. The positions held by the speakers are also reversed. Ironically, Satire's dismissal of poetic invention contains that very form of fiction:

> As Satire was reciting these lines, I succumbed again to the mood to banter, despite her prohibitions and stern rebukes. "A fine performance, my Satire," I said. "Has your choler made a poet of you? . . . What has suddenly happened to your ever-ironical and subtle contempt for the bombast and conceits of the poets, whereby you content yourself with chaffing and witticisms while consigning their poetry to the realms of absurdity?" (809)

In a sudden reversal, Satire's seriousness goes hand-in-hand with poetic delirium. From this point on, the reversal of positions becomes a reversal of textual mastery: Martianus now holds the dominant place. The switch is illustrated in the following diagram:

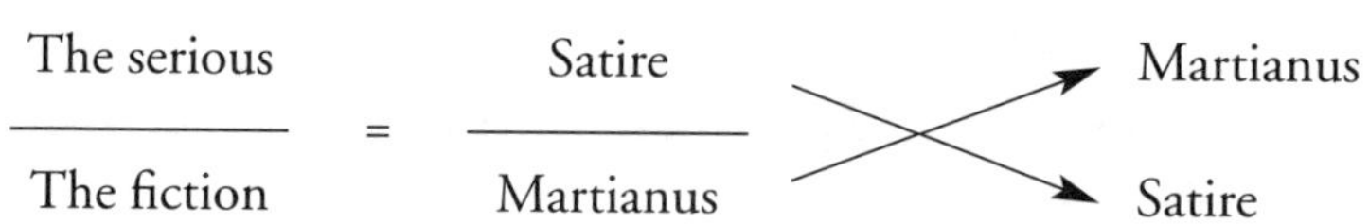

This alters the standard distinction between the types of speech, along with the one between the seriousness of knowledge and the playfulness of fable. The *Marriage* proclaims that the creative space of the mythological fable necessarily dominates the demands of rationality and of meaning. Silenus's drunkenness demonstrates allegorically the collapse of rationality into fiction's childish playfulness.[4]

In knowledge, there is the game; in playful fiction, a science. This shift is confirmed at the end of the second book and at the beginning of the third, an interlude where the text moves from allegory to doctrinal essay. Once again, the positions are reversed. Martianus declares with finality that his mythological discourse has been set aside. Although the role of entertainment is reduced, a new permutation appears. This time, the poet comes down on the side of the austerity of doctrine: "So now the mythological part is ended; the books which follow set forth the arts. With true intellectual nourishment they put aside all fable and for the most part explain serious studies, without, however, avoiding entertainment" (220).

Yet at the very opening of book III (about grammar, the key to all sciences), this virtuous resolution collapses. The muse, ordinarily a severe critic, is now a drunken poet: "Once again in this little book the Muse prepares her ornaments and wants to tell fabricated stories at first, remembering that utility cannot clothe the naked truth" (221).

According to Satire, the doctrine quite literally cannot be exposed to view. It must first pass through a metaphor. Furthermore, she conceals her own call for rationality (transmission with no remainder) and shows herself to be complicit in the baroque Asiatic aesthetic of the *Marriage:* "She regards it as a weakness of the poet to make straightforward and undisguised statements, and she brings a light touch to literary style and adds beauty to a page that is already heavily colored" (221).

Martianus's Asiatic aesthetic opposes the classical demands of an Attic style that privileges brevity, clarity, and propriety of terms. He relies instead on superfluity, addition, detour, and ornamentation. One need only look at book V ("Rhetoric") to find, in a mirror, Martianus's theory of style, under the heading of the *ducti* (direction, conduct) of legal cases (470). He distinguishes five styles: simple, subtle, figurative, oblique, and mixed. The first of these is never used as such anywhere in the *Marriage,* unless it appears as a secondary rhetoric to demonstrate the effects of propriety. The others all rely on equivocation, double meaning, dissimulation, and meaning's metaphorical clothing *(integumentis vestitia).* We must note in passing that the allegorical, Asiatic style was the very one that guaranteed the success of the *Marriage* with medieval audiences, at the expense of more sober writings.[5]

Paradoxically, Martianus the poet balks at Satire's prohibition of the use of metaphor, even though she does little more than restate the author's aesthetic principles: "'But,' I cried, 'in the previous book notice is given that the myths have been put away and that the precepts in the volume which follow are a work of those Arts which tell that which is the truth'" (222). Satire responds, "Let us tell no lies, and yet the Arts are clothed. Surely you will not give the band of sisters naked to the bridal couple? . . . To say no more about embellishment, what is to be the program?" (222).

Martianus's answer follows a logic that, if it were to be carried through completely, would be that of a modern, Christianized science: A doctrine or a knowledge, if it is theoretically true, does not need the ornaments of either persuasive rhetoric or of a body (of an individual) to sustain them. Their usefulness is not tied to a particular enunciation: "Surely let them speak on their own teachings, and let them be clothed in incorporeal utterance" (222).[6]

Martianus here approaches Tertullian's statements about the *cultus,* linking it here to the nudity/truth (meaning, knowledge) of a body. But Satire's call for sexual abstinence has nothing to do with the Christian chastity of *On the Apparel of Women.* Satire ends the dispute once and for all and at the same time justifies the fables dear to her scribe: "Now you are deceiving me *[ficta]* . . . and are not consistent with your promise; why do you not admit that your work cannot be composed except by the use of imagery *[figminis figura]*?" (222).

At these words, the one who adheres to pure doctrine surrenders to the muse's reasoning. But to whom, exactly, does he surrender? Not to a model of knowledge that presupposes a (naked, obscene) first meaning, clothed afterward with rhetorical ornament, a secondary clothing. Instead, the surrender is to a theory of meaning that claims there cannot be knowledge independent of the framework of a rhetorical fiction. In such a system, nudity/truth has no existence or essence of its own. Always and forever, it is metaphor; and obscenity, no longer attached to nudity, moves to the arabesques of the Asiatic style. Correctly speaking, there is no doctrine, nor is there a doctrine of correct speech, because this always depends on what comes before and what dominates it. Without contorting the text beyond recognition, one can even state that for Martianus the essence of language is fiction, so it is all the same whether one produces a doctrinal exposé or a mythological allegory. Whether the author is aware of it or not, his writing or speech comes from the absence that founds language, and this absence drains discourse of its contents, no matter what they may be. The muse is telling us that nothing escapes the law of fiction: "Your work cannot be composed except by the use of imagery" *[figminis figura nil posse comparari]* (222).

This foundation has repercussions for the status of the ornament. As was the case with the Sophists and the Latin rhetors, *vestitio* is the locus of thought and truth, the *plasma* of a world of seductive statements that need not refer to anything else so long as they are plausible. To make such a claim in the middle of the fifth Christian century is to rebel radically against the thingism of the Incarnation.

DESIRE, THE SOURCE OF KNOWLEDGE

To read the *Marriage,* one must assign a meaning to the text's two most prominent mythological figures, Mercury and Philology. One must also take into account the nature of their relation, their fictional courtship and marriage. Fortunately, the Carolingian commentators have cleared the way for us. To them, Mercury was the allegory for eloquence, and virgin Philology represented the love of reason (too readily identified with a theological *ratio;* I will come back to this).[7] Just as for Cicero, the need for their marriage arises only because they have been separated.

On the level of the fictional structure, the Mercury/Philology couple in the story mirrors and repeats the couple Martianus/Camena (another name for his muse, Satire), the couple of the framing fiction. Because it concerns precisely the divine Mercury/Philology couple, the writing of the *Marriage* places its entire project back into question in a reflective movement. With this in mind, we see that Mercury reinforces the "lustful," "capricious" side that Satire has already brought to light in the name Capella. Mercury thus stands not only for the transmission of meaning in the seductions of eloquence, but also, even more, for the circulation of a phallic desire (which amounts to the same thing) that his mother tries to master:

> She [Juno, Mercury's mother] was concerned about him, especially because his body, through the exercise of wrestling and constant running, glowed with masculine strength and bore the muscles of a youth perfectly developed. Already with the first beard on his cheeks, he could not continue to go about half naked, clad in nothing but a short cape covering only the top of his shoulders—such a sight caused the Cyprian [Venus] great amusement. With all this in mind, he decided to marry. (5)

He must, then, marry sapience, because if desire and the transmission of meaning are left with no control over their wanderings, they breed monsters: "She [Juno, goddess of marriage] urged that the marriage take place quickly, before the Cyllenian [Mercury], enticed and inflamed by the Cyprian [Venus], was impelled to father a brother for Hermaphroditus" (34).

With impressive self-certainty, Martianus moves to join the quicksilver of desire not only to the persuasions of eloquence but also to all of artistic activity. Mercury's sublime love for Philology has inspired him to excel in poetry, painting, music, and sculpture (36). In the *Marriage,* the forbidden desire for pleasure is the origin of art. With good reason, Jupiter worries about the outcome of the marriage: Will the zeal of the artist disappear in nuptial languor? Juno reassures her noble husband. Philology, symbol of the world of knowledge, whose face bears the praiseworthy pallor of the scholar, will be able to reestablish the prohibition necessary for desire's survival (37). Mercury is the symbol for a poetics that the *Marriage* soon develops more fully, and he is an image *en abyme* for Martianus's activity as a writer.

After much deliberation, Jupiter invites the goddess Fraud, Mercury's companion, to the wedding (51). Ereainus later draws attention to the way Martianus is using this allegory to lay out his text's essential relation to lying and to the essential equivocation of language.[8] By choice, the writing of the *Marriage* places itself under the sponsorship of a symbol that is neither good nor evil because it hides both the true and the false equally. Mercury is also the god of commerce and so controls the wealth produced by the circulation of both merchandise and meaning (*lucorum potenti,* 180). This vignette invites us to decode its *copia,* the abundance of its discourse, which is one of the basic elements of Martianus's Asiatic aesthetics. This *copia* also refers to the infinite circulation of signifiers in the *Marriage*'s theory.

Philology herself invites us to identify Mercury with the text when she turns to mathematical speculation to determine whether the auspices are good for her marriage. In her Pythagorean system, each letter of the alphabet, by its position, corresponds to a number. Applying this to Mercury's secret name, Philology comes up with the number associated with Theut or Thoth, the Egyptian god who invented writing.

In addition, Mercury circulates as a signifier in all the domains of knowledge. As a planet, he has a place in astronomy/astrology; and by virtue of the music of the spheres, he is also a note on the scale. This god, who is both the object of a doctrine and a desiring, acting subject in an allegory, is the perfect symbol for Martianus's project.

AN INCONSISTENT HIERARCHY

How must we understand Philology, the exact opposite of the desire to write? The feminine sex assigned to her is just as significant as Mercury's masculinity. In Martianus's system, the woman has a mastery over masculinity. For example, Jupiter, whose will ought to be the law of the world, is dominated by Juno (3). It is she who gives final sanction to the marriage (30). Philology, a woman, knows more than Mercury and thus knows things that the gods do not, things that extend from heaven to hell. She also has the gift of prophecy (22).[9] Her spirit is as swift as the planets (93), and the *septennium* of the liberal arts are this masterful woman's servants. These seven allegorical virgins, in Philology's train, frequently declare their dominion over the whole of the cosmos. In a most Pythagorean conception, Arithmetic not only produces a world, but she also produces the number one, which gives birth to Jupiter's unique and primordial nature (730). As a result, the divinities recognize her as the mother *(parentem)* of their essence (803). As for Rhetoric, she upsets a fundamental concept of Greek theology when she frightens all of Elysium with her blaring trumpets, placing the gods' impassivity in question.

The *Marriage,* which describes the celestial hierarchy, also contains a deep-seated instability. On the one hand, the arbitrary will of the gods is presented, as it should be, as the law of the entire cosmos: "What the gods decide is law" (21). On the other hand, Philology and the *septennium* control divine law. This seems inconsistent, but it is not incoherent. The fundamental irony that underlies the treatise also permits a description of a divine hierarchy in constant turmoil (just as does the relative positions of Martianus and Satire).

This turmoil is confirmed in the stratifying of the various domains of knowledge. In the opening preamble to each book, each of the arts claims to be the unshakable foundation of the others. Martianus takes no pains to state otherwise, except to start with Grammar and finish with Music. This instability in the overall structure effects the very organization of knowledge.

At a distance of five centuries, the *Marriage* repeats Cicero's model of knowledge (I will decode it below when I discuss the harmony of all knowledge), but it radicalizes the model's consequences. Cicero's hierarchical system is replaced with anarchy.

REPETITIONS AND LACUNAE

One could easily think that Hymen, the god of conjugal union, oversees both a sexual and a creative coupling between the two poles of an opposition (1). On one side, there is masculinity, desire, rhetoric, art, play, and the comic; on the other side, femininity, sublimation, suppression, science, and the serious.

But Hymen does nothing of the sort. Taking a closer look at the figure of Philology, one discovers that she moves in a sphere very close to Mercury. Among other proofs of this is the elegy by Clio, the muse of history, who praises Philology's talents as a rhetorician. Ironically, all the ambiguities of rhetoric now hold sway over wisdom:

> You sound forth in the guise of a rhetorician and set free by your passion the man accused, you link together contrary sentiments, building up sophisms by heaping together arguments, now binding something together by the rule of grammar, clever at using your gift of fine speech to play with words that by their double meaning destroy the ordinary sense. (122)

Philology's connection, first and foremost, is to words, and she thus has no connection to the thing (which would make the study of philology a science). She influences the whole *septennium* from books III to IX of the *Marriage.* Philology has a role in the obliqueness, irony, and equivocations of knowledge, which make this knowledge the double of sophistry. The doctrine must be read first as a metaphor (the work of words) and only then as knowledge (a writing about things).

Everywhere there are clues that knowledge gives itself voluntarily to metaphors. The purpose of Rhetoric's argument in the book devoted to her is not to find a path toward certainty; rather, it is "a means of producing credence in a matter of doubt" (474). This definition is typical of those arguments from the fields of legal or political speech, where the demonstration never claims to establish a truth, but instead claims only to create a plausibility. Only by turning to Lady Dialectic could one find a theory of philosophical argument or scientific demonstration. One of Dialectic's primary attributes ought to be reason, yet the allegory in which she has a role contradicts this. Dialectic carries a venomous serpent in her left hand, which she keeps hidden under her cloak. She is not the procedure leading to reason, but a magician and a sorceress, associated with fraud (328). The *Marriage* transforms Dialectic into the double accomplice both of deceitful persuasion and of rhetoric.

Similarly, Martianus's linguistic theory does not escape irony. The definition of proper meaning that he proposes is obviously straight out of the classical tradition (proper meaning is that which distinguishes one thing from another). He repeats this definition in his chapters devoted to Grammar, Rhetoric, and Dialectic. But each time he illustrates the definition, he chooses an example with a double meaning: "[N]o one can laugh unless he is a man" (348). Everything associated with knowledge of the thing (the very property of language) seems to have changed into a farce. It is a comedy of metaphors, a *gaya scienza,* a parody of science. In the same (il)logic, Dialectic does not care about propriety, the contrary, or the analogy, even though it is their usage that she ought to regulate (360). In a knowledge where everything is irony and metaphor, these distinctions have no relevance.

Martianus's work goes a step further. All the books on doctrine demonstrate a refined practice conscious of their lacunae. None of Philology's disciples succeeds in laying out a complete knowledge. The gaps of the (false) encyclopedia are, every time, deeply indicative. Grammar begins to bore the Elysian audience, and so Minerva prohibits her from discussing tropes, ornamentation, or barbarism. These are precisely the sources of Martianus's baroque art (326). Minerva also interrupts Dialectic precisely at the moment where the latter would have unveiled the recipes for lying and thus would have confirmed her solidarity with Rhetoric: "The matters that remain are founded on great deceit, and false deception encompasses those who are caught by them, while you prepare sophisms fraught with guile, or seductively make sport with trickeries from which one cannot get free" (423).

Minerva thus censors both the lying equivocations of fiction and, more important, Martianus's very art of writing, insofar as it is fictional. Everything that the *Marriage* condemns comes back to it on the level of practice.

In another aspect, Martianus, in copying knowledge, does not simply repeat what has come before. He truncates, mimics, and apes this knowledge, accentuating the carnivalesque effect of the gay science.[10]

There is one very important lacuna that ironically gathers together all these incomplete knowledges. Martianus pays a great deal of attention to the courtship and the wedding preparations, yet he is silent when it comes to the wedding night. It is here that the *Marriage,* as a book and as a fiction, should come to its logical conclusion. The coupling of knowledge and delight is eliminated from the text. Martianus "cuts off" *[decidit]* his work.

There are two main pretexts for the repeated interruptions in the doctrine: Either the listeners are bored, or the exposé is delaying the marriage. Voluptas (Pleasure) cuts off Arithmetic at the very beginning of the latter's treatise because she feels that the mathematical mysteries are a poor introduction to a wedding night (725). In the opening to book IX ("Harmony"), Venus, the goddess of love, repeats this theme when she proclaims her disgust for compendia. One could deduce a real contradiction between knowledge and pleasure, between Philology, on the one hand, and Mercury, on the other. Very much the contrary: The *Marriage* proposes not a real antithesis but a diacritical opposition that latches onto the implausibility of the fictional framework. The difference between Mercury and his bride is a ruse; Mercury as a figure stands for the continuation of desire, and Philology (and with her each of the sciences) secretly symbolizes this as well. All of Martianus's efforts tend to make knowledge into a celebration in which Voluptas participates wholly. Visualizing the entire field of knowledge as an expansion of fiction (of literature), the *Marriage* produces a knowledge without sublimation. Let us recall that the Latin rhetor Quintilian limited delight to literature. Martianus surpasses him and makes knowledge in its entirety the pursuit of delight. For Martianus, then, all of ancient science has become literature.

Given that knowledge contains lacunae, can we then conclude that for Martianus, knowledge cannot be totalized? If it cannot, he would be a "modern" scientist (since Lacan's "nothing is everything" is the very definition of Galilean science). This is not the case. In the *Marriage,* the lacunae of knowledge in no way represent the scientific ideal; instead, they result from an ironic writing. Although each specific knowledge fails explicitly, the compendium as a whole, through a leap in logic, makes a claim of totalization that combines and subsumes all fields of study.

A GENERALIZED SYNONYMY: HARMONIZED KNOWLEDGE

Ancient (pre-Copernican) cosmology divides the universe into two realms. First there is the sublunar domain. This is the realm of change, instability, uncertain opinion, and work; no precise calculation can describe this world. Then there is the heavenly vault of the fixed stars. This is the realm of the eternal, the gods, certainty, and contemplation; this universe can be precisely measured and bears no relation to the sublunar world, other than analogy (in particular, that of the microcosm/macrocosm).

Taking up Heracleides Ponticus's (d. 322 B.C.) cosmology, Martianus very obviously remains close to this fundamental partition of the universe. For him, there is a *discidia,* a fundamental separation between human and divine things (893). But in what seems to be a paradox, this separation will give him the means to totalize his encyclopedia in spite of its lacunae.

Philology's role is crucial for this totalization. She must become immortal before she unites with Mercury, otherwise the union with the god would kill her. Through her, all knowledge of the sublunary world changes status. From being imprecise and unstable, it assumes the fixed certainty of immortality. Philology must literally vomit all the books of science before she can begin her voyage into the celestial spheres to be judged by the Elysians. If Martianus's writing is a knowledge-filled horn of plenty, this representation of it is very striking. It is as if all of Martianus's knowledge were being labeled as filth. To compare knowledge to a foul liquid is an offense that the text makes up for immediately through Athanasia (Immortality), who carves these books in stone. In so doing, she also changes the uncertainty of the sublunar into eternally fixed and correct ideas (136–38). In order to withstand her celestial voyage, Philology drinks an immortality potion that her mother, Phronesis (Wisdom), gives her:

> When Philology received this, being extremely thirsty after such physical ordeals and seething of her mind [the vomiting of knowledge] once the secrets of the sphere [which is a "living sphere"] had been revealed and she had discovered its extreme sweetness, she drank it in a draught:
>
> and straightaway her limbs are strengthened with new vigor,
> her fragile thinness passes, the power of earth leaves her,
> and there comes to her the immortality of heaven,
> free from the laws of death. (140)

Philology's metamorphosis is from transitory to eternal, from uncertainty to truth. This scenario, appearing as it does in the fifth century A.D., is strikingly anti-Christian. Even more important is Martianus's sleight of hand. Before our eyes, he transforms Philology, and thus all the knowledge contained within the *Marriage,* into something immortal and immutable. By design, this metamorphosis is of the order of myth, of fiction, since it depends entirely upon a *pharmakon,* a (verbal) magic that reveals its results to be a phantasm.

In the final analysis, Philology, through her transformation, becomes the disincarnation of the knowledge she represents. By becoming a goddess, she loses her body, and in a very Greek fashion, she begins to appear in a simulacrum. Martianus's move repeats that of Christian Docetism (in an entirely different spirit). His knowledge also takes on the structure of a simulacrum when he confers divinity on Philology. It is entirely possible that the goal of this move is to produce an ironic reading of the Christian Resurrection. It may also be Martianus's way of twisting the Resurrection, in the manner of the Gnostics, back into a pagan knowledge.

On another level, the whole of the treatise repeats this trajectory. It succeeds in totalizing all the fields of knowledge by starting in a science of the letter and winding up in music. If our goal is to understand Martianus's method, we must go to the core of his deeply analogical thought. Martianus begins with a unique conception of the signifier.[11] In the *Marriage,* the signifier (discussed by Grammar, Rhetoric, and Dialectic) is also a number based on its position in the alphabet, so it is also part of the field delimited by Arithmetic and Geometry. Furthermore, because signifiers/numbers allow one to calculate the positions of the planets in the celestial spheres, they also come up in Astronomy's field. The planets are also gods, and so mythology as well has a part to play in the knowledge of the signifier, even if Martianus does not give mythology its own book. Finally, the planets correspond to musical notes (the harmony of the spheres), which means that the signifier also has a place in Music's domain. The signifier thus harmonizes things and discourses.[12] It is the *stoichion* (basic element) both of the cosmos and of the knowledge of the cosmos. Universal analogy is thus the cause of inconsistency both in the system of knowledge and in the celestial hierarchy. The anti-Christian goal of the *Marriage* is to make each of its mathemes and each of its letters into a symbolic signifier. Words and things are absorbed in a general process of synonymy without a care for their distinctions. Step by step (from synonym to synonym, analogy to analogy), this system moves from the notion to the thing and from one thing to another. There is no master signifier, no Christian thing that has the privilege of giving order to words and things. One need not establish a continuity to move from one field of knowledge to another, from one type of reality to another. Everything leads back to the same principle. In Martianus, metaphor is a law of synonymy; it is constant and universal; mercurial quicksilver is its best possible illustration.

However, there is a specific order at work in the doctrinal exposés. They are introduced by Grammar, which clearly highlights the preponderance of the signifier in the *Marriage*'s system. Harmony comes last in the sequence, and so the encyclopedia's crowning her over the others is justified. Very specific clues to this precedence arise before the conclusion. For example, in Arithmetic's speech, Martianus indirectly justifies the division of his work into nine parts: "The number nine is also the last element of harmony" (741).

Although Harmony introduces a new inconsistency into the text by attributing the movement of the planetary spheres to Jupiter (in the heaven of the true ideas) (911), she is in fact the true commander of the stars (they correspond to musical and mathematical intervals). She claims dominion not only over the other disciplines but also over the world (and hell) and knowledge: "O Harmony, verily surpassing the great divinities whose praises you have sounded; you have been able with your song to subdue Erebus, the seas, the stones, the wild beasts, and bring sensation to rocks" (908).[13]

Harmony also defines the different arts represented by the Muses, who have sung Philology's praises in book II. They are also nine in number, and each has been assigned her respective zone in the universe (seven belong to the gods, two to the terrestrial sphere) (see 741).

Furthermore, through the analogy of the microcosm to the macrocosm, Harmony governs man, assigning proportion to his members (923–24). Man, for Martianus, is a musical being first of all.[14] Harmony thus eliminates the distinction between mortals and divinities, and by so doing, she permits the marriage of Philology and Mercury.

As Arithmetic's twin sister, Harmony organizes the doctrine that unites knowledge of the signifier with that of numbers.[15] It is she who gives the encyclopedia its organizing principle.

Harmony, the orchestral director of the cosmos, man, and knowledge, binds together all the lacunae in the compendium and permits

Martianus to bring about the aesthetic totalization of his discourse. Although Harmony's dominion over knowledge takes place in fiction (analogy, myth), her position is confirmed in the *Marriage*'s stance toward philosophy. Camena, Martianus's muse, accuses him in Geometry's book of having omitted philosophy from the catalog of the sciences (576). Martianus responds that this is because philosophy's knowledge is not reasonable; rather, it is a confused, obscure, uncertain mass whose form resembles a labyrinth (580). Aristotle is ridiculed when "Entelechy" (Aristotle's "Final Cause") is driven out. The obscure and noisy disputes of the philosophers are a cacophony that the Muses' songs reduce to silence (213). Purely rational (and discordant) knowledge is summarily dismissed, to make way for Harmony's supremacy. The positive knowledge of the treatise may not have been its reason for existing, even if the medievals did think so when they repeatedly copied the content of the exposés. Instead, this knowledge may have a rhetorical effect as its goal. Martianus's seriousness calls the reader to assent to his doctrine and hides his ulterior design: to promote an aesthetic and musical conception of the world.

Harmony, the supreme goddess of the *Marriage,* strengthens Martianus's intense opposition to Christian discourse on two key points: its origin and its form. Martianus creates a new, not involuntary, inconsistency when discussing Harmony's genealogy. On the one hand, she is Venus's daughter (909), a fact that unites the cosmos and all knowledge in one goal: the pleasures of love. On the other hand, she declares that the revolution of the spheres is her mother, and the matter of the universe is her father (as they are for her twin, Arithmetic). This origin obviously contradicts her role as the world's harmonizer. The treatise therefore assigns her to two antithetical positions, that of the creator and that of the creation. Harmony, commander of the world, refers back to the uncreated universe of Greek theology. Her unstable genealogy runs counter to the Christian discourse on music and creation, for which Saint Augustine, Boethius, and Cassiodorus are the principal sources. They certainly agree with the concept of the music of the spheres *(musica mundana)* without questioning it.[16] But unlike Martianus, these thinkers deduce from it a proof of the existence of the Creator. Furthermore, they see this proof as being reinforced by the harmony of the world. As the heirs of the *Marriage*'s pagan viewpoint, the church fathers produce a complete homonymy in this proof of the existence of the

Creator. Although their doctrines bear a resemblance to one another, Martianus and the church fathers give what seems to be a common element different meaning. Martianus tries to make a pagan doctrine survive, and the church fathers try to destroy it.

Martianus's repugnance for direct discourse, the right word, and Attic aesthetics has its reflection in the very form of his encyclopedia. The circular, cyclic character of the music of the spheres *[curvatio sphaerae]* is a marvelously apt metaphor to describe all oblique aesthetics. There is a "curvature" to the *Marriage,* just as there is to the profound nature of the knowledge it brings forth. The disciplines are cyclical [*cyclicas,* 998], or, if one prefers, they are etymologically en-cyclo-pedic, encompassing all teaching. Martianus finds several meanings in the circle of the disciplines. We take our cue here from Remigius of Auxerre, who saw the circle as a symbol for perfection.[17] It also stands for the difficulties of the unmasterable arts, which, for this reason, have "no beginning or end." This serpentine knowledge (swallowing its own tail) furthermore points to the pagan great year, the eternal return of the same that can be demonstrated to be the profound structure of thought in the *Marriage.* Through this doubling back, Martianus refers to a circular structure of knowledge, a structure that the church fathers attempted to banish definitively in the name of the Incarnation. The Incarnation presupposes the linearity of time and of the concept, which is to say, their historicity. Martianus, breaking with Christian discourse, constructs an aesthetic of knowledge in which the same eternally returns to the same place, producing a celestial music in its circumlocutions. This production has nothing of the gratuitous or trivial, since, like literature for Quintilian, it is part of a generalized economy of desiring impulses. It is the aesthetico-erotic evaluation of the world and its representations.

THE CAROLINGIAN REREADING

To interpret the *Marriage* as merely rewriting pagan knowledge would be an abuse of the text. Five centuries after the Incarnation, it takes its place in the dialectic created by the production of Christian dogma, and it represents a profound disputation of all that the church taught. The medieval school (which is ecclesiastical in origin and spirit) took the *Marriage* to heart as a reference work. And yet, as far as we know, only one theologian denounced this falsely canonical text as satanic. Prudence of Troy, polemicizing against Johannes Ereginus in a debate over predestination, attacks his opponent for making frequent references to Martianus's text. For him, it reeks of the sulfur of the labyrinth; one would be better off meditating on Scripture or on Augustine's *De civitas dei.*[18] In Prudence's rigorous vision, there is a striking antithesis between the *Marriage* and Christian teaching. Even though Prudence's attack only has a small effect at the time (Martianus was immensely popular until the Renaissance), he chooses its target well. Ereginus and Remigius of Auxerre are the ones most responsible for the integration of Capellian disputation into Christian discourse. This absorption of a discourse occurs in a fundamental hermeneutic move (which the followers of the Scottish doctor will apply to all the literary movements of antiquity). In the preamble to the *Annotationes in Marcianum,* Johannes Ereginus draws a distinction between mythology's apparatus of fable and the apparatus of the truth. On the one hand, there is lasciviousness, poetic petulance, and instability. The author of the *Marriage* gives free reign to knowledge, but in accord with his cognomen's fantasies. On the other hand, allegory conceals the "true philosophy," understood as a knowledge in accord with the message of the biblical revelation. Beginning with this fundamental distinction, Ereginus sets about trying to separate the wheat of wisdom from the chaff of fiction. With great caution, he points out each occurrence of the fable with *finxerat,* "he invented." With equal care, he also comments at length on mythology, thereby producing one of the Middle Ages' most important reference works on ancient culture. Christian interpretation, as we can see, begins its work by distinguishing fiction from doctrine. This procedure is a clue to its weakness (since it unravels what Martianus, as we have shown, knits together, "marries") but also to its ability to absorb contradictory views. To do this, it suppresses what does not match Christian doctrine; what is suppressed reveals itself in fictional literature. Subsequent commentators see no use in coming back to this point. Once the mythological and pagan bases of his text are neutralized by the arrival of fiction (which becomes literally "incredible" under the pen of the church fathers), Martianus assumes the function of an "official" and admired writer.

As a result of Ereginus's reading, the phylogenesis of medieval culture appears in its full schizophrenia. Under its apparent harmony lie two fundamentally opposing currents. One can follow their traces as they reemerge through the centuries. On the one, canonical, hand, there is the referential rhetoric of the Incarnation; on the other hand, we find an aesthetic and an erotic of the world that has no limit in the pleasure of its infinite metaphors. Isidore of Seville, an heir to Martianus and a predecessor to Johannes Ereginus, attempts to synthesize these in the seventh century.

5

A Divine Harmony: Isidore of Seville

Bishop Isidore of Seville takes up the encyclopedic project two centuries after Martianus, his pagan predecessor, from whom he borrows heavily.[1] His compendium, the *Etymologies,* more complete than *The Marriage of Mercury and Philology,* assembles the shreds of knowledge left over from late antiquity.[2] Like the *Marriage,* it also enjoyed immense popularity in the medieval *schola,* where its Christian conceptual framework distinguished it formally from the *Marriage.* So in keeping with my working hypothesis, this difference cannot help but be felt at every level of knowledge that comes to light.

THE REALISM OF THE *ETYMOLOGIES*

On the first level, Isidoran thought seems to rely on the fictional and mythical prestige of an absolute realism very close to Martianus's use of metaphor and analogy. For Isidore, the name is precisely adequate to the understanding of the thing: "The name of a thing is a notation *[notamen]* that, in its naming, gives us knowledge of the thing. If one does not know the name, knowledge of the thing perishes" (I, vii, 1).[3]

Using etymology, Isidore can then unfold the order of the world and its causes. This entails a hermeneutic thinking of origins, similar to Tertullian's *praescriptio.* The precedent, that is, what came first, is always privileged and is held to be closer to being: "When you know where the name comes from, then you will more fully understand it. The study of all things is made easier with knowledge of etymology" (I, xxix, 2). One need only reduce words (and even letters) to the simple, the first, the one, or the elementary. Isidore here proceeds by an analogy of the unknown to the known: "Analogy, a Greek word, we call in Latin the comparison or proportion of similarities. It works by comparing what is doubtful to something similar that is certain and by demonstrating the uncertain by the certain" (V, xxviii, 1).

Isidore's thought, with its doctrine, founds an entire segment of medieval fictional writing, and like fiction, it is guided by language. Because it is structured in accord with language's echoes and phonetic resemblances, Isidore's etymology is thus poetic etymology (which has nothing to do with that of philologists).[4] Grammar, etymologically the science of the letter (or in our terminology, of the signifier), is both the key and the door to the *Etymologies.* It has this in common with the *Marriage:* "Grammar is the science of speaking rightly *[recte]* and the origin and foundation of the liberal arts" (*Etymologies,* I, v, 1).

What needs to be clarified, then, is how Isidore's literal (and literary) ontology differs from Martianus's musical knowledge. First of all, we can point out certain superficial differences between the *Etymologies* and the *Marriage.* On the level of style, Isidore has a taste for an impersonal Attic style emphasizing clarity, precision, and brevity in opposition to Martianus's baroque Asianism. Isidore privileges "direct" discourse over "African" curvature and ornament. "The direct [without detour] that walks in rectitude [in a straight line]" *[directume, qui in rectum vadit],* he writes in book X, 69. His very clear-cut decision in favor of the propriety of language runs counter to Martianus's use of equivocal metaphors. The *Marriage* has an aristocratic spirit, and it includes only the liberal arts (those that "liberate" one from physical activity). The *Etymologies,* on the other hand, include the most humble manual arts, no doubt under the influence of Christ the carpenter. All this has little influence on linguistic ontology, which for both authors is the domain of rhetorical poetry rather than of science.

The radical opposition between these two comes from what each uses as the totalizing force of his encyclopedia. Martianus incorporated the voluntary incompleteness of his knowledge with and through Harmony. But Isidore, despite his stated goal of completeness, makes no pretense to having achieved a totality. There are four principal reasons for this.

First of all, language has arbitrary words, whose etymology cannot be determined: "The ancients did not name everything according to its nature, but some were given names in according to their wishes *[placitum]* just as we give the names we wish to our slaves and our possessions" (V, xxxix, 3).

The master's (language's) arbitrary will outmaneuvers the master encyclopedist's desire. Naming things *ad placitum* fundamentally disrupts the possibility of a totalized compendium.

Second, the method of etymology always ends in a confrontation with silence. Its goal is the unknown ur-language that has no written record. It is then compelled to fall back onto a fiction of origins to recapture what is lost and to speak the first word.

Third, Isidore is aware that his method limits him to the Latin (and, to a much lesser degree, the Greek) world: "Place-names are indicated with many words because of the diversity of peoples. There are a great many barbarian names unknown to the Greeks and Latins" (I, xxix, 5).

The encyclopedia thus only covers that part of the world that speaks Greek and, of course, Latin. It admits its own inability to grasp the alterity of its "barbarian" exterior. In particular, the *Etymologies* excludes the Visigothic languages of Isidore's political masters by taking a secret cultural revenge on them. The Germanic language names nothing in the work, neither slave, possession, notion, nor thing. Even Isidore's dedication to King Sisebut is in Latin. He calls him both "master" and, as befits a Catholic bishop, "son." This of course means a spiritual son, but it also means a barbarian child (although from what we know of Sisebut, he was well-read), to whom Isidore demonstrates the wealth of the Latin culture.[5] However, this is not only a rhetoric of cultural superiority. By limiting itself to Greek and Latin, the *Etymologies* modestly, one more time, admits its incompleteness.

Finally, Isidore, despite his resemblances to and his borrowings and copying from Martianus, breaks completely with his forebear by introducing the Christian God into his work. This God is first conceived (unlike in ancient theology) as the Creator of the world—that is to say, at the same time, as the first etymological cause or thing: "There is nothing that does not have its origin in God.[6] He is called the Creator because He creates the whole of the world" (VII, i, 33). This privilege also extends to Christ, or in other words, to the Incarnation: "He is called Life because

He created. . . . Source because he is the origin [*origo,* or etymology] of things" (VII, ii, 21 and 28).

The difference is not merely metaphysical, arising in the cause or causes of physics and cosmology; it also touches on the origin and ontology of language. Faithful to the canonical tradition of negative theology, Isidore declares that no name can adequately describe the divine: "He is called ineffable not because he cannot be spoken of but because he cannot be in any way described by human intelligence or soul" (VII, i, 17).

The *Etymologies* find the limits of their knowledge in God because there is no etymological method that can describe him. This is the one notion that cannot be voiced in any language because God lies at the origin of words as well as of things. He is the absolute and limitless beginning. For Martianus, everything seems to be sayable in the bedlam of the *gaya scienza.* In the *Etymologies,* by contrast, writing works toward that which cannot be spoken and which thus forces writing to fall silent. The letter, words, and language become the traces of the Other, of a radical difference that they cannot indicate while speaking of it. From this, the *copia* of words and the superabundance of etymological glosses always refer back to and are reversed by the *inopia humana,* the failure of human language to name God and his properties: "Human imperfection makes us unable to speak [the true name of God], just as it does his other names, to the extent that that which is ineffable can be said in a variety of ways since no human word says anything appropriate to God" (VII, i, 32).

God opens holes in language. This origin of all etymologies cannot be comprehended in any of them, and so the encyclopedic cornucopia develops in inverse proportion to its ability to arrive at the first word.

Isidore uses God's ineffability to produce a homonymy between his Christian knowledge and the pagan knowledge of Martianus. It is noteworthy that this bishop of Seville devotes an entire treatise to this difference, a treatise in which he eliminates improprieties of usage and—what is more important for our purpose—the incorrect usage of "the pagan poets who bowed before the necessity of verse."[7] It is indicative that this distinction is drawn at all. Everything he writes seems to indicate that "poetry" and "paganism" were two words for the same thing, as if thought had to separate itself from one as well as from the other if it were to become truly "proper," or in another word, "Christian."

In the *Etymologies,* difference is a "subspecies of definition that the authors of theoretical treatises propose about similarity and difference" (I, 31). Synonymy and homonymy are glossed thus: "Synonyms, that is, plurinomy *[plurinomia]*, when there is one meaning in several words. Homonyms, that is, uninomy *[uninomia]*, when one word has several meanings" (I, vii, 14–15).

These are entirely scholarly "differences," and it goes without saying that they are strictly grammatical.[8] Yet in relation to Isidore's entire project, these etymologies take on an entirely new meaning. At stake in this difference is distinguishing between the same (that is, the ancient) of pagan thinking and the other (that is, the new) of Christian knowledge: the production of homonymy. Homonymy places the core of Isidoran thought *en abyme.* We cannot decode it by comparing it with other sources, either hypothetical or real. Just as Tertullian is, Isidore is caught in a contradiction: His etymological method, which reveres the ancient, the original, is in conflict with his vocation, which is inspired by the evangelical message that breaks with ancient tradition. He quotes Saint Paul (2 Cor. 5:17) on this point, and thus affirms his radical novelty: "Old things are passed away; behold, all things are become new" (VI, i).

Unlike the *Marriage,* the *Etymologies* cannot be considered only as poetic knowledge of the world (or more precisely, as the fiction that structures a science); even the fiction writers of the Middle Ages tapped heavily into it (probably in a calculated manner). Martianus ironically indicates the difficulties (on a scientific level) of a knowledge of the signifier culminating in metaphor and the aesthetic. Of course, the *Etymologies* in their turn also appear as a poetic in search of a first and secret language (that of literature), although the search admits that it has limits. For this reason, the encyclopedia is in touch with theology's Real and cannot be completely interpreted as literary. Isidore repeats the decisive break accomplished in the Incarnation, so in spite of his work's mythological realism, and because of his conception of the created world, he is a forerunner of modern science.[9] To demonstrate this, we need only replace the *Etymologies'* First Cause with the material universe of modern science. In other words, we need only prohibit any reference to God as the cause or the explanation of phenomena (in the seventeenth century, Galilean science makes just this move).[10] It becomes immediately obvious how Isidore's work goes beyond Martianus's: The absolute realism of language finds its limit in the ineffability of God.

Many centuries later, this limit allows modern science to emerge. In the *Marriage*'s system, language is unbounded (even if the *Marriage* does present a functional knowledge in its allegory). Isidore's step beyond his predecessor presupposes a necessary corollary, the letter *X*, the physicality of the Incarnation. Through it, the body, matter, work, and world become sanctified, worthy of interest, and capable of investigation. The gloss on the Eucharist makes this clear:

> Although the body and blood of Christ are made of the fruits of the earth, they are sanctified and become a sacrament in the invisible working of the spirit of God. Thus the sacrament of bread and wine is called "Eucharist" by the Greeks, which means "good thanks." And what could be better than the body and blood of Christ? (VI, xix, 38)

Seen in this way, Christ's *X* (the first letter of his name in Greek) is not merely a "signifier referring to another signifier." This letter also indicates a mysterious cause, but one that can be potentially calculated.

Isidore's legacy is crucial to medieval thought. It is not because he thinks there is a propriety to language that he is a realist (the *Etymologies*' realism is mythical, and poetic etymology immediately overtakes it); rather, he is a realist because he declares totalization to be impossible, in contrast to Martianus, for whom music is the totalizing force. Isidore gives the medieval tradition, before its time, the possibility of thinking in "modern" terms, of developing a system of knowledge in which "nothing is everything."

THE COMPILER'S TOPO-GRAPHY

Isidore claims to transmit preexisting knowledge as a copyist who, although he does annotate, does not refer to anything he himself has discovered. He continually points to other, more ancient ways of knowing.[11] This enunciative position, always in reference to something else, seems to keep its paradigm hidden and thus to prevent us from defining it with any precision. The encyclopedist's identity disappears in the recopying of knowledge's commonplaces, and the Attic style gives him the mask of neutrality; he takes shelter behind a mass of scholarly writings, glosses, extracts, and compilations (late antiquity held all of these forms in high esteem). In addition, the gesture of etymological discovery itself is already discussed in ancient rhetoric, and so it is a repetition of what has already occurred. Just as a word derives its propriety from its antiquity, the more a fragment of knowledge is copied, the further it goes back in time, the more authority it accrues.[12]

Also adding strength to Isidore's rhetorical position is the fact that the privilege of creation (of producing what is radically new) is reserved to God, as we have already seen. As Tertullian would have wanted it, not only is the encyclopedia's compiler deprived of the prerogative of invention, but also, and for the same reason, scientists and artists must repeat rather than create.

The precise image that Isidore held of his own writing becomes clear when we interpret, as in a mirror, the *Etymologies'* definitions as so many examples of his gesture of writing. The text itself authorizes just such a critical move. First of all, the word "mirror" is assumed in a logic and an aesthetic of addition: that of rhetorical ornamentation. The compiler also has an interest in this aesthetic, since he "reflects" ancient knowledge and gives it a supplementary beauty in the act of copying it: "Women look at their own faces in mirrors *[specula]*. They are thus called either because they reflect their splendor, or because women inspect the state of their face and add the adornment that seems to be lacking" (XIX, xxxi, 18).

And then, in the definition of his own title in the city of Seville, *episcopi,* Isidore discusses *en abyme* his own encyclopedic function, both in particular and in general. In effect, the bishop is a *speculator* who reflects another (for example, knowledge) and redirects it for future use by giving himself over to ethical, scientific, or philosophical speculation: "The Greek word *episcopi* is translated in Latin as *speculatores;* a *speculator* stands before the church. He is called this because he observes *[speculatur]* and he oversees the morals and the lives of those sheep in his protection" (VII, xii, 12).

Although each definition potentially refers to the work of the compiler when it reflects this work, I will focus my commentary on certain key words that frame the concept of writing.

In the first place, Isidore is a *lector:* "He who gathers in his own soul *[colligendo animae]* all that he reads is a collector just like one who hoards" (VII, x, 154). To decode traditional knowledge is far more than simply to become familiar with it; it is to internalize this knowledge actively. Again, encyclopedic activity is not at all the simple amassing of disparate facts; rather, it is an act of profound linkage, the unification of the diverse. The fragments of antithetical knowledge available to late antiquity are made uniform and clear.

Logically, this gives rise to the definition of the *compilator:* "He who mixes foreign speech with his own is like a paint merchant. He piles together many colors in one mortar" (X, 44). The compiler fuses same and other. If he is skilled, he makes their boundaries invisible. From mixture and diversity (these are rhetorical and poetic, but also metaphysical), a new coloring is born, one that amalgamates the hetero- and homogeneous and hides their construction.

And finally, the *inventor* is as described in traditional rhetoric: "He who finds what he has sought" (X, 122).

Isidore does far more than copy the commonplaces *(topoi)* of knowledge as he takes inventory of them in his textual warehouse. By combining them anew, he at times radically reinvents the cultural tradition that he has before his eyes.

For centuries, the Middle Ages practiced writing (both fictional and doctrinal) according to the definitions of the *Etymologies.* Theology prohibited the age from creating, so it found its inspiration in the inventive rereading of what was already written. It actively produced a collage of heterogeneous knowledges, of rhetorical and fictional topoi. These practices must be thought of as powerful means to novel creation, and not as pale imitation or sterile repetition (as the romantic dogma of originality would have it). Through his invention, working through the gaps in the pre-text, the "author is he who augments" *[auctor est qui auget]* (X, 2) by redeploying what is already known and has been said a thousand times.

PAGAN FICTION

Isidore, as a worthy heir to Tertullian and Augustine, is everywhere hostile to the poetics and mythology of antiquity. He writes in the *Sentences,* "Christians must not read the inventions of poets *[figmenta poetarum]* because with the bait of vain fables they catch the spirit on the hook of the passions."[13] This is a stunning, even contradictory statement (that Tertullian or Augustine could have signed) from the pen of a bishop who returns repeatedly to precisely this source of cultural wealth.

The *Etymologies* continue and intensify this condemnation. First, the doctrine of the simulacra that it develops comes from a Christianized Platonism: "Simulacra are thus named either because they are similar *[similia]* or because they are simulated *[simulata]* and fictional *[conficta];*

because of this, they are false" (VIII, xi, 6). The position that the poets, these makers of simulacra, occupy in the Isidoran structure is equally revealing. In book VIII, he discusses poets after Christian heretics. The "pagan philosophers" and the "sibyls" frame them. They also appear side by side with "magicians," "pagans," and other "pagan gods." In fact, the origin of the poet's art places him with the idolaters and in a way that seems irreversible. A quotation from "Tranquillus" (an unknown author) justifies this condemnation:

> When men drew themselves up from savagery and for the first time attempted to run their lives by use of reason, knowing themselves and knowing the gods, forming a reasonable cult and the necessary speech, they thought they had made a magnificent cult to their gods. Thus, as they built for them temples more beautiful than their [own] homes, and they made simulacra larger than their [own] bodies, they also thought to do them honor with more august eloquence, and they sang their praises with more illustrious words and more joyful rhythms. (VIII, vi, 6)

Therefore, the origin of poetry is idolatry. Pagan religion becomes literature, and literature becomes religion (both are "false," both are simulacra, but nevertheless they are signs of progress in the human spirit). This is the opposite of Tertullian's rigor.[14]

The view that the lying simulacrum conceals its own real basis reemerges in the distinction of the genres of discourse (many critics have commented on the following passage):

> These are the differences between history *[historia]*, argument *[argumentum]*, and fable *[fabulam]*. History is of true things that took place. Arguments are of things that did not happen, but could happen. And fables, assuredly, are of things that did not and could not happen because they are against nature. (I, xliv, 5)

As Fontaine emphasizes, the criterion of this difference is neither one of genre nor one of form.[15] It is the content, the signified of the discourse, that forms the *discrimen* of the types of discourse. It is a logical criterion taken from reality. To grasp those distinctions, we must imagine the difference according to the aim of the *Etymologies* as a whole. History must above all be grasped as "holy history," with Moses as its first author. It is defined insofar as it brings together the various histories of humanity. Furthermore, according to Isidore's text, it is the only kind of discourse having to do with the Thing and with reality. The *Etymologies* are thus a particular subcategory of this discourse.

Argument is the art of the plausible. It thus includes rhetoric. As for the fables, we can assimilate them into literature as pure speech without relation to an event or to the Thing. Elsewhere, Isidore clarifies this: "Poets draw their fables from the spoken *[fari]* word, because they do not happen but are created *[fictae]* by speaking" (I, xl, 1). Furthermore, since the essence of poetic fiction is to be nonnatural, Isidore emphasizes its identity with Lucifer's work.[16]

Servius, a commentator on Virgil and witness to late antiquity, allows us to note the radical opposition between Christian discourse and the pagan conception of fable. Although Servius believes fables to be against nature, for him they can either be allowed or not. History, which does follow nature, also can either be allowed or not. The criterion for discrimination is aesthetic. Conformity to nature, or the *discrimen* of the thing that the discourse is about, plays no role.[17] This is fundamentally different from Isidore's position, in which the sanction or the nonsanction of the thing comes first.

How, then, are we to explain Isidore's practice, which often turns to the fables of mythology and to citations from Roman literature? He seems to contradict his own theory/theology of pagan culture. However, even though fabulae have been rejected because they have no link with the Thing, they are nevertheless not devoid of semantic content. The fable is rehabilitated in a very particular way. Its goal can still be to produce pleasure, to interpret human actions, or to allegorically describe natural phenomena (I, xl, 3). For example, a crippled Vulcan stands for the nature of the flame, which is never straight. There also exist narrative fictions *[ficta narratio]* that have no relation to reality, but they are nevertheless less "carriers of true meaning" (I, xl, 7). Fiction thus equivocates between the reality that it shunts aside and the true meaning that it allegorizes.

UNIVERSAL HISTORY

Isidore's recourse to the whole of pagan knowledge finds its legitimacy elsewhere. The *Etymologies* divide human history into six periods and take great care to make them coincide with the birth of the great branches of Western culture (which for Isidore are the Hebrew, the

Greek, and the Roman cultures, and afterward the Christian culture, the only one with a universal vocation, for it no longer depends on a particular people or a particular language). These periods are

1. From Adam to Noah (the birth of Hebraic culture)
2. From Noah to Abraham
3. From Abraham to David (the birth of Greek culture)
4. From David to the Babylonian exile
5. From the Babylonian exile to the Incarnation (the introduction of rhetoric to Rome)
6. From the Incarnation to the end of time (V, xxxix, ff.)

The history of humanity is thus entirely related to a biblical genealogy. This chronology emphasizes the rupture of the Incarnation. After the break, no more ruptures (*aetas* is Isidore's term) are possible. This does not mean that nothing happens anymore; on the contrary, our historically eventful age is defined by just such a break. Instead, everything that happens is stamped with the seal of the Incarnation. History continues in a series of ruptures, but in a sense obviously different from the one I propose in this book.

Isidore knowingly takes up a myth of cultural becoming that focuses on discoveries. For example, he holds that the arts and technologies were invented by the Hebrew people.[18] In art, Moses invents the hexameter of epic poetry before Homer; the hymn is discovered by David, and the epigram by Solomon; rhetorical prose belongs to Isaiah; and before Apollo, Tubal creates the zither and thus music. In the domain of the sciences, Abraham discovers astrology before Atlas; and Genesis founds philosophy, ethics, logic, and physics and thus displaces the Greeks. The first historian is not Herodotus but Moses. Finally, Hebrew is the mother of all languages (X, i, 1). The Jewish people are the model for each encyclopedic project (especially Isidore's), and the compendium and its contents proceed from a divine origin at work on the chosen people. The Hebrews came before the Christians, but they also came before the Greeks and the Romans. They are the unique source of knowledge. The diversity of cultures that followed them shattered universal history. Isidore's task is to bring everything back together under the umbrella of a theocentric signified. The extension of his curiosity to all domains of knowledge is also justified. Using this fiction of Hebrew origins, Isidore is able to harmonize the schizophrenia of medieval knowledge that was discussed above.

There is no "thought" that unifies medieval knowledge. Rather, it is brought together by two formal acts of writing (two practices of fiction). To bring the various elements of medieval thought together in harmony requires that they be juxtaposed. If some of the fragments then appear to be antithetical, there must follow a discovery of their common origin in the Hebrews.

This gesture is elemental for medieval civilization. Through it, medieval Christians gain an orientation from which to reread pagan antiquity. Furthermore, every erudite Christian is now permitted to refer to the pagan basis of culture.[19] A perfectly adequate emblem for this harmony is the symbolism that Isidore confers upon the instruments of writing. Significantly, this is the only illustration that is of biblical origin:

> The pen comes from a tree [*calamus,* the rosebush] or from a bird *[pinna].* Its point is split in two *[dyade],* while keeping the unity of the whole. I think it is a sort of mystery, after the fashion of the Old and the New Testaments divided into two peaks, from which the sacrament of the word flows in blood and in the Passion. The pen, furthermore, puts ink upon the page. (VI, xiv, 3–5).

Christ's blood-writing is a model for all writing, past or future. Symbolically, it binds the *concordia discors* of the two Testaments. It is also the image of a continuity in the transfer of cultures. Truth moves from the chosen people to Greece and Rome, then to the universal community of Christians. More secretly, blood-writing connotes the erasure of the split that Isidore brings about between pagan and Christian knowledge. The *Etymologies* bring an accord to what seemed to be in complete discord in an eternal dyad. This is visible in the definition of *concors,* which underlines the interiority of this operation: "'Concordant' is said of the conjunction of the heart *[coniunctione cordis].* That is concordant that links with the heart" (X, 37).

THE COMPILER AND THE POTTER; OR, DIVINE FICTION

In the *Etymologies,* an absolutely crucial notional and semantic flood sweeps over the verbal roots of fiction. Its definition appears in the terms of the modest art of the potter: "To fiction is in fact to make, form, and fashion" *[fingere est enim facere formare et plasmare]* (XX, iv, 2). "Fictioning" indicates an activity that is not of the order of fantasy or lie and that differs radically from the sophistic *plasma* as it appears in *The Marriage of Mercury and Philology:* "The clay *[fictile]* vase is said to be made *[fictum]* not because it is a lie *[mendacium]*, but because it is made to have a certain form" (XX, iv, 2).

Starting with preexisting matter (clay), the potter forms something new (the vase), a pure container. That is, each signifier refers to the equation "vase = word" that appears in Augustine. For this reason, pottery is a very precise emblem for the art of the encyclopedic compiler. By leaning on the already-written, he produces a new cultural object through juxtaposition. It is framed and developed by a true fiction.

The gesture of the potter and that of the encyclopedist are placed under the care of a very high and very holy patronage, the potter par excellence in Paul's letter to the Romans (9:20–21). It is God: "Will the clay vase *[figmentum]* say to him who formed it *[finxit]*, Why did you make me thus?" (XX, iv, 2).

The encyclopedia is a third term between fiction and creation. It thus receives a dignity that is only one step below that of the one true *plasmator*. By juxtaposing and harmonizing, the encyclopedia invents the myth of a unified human culture. Its act is a repetition of the model of Genesis, to which it is related by analogy. Nothing more was needed to make the *Etymologies* the birth of "medieval" culture.

The *Etymologies* are far from being a disparate hodgepodge assembled by an obtuse, confused, and ignorant mind.[20] They are a completely coherent foundation for what followed, and they legitimate the rereadings the Middle Ages made of the classical authors. They found the myth of the cultural continuity from Greece to Rome and from Rome to France (the *translatio studii*) illustrated by Chrétien de Troyes in *Cligès*. The scriptural practice of the Middle Ages finds its Christian pedigree in Isidore's work. It is now permitted to create something new by juxtaposing what has already been written, the commonplace. And finally, the letter that makes all totalization impossible troubles knowledge, no matter what its field, with its creative unease.

Through his contribution, Isidore becomes an *auctor* in every way. He augmented the knowledge that he transmitted with an essential addition, and he is very conscious of this. In an anecdote, the *Etymologies* declare the inherent dignity and nobility of the creative work of compilation:

One day, this Mantuan magician was accused of the crime of compilation because he confused several lines of Homer by putting them in his own work, and his ancient rivals denounced him as a compiler. He responded, "It is a sign of great strength to have wrested the mace from the hands of Hercules himself." (X, 44)

6

"Sancta Simplicitas": The Old French *Sequence of Saint Eulalia*

And they were all filled with the Holy Ghost, and began to speak with other tongues, as the Spirit gave them utterance.

—Acts 2:4

Until now, I have chosen to analyze only Latin texts in my study of Christian writing. These cultural objects are conceived in a dual centrality: that of a language and that of the church. This duality guaranteed a potential "universality" to the diffusion of the Christian homonymy of paganism that occurred over the Roman roads, a vast network for the transport of meaning as well as of goods and people.[1] What happened when this network was damaged by invasions from the east, when it collapsed and gave birth to the linguistic units of *Romania*? The clerics of the Carolingian age were forced to deal with this problem.

The great barbarian invasions from the east destroyed the highways of Roman/Christian symbolism. This destruction might have been a deliberate strategic objective of the eastern conquerors.[2]

This collapse was not just economic, social, or political. It had a direct influence on language. The *koiné* of a common Roman speech was overthrown between the fifth and ninth centuries, and two separate written language systems moved into the vacuum. On the one hand, there was the language of the Bible and of church intellectuals, and on the other, regional dialects developed that were no longer mutually comprehensible. As a positive result, the chaos that overcame the centrality and generality of the Roman Empire gave birth to the individual nations of modern Europe. On the political level, the linguistic situation gave sanction and form to the opposition between the language of the people (Gallo-Roman) and the language of the masters (Latin or German), an opposition that did not exist under the empire. The social differences in feudalism literally find their voice here. My theme is thus the recognition and articulation of the diverse oral languages of the people in the written languages of their masters.

In about the fifth century, the Roman notion of *universalitas* began to move from the political realm to the collective imagination. Charlemagne, for one, intended to make this dream live again. To do this, he had to rely on the clerics of the only worldwide institution that survived the fracturing of languages and peoples, the Catholic (which is to say "Universal") Church. Both the church's hierarchy and its language, "Church Latin," gave it coherence, but these two seemingly different things are actually one.

A small handful of clerics from the four corners of Europe (Peter of Pisa, Paul Diavre, Rabanus Maurus, Alcuin) established the legitimacy of the imperial ideal. With extreme intelligence, they mined their knowledge to create the imagination of Christian Romanity, for as monks, they had never let go of the notion of *universalitas.* Their work was influential in four basic ways: First, they brought about the scientific and artificial reconstitution of classical Latin, with the objective of restoring the universal language. This time, however, the language was restricted to a very small group of international intellectuals, the literati. Next, they produced the idea of empire, a synthetic and eclectic collage of Roman, Byzantine, and Germanic sources, legitimizing the concept of an emperor whose power is simultaneously universal and sacred. With his power dependent on the pope, such an emperor would be the "sword of the law," a secular reflection of the "sword of faith." Furthermore, with the Oaths of Strasbourg (A.D. 842) these clerics set up a territorial division based on a completely original idea: linguistic difference. Going beyond vassalic homage, this was also the induced birth of language-based nationalities, in particular German and the French.[3] And finally, they invented a new, more rapid and more economical calligraphy, the Carolingian minuscule. This facilitated the circulation of meaning, of the classical heritage, and of the decrees of power. Erudite Italians rediscovered this form of writing in the fourteenth century, and it has been the basis of calligraphy and printing down to our own time. This fact alone establishes its importance, yet this script also gave rise to an intense creativity in the domain of writing (in every sense of the word). These four developments had extreme historical and cultural importance for the Carolingians, since they implied a complete mastery of the political, linguistic, literary, and theological knowledge of the time. In addition to their individual competencies, it must be supposed that each cleric was quadrilingual. He has to have known Greek, Latin, German, and Gallo-Roman.

Greek was the language of diplomatic exchanges with Byzantium, the government that kept the notion and ideology of empire alive in the east.[4]

Latin was the international language, reestablished in its classical glory by these clerics. This is a completely re-created language, and not simply the result of a "return" to Latin. The clerics promoted Latin to the rank of a formal and artificial language that served to spread the idea of Roman centrality. It was also the language of the church, of theology, and of letters, and it was the language in which all knowledge was transmitted in the schools. Furthermore, Latin was the language of the law, being the only language employed at the time for any legal action, even the most modest. Finally, by extension, it was the language of the state and of power. Because this language was the exclusive domain of the clerics, they were guaranteed a monopoly over the exchanges within the civil state, whether these touched on the symbolic, the economic, the juridical, or the political.

German was situated just beneath Latin in the hierarchy. It was the language of the Frankish masters who came from the east to dominate the remnants of the ancient Gallo-Roman space. It was also a language of culture, schooling, and law: Charlemagne had the Frankish epics and German law put into writing, but they have since disappeared. The Carolingian poets are very conscious of this three-dimensional linguistic context. They make a practice of combining German (as with the *barbbarolexia* of the classical rhetors) or Greek (see Theodulph of Orléans and Ermold the Black) with Latin (Johannes Erigenus).[5]

Gallo-Roman was an exclusively oral language of the people and of serfs. The clerics and their masters had to use it in their daily lives, but it had no other sphere of cultural existence. The ruling classes only used it to make their laws understood to their subjects; what remained of the Gallo-Roman aristocracy used Latin in their relations with the Carolingian court. The Oaths of Strasbourg promoted Gallo-Roman to writing, where it eventually became Old French. This move to writing must not be interpreted according to a modern democratic schema, which would be an anachronism and an illusion. In 842, Charlemagne's grandsons Charles the Bald and Louis the German did not need the understanding or approval of those they dominated. Rather, the Oaths of Strasbourg were concocted by the quadrilingual clerics to articulate, as did Latin, a message of political submission whose link to language was unbreakable: "You speak Gallo-Roman, and so you will be a subject of Charles the Bald. You speak German, so your master will be Louis the German."

This decisive break in the forms of power was planted in the ninth century, and it would only begin to bear fruit much later. Before 842, the respective languages of suzerain and vassal were of little importance. The bonds of man to man were not based on the languages spoken by either one. Slowly, the Oaths upset and replaced all the codes of the circulation and transmission of feudal power (for example, vassalic homage). No longer would the people be the subjects of a man; they were subjects first of a language, and only then of the master who spoke it.[6]

Ruling-class Gallo-Roman children were thus raised in a metaphorically sexed Carolingian context. On the one side, there were the male languages of culture and power (Greek, Latin, and German).[7] On the other, there was the oral vernacular, the mother tongue, placed under the sign of the woman.[8] The sons, whether political heirs (suzerains) or cultural heirs (abbots and intellectuals), could only accede to culture and power by breaking away from their servile and feminine language, and clerics were at the center of this separation. They were at once masters of this linguistic game and caught in a triple bind with regard to power (they did not fight), to sexuality (they took a vow of chastity), and to speech (they took a vow of silence); this complex relationship can be seen in the marginalia of their manuscripts. The monks' primary vocation was that of writing, and they often used it to communicate in the silence of the scriptorium. As symbolically castrated, they were limited to a triple abstention that was reversed through the cultural intervention of the pen. Thus, they were permitted to accomplish the task that was assigned to them in the Oaths of Strasbourg: to produce a symbolic *written* place that both recognized and subjugated the oral mother tongue.

REHABILITATIONS

The juridico-political operation of the Oaths has a parallel in another domain. What the monks accomplished for their kings is masterfully and decisively repeated in what we will call the liturgical literary domain. In part, the *Sequence of Saint Eulalia* (circa 881) puts into practice the decree of the council of Tours (813), which enjoined priests to transpose for the *illiterati,* the *idiotes* (those who spoke only the local vernacular), "Latin sermons into the rustic Romanic or German language so that all may understand what has been said." The *Sequence* crystallizes a system of linguistic apartheid wherein the clerics renounce giving the people access to the languages of culture and power.[9] As Renée Balibar notes, we must speak of the situation in the Middle Ages not as a bilingualism but as a colingualism. Only a small, literate elite was bilingual, and their bilingualism excluded the large peasant majority. Yet by bringing the vernacular once more to the level of a written language, the clerics recognized the literary fiction of hagiography and authorized it as a vehicle for the transmission of a theocentric signified. But in the same move, they also brought into play a new way of relating the language of the international elite to the local vernaculars. The *Sequence* is just as important as the Oaths and must be thought of as symbolically symmetric to them.

Classical historical philology has ambiguously recognized the importance of the *Sequence.* In the question of the evolution of phonemes from low Latin to French, the discipline has recognized that there is no more important text outside the Oaths, and so there have been innumerable philological studies of the *Sequence* (and let it be said that these studies are entirely justified by their own results).[10] Given the importance accorded to this poem, there has been a curious indifference to its literary quality. This indifference is associated with a set of unquestioned assumptions as to the conditions in which the work was written. When one reads this accumulation of knowledge, one is aware of a lively contrast between the rigor and detail of phonetics and the paucity of general conclusions.[11] I shall briefly review several elements of this phenomenon, whose extent calls for an explanation that is as general as philology's conclusions. In my opinion, the reason for this neglect resides in a teleological metaphysics of origins that has been projected onto a Carolingian past that resists such a way of thought. This metaphysics holds that the *Sequence of Saint Eulalia,* an original and primary text, could only be historically, linguistically, and statistically a stuttering first attempt, and therefore clumsy by definition. To say this is to forget that in linguistics, just as in art, a "beginning" has always been preceded by a cultural accumulation (and so it is always a rebeginning). Also forgotten is that those who produced the *Sequence* had a highly refined cultural and linguistic education. Paradoxically, phonetics (a positive science if there ever was one) obscures the readings of the story, and so there needs to be a positive reexamination of its historical context. Alongside this, I will reinterpret the literary aspect of the text itself, to give it what I think is its true importance.

Linguistic Mastery

Philology's first presupposition is the linguistic awkwardness of the copyist or the author of the *Sequence.*[12] In order to evaluate the credentials of this maker as a philologist, one need only examine the material and linguistic context of the manuscript that preserves the *Sequence.* The only known manuscript (which can be dated to 881)[13] contains three separate languages: the German of a poem to the glory of Louis III, the Latin used for another sequence devoted to Saint Eulalia, and finally, Old French.[14] He who made the text was doubtless a member of the very learned and very cultivated Carolingian clerical elite. These men could all write in three separate languages, and they were very familiar with the culture of each.[15] At the very least, if three separate individuals collaborated on the manuscript, they each had a linguistic sense so highly developed as to effect a circulation of meaning among the three spheres. So whether one assents to one or the other of these hypotheses, the linguistic anomalies of the sequence in Old French cannot be attributed to error, clumsiness, or the inherent groping in the dark of the first transcription of an oral language. On the contrary, one must suspect that the "abnormal" spellings indicate deliberate calculation in the use of language.[16] By transferring this reasoning to the literary and aesthetic levels, one no longer thinks of the *Sequence* as the first stammerings of childhood; rather, one sees it as a polished and masterfully wrought work of art.

Let us take an example that touches both the level of linguistics and of aesthetics (one of the faults of linguistics is to separate them radically; the textual practice makes this division inoperative).[17] The *Sequence* contains many "Latinizing" characteristics. The first line offers no fewer than three:

Buona pulcella fut Eulalia[18]

By the end of the seventh century, the Latin final *a* had muted into an *e*, so the manuscript's spelling does not coincide with that of its probable date. This anomaly is frequently interpreted as a hesitation on the part of the copyist, who still has the Latin of his liturgy and his education ringing in his ears. As a working hypothesis, this cannot account for an important contradiction: Elsewhere in the poem, the maker's ear is tuned finely enough to write the final *e* "correctly." There are seven examples of this in the *Sequence*. An explanation for this apparent incoherence is needed. Once we have set aside error as a hypothesis, only one plausible explanation comes forward. There is an intentional dialogic game being subtly played between the masculine liturgical language (Latin) and the popular maternal language (Old French) in the modification of the feminine declension. In these irregularities, the very speech of the *Sequence* takes note of the overhanging presence and absence of the sacred masculine language. The opposition of the Latinizing *a* and the Romanizing *e* evokes an entire drama of birth and severance played *between* sexes and languages and foresees the possibility of a new inscription.

With regard to diction, this effect is pursued coherently. Abstract scholarly terms (*clementia, virginitet,* "clemency," "virginity") and popular words (*pucella,* "maiden") are set in contrast. The text even goes so far as to give two spellings for the same name, a name central to its project and its problematic: "Christ" is spelled in a Latinizing form (*Christus,* line 27) and elsewhere in a vernacular form (*Krist,* line 23). It seems as if the text is making note of the identity of the concept and of its verbal differences whenever it is translated, transposed, or transferred into another linguistic sphere.[19] In Latin, both the cleric and his protagonist, Eulalia the Martyr, can imitate the passion of *Christus* in close proximity to the linguistic experience of it. In the vernacular, the writer must make the effort to transpose (that is, alter) this experience, in which the masculine sphere of the sacred and the feminine sphere of the vernacular are both married and separated.

It is essential that the concept of Christ Incarnate should be at the center of the difference between these two spellings. Obviously, the problem is not one of homonymy in relation to paganism. Success on this front had already been won by the time the text was written. The purpose, rather, is to show that though the Incarnation can have many spellings in many languages, these spellings are actually synonyms, and that these synonyms' meaning is transnational. It depends upon no existing speech. The transliteration necessarily presupposes a passage through blank language, the "language of truth" devoid of signifiers posited by Saint Augustine in the *Confessions.* In its transfer from the low Latin *Kristus* to the *Christ* of all vernaculars, the knowledge of the Incarnation comes to light through a silence. The possibility of all transliterations is mute, which means that truth is only incarnate everywhere because of a fundamental absence.

Transcription or Creation?

Criticism of the *Sequence* makes another commonplace assumption that the preceding remarks lead one to question. The *Sequence* has always been interpreted as a sort of stenography, a more or less skillful attempt to record a living language, spoken in a given place at a given time.[20] But is it a question here of an oral language that clumsily seeks to be written, or of a writing that creates itself, almost ex nihilo, to assign a place to the vernacular? In the second case, the *Sequence* (along with the Oaths) would be an example of an *invented* language that, though respecting orality (if only to make itself understood), would impose its own norms upon it, independent of what is spoken, because it obeys other conventions, those of a written and cultivated rhetoric. We must review an entire set of presuppositions that are brought to bear not only upon the *Sequence* but upon the birth and evolution of the French language.

First, the *Sequence* must no longer be thought of as the elevation of a spoken language; rather, it must be seen as a skillful compromise between the sometimes opposing demands of popular and literate culture, among the constraints of orality, of writing, and of literary fiction.

For the same reason, it might also be necessary to push back the beginning of normative grammar and spelling. It was not in the sixteenth century but well before that this very French phenomenon occurred, that the "natural" evolution of the language was delayed and submitted to a collection of rules devised by clerics.[21]

Next, the Carolingian clerics, through their willful intervention, also affected the random nature of linguistic change. No longer would it proceed from the heterogeneous chaos of phonetic evolution; now the logothetes (creators of language) would have a hand in it. The relation to the linguistic norm is no longer subconscious; it is partly voluntary and aesthetic. As a result, medieval writers would also develop their own norms, to the degree allowed by their poetic talent, and find legitimacy for their moves in the innovation of their great Carolingian predecessors. Its own phylogeny gives theoretical justification to writing the history of Old French as the history of a writer's language.[22]

Finally, the hypothesis of the erudite invention of Old French in a compromise with a "natural" and "popular" language leads to a review of each document. The Middle Ages were the departure point of a long tradition, which passes through Joachim du Bellay and François de Malherbe and is continued in the examples (almost always literary) of the Grevisse French grammar and the *Grand Robert* dictionary, a tradition in which the masters of the language are those with the greatest claim to control it, for theirs is the finest ear. I speak here of writers.

"SOURCES"

The *Sequence*'s literary history is as complex as its linguistic framework. By the time the Carolingian clerics introduce Eulalia into French, she has been a Latin literary object for at least five centuries. Our creator/poet, familiar with Christian sources, knows very well that the Christian writers Augustine and Prudence each consecrated a hymn to the little martyr. The latter "source" must be interrogated carefully, since the ninth-century Latin sequence quotes it directly:

> Spiritus hic erat Eulalaia
> Lacteolus celer innocuus.[23]
>
> This was Eulalia's unstained soul rising to heaven.

These lines correspond exactly to lines 164–65 of Prudence's hymn. The Latin sequence of the Valenciennes manuscript deliberately establishes an intertextual play whose extent is measurable in relation to Prudence and the two readings of him in the ninth century.

More generally, Prudence's work is caught between the demands of state and church, and so it carries political, religious, and linguistic implications.

First, there is Roman "nationalism" or "imperialism," which functions independently of one's race or national origin. This creates a profound link to the idea of the empire's centrality: "God, wishing to bring into partnership peoples of different speech and realms of discordant manners, determined that all the civilised world should be harnessed to one ruling power."[24]

The principal binding force is a single language that homogenizes the different people and allows them to communicate. The barbarian invaders oppose this force, representing the threat of a fragmentation of language and thus of society.

This radical *discrimen* repeats itself on the religious level. According to the Christian apologists, the Roman Empire is only a network of meanings unified by its laws and by a language that allows the Gospels to be spread everywhere. Rome is the space of a logic, an economy, and a highway policy. Prudence expressly uses the word "highway," and it must be taken both in its metaphorical sense and utterly concretely, as meaning the Roman Road: "For the time of Christ's coming, be assured, was the way *[via]* prepared which the general good will of peace among us had just built under the rule of Rome" ("A Reply to the Address of Symmachus," II, 620–22).

In this view, the antithesis of the Roman Christian is not just the barbarian but also the Roman emperor who persecutes his Christian subjects. Prudence thinks of Maximian, whose prefect martyred Eulalia in 304, as an interior enemy. The pairing Christian martyr/pagan persecutor deposes and replaces the Roman/barbarian antinomy. Language is the controlling factor that brings all these things together. The Christian Roman is confronted by the pagan or barbarian, whose discourse is contaminated by the void to the point of being silent:

> Yet what is Roman and what is barbarian are as different from each other as the four-footed creature is distinct from the two-footed or the dumb from the speaking; and no less apart are they who loyally obey God's commands from senseless cults and their superstitions." ("A Reply to the Address of Symmachus," II, 816–19)

The barbarian's muteness and animality are, of course, metaphorical. His native language is devoid of meaning because in Prudence's time it cannot articulate either the signified of Roman centrality or that of theocentric monotheism. Similarly, if the Roman persecutor is not a Christian, then his Latin is likewise "mute"—meaningless.

The hymn to Saint Eulalia fictionalizes the entire problematic of the emptiness of non-Christian speech. Maximian and his henchmen are nothing more than barbarians. Theirs is not a complete language (the special privilege of the Christian Roman) but rather a discourse (which carries the curse of the pagan and the Roman) whose essential vacuity stands in contrast to the language of the little saint:

> Isis, Apollo, Venus—they are naught; Maximian himself too is naught; because they are works of men's hands, both worthless, both naught. Though Maximian, lord of power and yet himself in vassalage to figures of stone, prostitutes himself to his gods and makes himself over to them, why does he persecute noble hearts?[25]

The conflict is one of linguistics. The figure of Saint Eulalia affirms a language of charity, that of the Christian empire, a meaningful language. As the universal and international language, it articulates the ideal (never brought fully into being) of cultural unity, of drawing all the particularities of the empire together under one cultural banner. This is what Prudence's text tries to achieve. Maximian's prefect opposes this movement by persecuting its language in the name of an empty and enslaving discourse of power. The polytheist nature of this discourse separates all the particularities and condemns them to struggle with one another without reference to a center. In a different context, the Carolingian clerics could not help but address this problematic because they intended to synonymize the different languages of their empire by reorienting them to theological notions.

The fourth-century hymn is entirely self-reflexive, first of all in its writing. Prudence compares his text to the crown of a martyr symbolizing his simultaneous death and victory (the entire collection of hymns is called *Peri Stephanon,* "Crowns of Martyrdom"): "Give her these gifts, you girls and boys, from the luxuriant leaves. But I in the midst of your company will bring garlands wreathed of dactylic measures, of little worth and faded, but still joyous" ("Crowns of Martyrdom, III," 206–10).

This *mise en abyme* occurs again in the fiction. Eulalia not only sings the universal language (Catholic and Roman) against the empty discourse of her persecutors, she elevates it to writing. Her gesture is an exact copy of Prudence's, one that is copied again by the Carolingian clerics. Eulalia's body and blood are the author's tools:

> In a moment, two executioners are tearing her slim breast, the claw striking her two girlish sides and cutting to the bone, while Eulalia counts the marks. "See Lord," she says, "thy name is being written on me. How I love to read these letters, for they record thy victories, O Christ, and the very scarlet of the blood that is drawn speaks the holy name." These words she uttered with never a tear or moan, cheerful and undismayed." ("Crowns of Martyrdom, III," 131–42)

The instruments of torture and her flesh and blood are changed respectively into the pens, parchment, and ink of a writing to the glory of Christ. Prudence loves these reflexive metaphors.[26] Medieval literature made them into a topos—hemographia, "writing in blood"—but such an image is not just a rhetorical figure.[27] According to the logic of the Incarnation, it must be read literally, not as a simulacrum but as Christian fiction supposing a real basis, in this case, the Passion. What does this mean? That Christian language requires not only a theoretical reflection but a practice, an incarnation by a martyr. It must pass through a writing of the body. Only a page empty of all writing, even the mark of sexual relations, is worthy to record a spiritual writing.

Prudence's hymn relies heavily on the theme of a virginity metaphorically linked to the language of a faith that must be purchased with one's life. From the second line of the poem on, Eulalia is a *sacra virgo,* a holy virgin.

The church fathers thought about virginity a great deal. For Gregory of Nyssa, it is the privileged means of approaching the beatific vision of God (in *De virginitate,* circa 371). However, Augustine indicates the relation of virginity to language in the clearest possible way in the "Ecstasy of Ostia" episode in book IX of the *Confessions* (see chapter 3). The language without a language has no signs and no articulation. Just as the Marian dogma produces an economy of difference by insisting on a special case, so does the inarticulate language; this is also a sexual difference. For this reason, this language can be called virginal. What the executioners write on Eulalia's virgin body represents the language's development through time. Her virginity gives her the power to avoid marriage with a pagan, to avoid marrying (and thus compromising and destroying) virginal writing to the empty discourse of polytheism.

CONTEXT FOR EULALIA

The suzerains of the Oaths of Strasbourg were not seeking the approval of their subjects and soldiers. They only wished to designate whose soldiers were whose, based on the vernacular linguistic region they inhabited, and it was the clerics who elaborated this model. In writing the *Sequence,* the same literati were necessarily motivated by different circumstances: They wished to transmit the good word in the mother tongue. The call to evangelize is universal, and so the universal democratic idea is born in the New Testament (see chapter 3). Its language must be naturally transglossic because the clerics are now addressing themselves not to subjects but to a community of believers, who have joined of their own free will. They are not interested in delimiting territories of political power without the consent of the governed; rather, they wish to transmit a message that transcends power relations. French literature is born under the sign of the book, a model that is both democratic and transnational.[28] The premise of vernacular fiction, that truth is not based in any one language, provides a principle for the widest possible diffusion of Carolingian thinking. Furthermore, in order to bring its listeners into agreement, the *Sequence* must assume the shape of persuasive rhetoric. With this as its goal (as we will see further on) the *Sequence* will draw upon the subtle resources of the Latin oratory art, which also aims to persuade. All the Romanic literatures are marked at birth by this initial paradox or compromise. They are an aristocratic creation whose goal is liturgical, so they all have the potential to become universal.

THE NINTH-CENTURY LATIN SEQUENCE

The Valenciennes manuscript also contains a sequence in Latin whose first ten lines are a hymn, in which the poem emphasizes the divine praise it contains (line 6) and its own poetic eminence (line 7), as well as its musical quality. The last ten lines are devoted to a prayer of intercession and thus insist on that quality of the sequence. By contrast, the narration, amply developed by Prudence, takes up only eight lines of the poem. Furthermore, as we have seen, two of these lines are quoted from the fourth-century text. It seems as if the purpose of the poem is to reflect on the means of its performance, on giving voice to writing, and on the making of music. For this reason, the story, and thus the martyr, are placed in secondary relation to the work and are dependent upon it. The entire stress is on a dialogue between musicians—male clerics—who continually use a specialized technical jargon to praise the excellence of their own poetic performance. The implicit reader of the Latin sequence is a member of the circle of the literati.

As for Eulalia, the writing of her body is no longer hers. She only reflects an act of communication as she becomes the exemplary vehicle for the prayer of intercession that the Christian community addresses to God. Setting the Latin and French poems side by side as two manifestations of the same text, we see that the unified international language of the literati stands in opposition to multiple vernaculars. In Latin, the narrative fiction is detached from the specific body of the saint. It is up to the Old French version to detach the fiction from its Latin foundation and return it to the incarnation of hemographia. The Thing of the Incarnation justifies this flowering of the diverse, rather than a discourse of meaning.

This is to say that the Latin sequence is an act of passage in the manuscript. Through its textual citation of Prudence, it forms a bridge with a Latin-Christian heritage in order to prepare the vernacular to accede to the dignity of the liturgy.

A VIRGIN REBIRTH

The Old French *Sequence* seems to follow very closely the prosodic and melodic structures of the Latin one. However, it actually only retained the musical aspect. In appearance, the Romanic text (twenty-eight lines long, as is the Latin text) only comes to its performative aspect—the prayer of intercession—in the last four lines. The rest of the text is entirely devoted to narrating Eulalia's passion. But it would be an error to conclude from this shift in emphasis that the Old French *Sequence* is somehow more spontaneous and naive than Prudence or the accompanying Latin poem. One cannot assume that developing the narrative at the expense of reflection is a sign of lesser artistic skill. It is insulting to the work to relate the suppression of specialized jargon (and thus of the cultivated reader) to the level of writing, interpreting such suppression as a result of the maker's relative incompetence. In fact, this interpretive presupposition does not agree with the material situation of the *Sequence* in a manuscript that contains three (at least) languages, nor does it agree with what cultural history teaches us of the Carolingian court. This supposition once more excuses the reader from examining the literary, rhetorical, and cultural implications of the writing of the vernacular.

I propose another interpretive conjecture: The explicit poetics and linguistics of Latin are doubly displaced onto the implicit ones of the French coming into being before our eyes (in the silent, virginal space of the truth, of Lacan's midspeech, or inter-diction). To strengthen this hypothesis, I need only note that Latin linguistics and literature had always been the subjects of treatises on grammar and poetics. This occurred even during the periods when classical culture was all but forgotten. Rabanus Maurus, a writer, theologian, and politician at Charlemagne's court, busied himself with just such rhetoric and grammar. In contrast, the first explicit theoretical reflection on French dates from the thirteenth century (Brunetto Latini's *Li Livres dou trésor,* 1260). As for the first French grammars, they came about in the sixteenth century.[29] Historical criticism has thus tended to conclude an absence of "reflection," but in reality, before these efforts, linguistic and literary specularity, so evident with Prudence and in the Latin sequence of the ninth century, hide themselves in the interior of the vernacular story. Beginning with the Old French *Sequence,* specularity becomes an integral part of the practice of poetic language. This text seems humble, but once again, this humility is a topos in the rhetorical repertoire, that of "affected modesty."[30] The poem establishes a principle of creation and interpretation that will be very closely followed throughout the history of medieval French literature. The specular function is delegated to the story, where it continually both hides and manifests a project of writing. These passages occur in addition to passages that openly reflect (upon) their essence and that must also be thought of as being part of the fiction.

Legitimately, this new poetic and linguistic practice can be called *Romance.*[31] This word does not just name a group of languages and literatures descending from popular Latin. In the twelfth century, it also came to be indissolubly linked to a mode of creation tied to the vernacular, a creativity that puts into practice the principles of a radically innovative poetic by hiding them in the detours of the narration. Between the ninth and the thirteenth centuries, there is no theory without incarnation in a practice of writing.

The Romanic *Sequence* is the first appearance of this, a monument both minimalist and complex, and so it is necessary to demonstrate the literary and rhetorical virtuosity of its maker.

The poem opens with a commonplace derived from Saint Paul: the opposition beween the letter and the spirit (*"Littera occidit, spiritus autem vivificat"*; 2 Cor. 3:6) in the form of the body and soul of the martyr:

Buona pulcella fut Eulalia:
Bel avret corps, bellezour anima

Eulalia was a good maiden:
She had a beautiful body, a very beautiful soul.
("Le Martyre de sainte Eulalie," 1–2)

The writer, guided by a certain medieval exegesis of the Bible, transposes the letter/spirit opposition to Eulalia's body and soul.[32] From this point on, the body can only be a Romanic letter, a body of new signifiers whose beauty is emphasized in the opening lines. The previously unknown letter veils and reveals the even more beautiful secret of the soul. The letter is thus not only a metaphorical veil but a real material support of martyrography. These two lines sum up the maker's entire creation. They will be opposed by the sphere of the rhetorical *vestitio,* the luxurious clothing *(paramenz)* that the emperor offers to the maiden in his effort to seduce her; these are a paradigm for the letter that kills. The maker of the text hides his astounding creativity under an evangelical simplicity. He also encodes the principle of interpretation that should govern future readings. The goal is to discover the lively subtleties in the beautiful *simplicitas* (simple language used for rhetorical effect) of the letter.

On another level, the *Sequence* again develops the function of virginity in the relation, or nonrelation, of languages and discourses. Just as in the Latin texts, paganism's empty discourse collides with the obstacle of Christian virginity, with Emperor Maximian in the role his prefect played in Prudence's text.[33] It is important to note that Maximian restrains his executioners from raping the saint. For the sake of power, virginity only has meaning if Eulalia sacrifices it *willingly,* through marriage to an unbelieving noble, which would symbolize the suppression of Christian speech through a compromise with a polytheist discourse. Virginity has no meaning or value for the persecutors beyond the free choice to be made by the virgin.

Furthermore, not only does virginity represent the uncrossable barrier between the language of transcendence and a discourse of unbelief, but it is also an image *en abyme* of the vow of chastity that was willingly pronounced by the clerics who lie with Eulalia in writing. Virginity is this blank space that permits the conjunction and assimilation of the masculine that writes and the feminine that is written.

If the breaking apart of languages between the fifth and ninth centuries foreshadows the emergence of a national identity, virginity implicitly symbolizes this break, the separation in the independence and sexual difference that dominates the creation of the new Romanic writing. The male masters that enunciate the new language are similar to this very language because of their virginity. Liturgical Latin and the German of Carolingian power are also entirely (sexually) different from Romanic. Metaphorically, Latin and German are masculine languages. They surround Romanic, but they cannot assimilate it or gain access to its Othered essence, its virginal femininity. Eulalia names an irreducible alterity, but in a new way. The languages of mastery cannot be brought back into a compromise with its apparent femininity and its seeming lack of power, but the chaste Latin clerics, when they write the name "Eulalia," come into contact with their maternal Other (the vernacular) in a new and subtle way. They now voice what they have repressed over the course of their ecclesiastical apprenticeship.

Furthermore, Eulalia's virginity is a metaphor for the blank page, the empty clearing where there never has been an inscription (aside from those of the Oaths of Strasbourg, in an entirely different domain). Only a virgin parchment is worthy to receive the trace of the absolute rebeginning, the passage from the spoken vernacular to the written that is also the author's own operation.

Finally, the *Sequence* repeats point by point the conditions that Augustine assigned to Christian truth. The martyr must die so that her words may live on (in the vernacular). The statement must pass through the obliteration of its specific enunciator to become general. Interestingly, the poem no longer refers to the powerful topos of blood-writing, and the connection between the torture instruments and pens is also silent. The martyr's beheading only indirectly represents these tools. The copyist's silence encodes the secret underlying his work. Pen and ink are his from now on. He hides them metaphorically in the fiction but displays them concretely on the manuscript parchment, where they are silently substituted for Eulalia's own writing. The maker's discretion is now understandable: His own relation to virginity has produced a prohibition that is fundamental to any such relation. By hiding his actions, he has concealed the transgression implicit in his writing when it marks the virgin parchment.

"ARTE CALLIDISSIMA ET OCCULTA" [A HIDDEN AND SUPREMELY SKILLED ART]

The *Sequence*'s story was preceded by a long literary and rhetorical tradition. First of all, the Carolingian clerics had at their disposal a large accumulation of works in a specific literary genre. Latin hagiography from the fifth to the ninth centuries placed all the resources of fictional writing into action.[34] Next, Quintilian's discussion in the *Institutio oratoria* of the figure of *simplicitas* could not have escaped these clerics' eyes.[35] The trope functions by imitating ordinary discourse with the purpose of persuading the judge. To disguise his verbal skill, the orator uses the words of popular everyday speech as if they were his (*"verbis etiam vulgaribus et cotidianis,"* writes Quintilian). In the Latin tradition from Cicero (from whom the *Institutio* borrows its example), "rustic" or "everyday" speech becomes a rhetorical figure deliberately used in culture's refined discourse (the *sermo urbanus*) to convince and manipulate. The writing of the *Sequence* obviously moves beyond the domain of political debate, yet it follows Quintilian's example in hiding its art—a marker of his supreme skill (*"arte callidissima et occulta,"* he writes). The *Sequence* pretends to be the stenography of a written language. In actuality, it creates the poetic, rhetorical, fictional, and linguistic writing of Romanic, understood both as a language and as a tradition of fiction (as literature). Having been made homonymous for a long time, rhetoric is put to a triple use here, at once edifying, literary, and institutional.

The name of the martyr also announces the emergence of Romanic poetics. The Isidoran tradition comes into play, allowing one to seek and to find the secret of the name in its etymology. The force of the *Sequence* is concentrated on the eponymous saint's name—which is to say that it invents its uniqueness and individuality in a move that will have a profound influence on the development of the French language.

To explain this effect, one must return to the living Greek of the Carolingian age. Greek is always present in the work of such Latin rhetors as Cicero and Quintilian, who bow to its influence by quoting Hellenic terms and attempting to translate them. The late Latin grammarians who compiled the works of their forebears also continued their practice. We see Marius Plotius Sacerdos and Flavius Sosipater, and even Isidore of Seville, referring to Greek sources.[36] In this regard, the *Sequence*'s maker/poet, whose fineness of ear has already been demonstrated, could not have overlooked Prudence's Greek titles.

No matter what literary history may have to say, it is possible to break apart the name of the saint into its Greek components:

Eu: "adapted, proper, appropriate to sacred ceremonies"

Lalia: from *lalein,* "to speak, chat, sing while speaking of birds," from which comes the Latin *lallare,* "to sing"

Eulalia's name encodes a "good speech." Not only does she refuse the seductions of polytheist discourse (a conflict that is no longer pertinent in the largely Christian ninth century), but also, and above all, she is the concealed virginal eponym of the writing down of Romanic "good speech." Her soul, a dove that flies from her at death, is the emblem of this birth and rebeginning. Not only does Eulalia die to witness her faith, but she also gives birth to Romanic writing:

Volt lo seule lazsier, si ruovet Krist.
In figure de colomb volat a ciel.

Wants to leave this earth and join Christ.
In the form of a dove, she flies to heaven.
("Le Martyre de sainte Eulalie," 24–25)

The word "figure," so rich in associations in patristic exegesis, stands here for the movement through which the text interprets itself. One is left to suppose that this encodes an allegory by showing it as minimally as possible. The Romanic language gives birth to its own writing at exactly the moment of the martyr's corporeal death (the death of the letter). The move is Paulian, emphasizing a living spirit stripped of its materiality but referring henceforth to an incarnation. In separating itself from its place of enunciation (Eulalia's soul, and more generally the pen of the Carolingian maker), the new poetic language invents, as does all writing, its possibility of flight, to extend its wings metaphorically over the entire Romanic "nation."

On no level (linguistic, poetic, political) can the work of the Carolingian makers/creators ever be called ignorant, clumsy, or hesitating. On the contrary, it is the fruit of deep deliberation by clerics who in our age would be paragons of culture. Taking their cue from the implicit universality of the Christian message, they invent a new way for this message's diffusion. Born in the ruins of a former centrality, it incarnates on the parchment the humble and fleeting orality of the mother tongue.

7

Axiomatic Fiction; or, Of Books and Heresies: Alain of Lille

In certain respects, medieval history seems to repeat itself point by point. Nine hundred years after Tertullian and seven hundred after Augustine, the twelfth-century Cathars contested Catholic dogma in terms that closely resemble Gnostic Docetism. I am not about to argue for rewriting a chapter of history. That Catholic institutional thinking had not yet settled this conflict is a sign, for me, of something deeper. It seems as though the thingism/realism of the fiction of a rigorous Christianity is unable to saturate the desires of an imaginary of fiction. On the contrary, being formed by the prohibitions of Christianity, these heresies continually move toward an antithetical rebirth. From the formation of the dialectic of modern culture down to our own times, the combat of Christian and pagan images (a *logomachia* of literature and philosophy) remains constant; only its avatars and names have changed. Pagan knowledge has always offered the poetic exception to dogma, and so the process of its homonymy is unending.

CHRISTIAN KNOWING

Alain of Lille takes up a fundamental problem in his fight against heresy: how to graft human reason onto divine reason. The goal is to draw a radical distinction between the imaginary discourse of heresy and the true discourse of faith. The task is difficult because "the faith that human reason verifies through facts *[experimentum]* is worthless."[1] Thus, the Incarnation, the virgin birth, the Trinity, the resurrection of the dead—in short, Christian discourse—are all unbelievable, foolish, and vacuous. It is the Cathars who express the discourse of "good sense" and explain the miracles and the sacraments as God's magic, sleight of hand, and the use of simulacra. How is one to prove them wrong?[2]

The first step in the struggle against heresy is to reaffirm the impossible state of affairs that lies at the center of Christian thought: God become man. Here we must quote and translate in full the *Rhythmus de incarnatione Christi,* which demonstrates that the seven liberal arts cannot comprehend (in every sense of the word) the paradox of the Incarnation:[3]

1. Grammatica	Grammar
Exceptivam actionem	The Word of the Father
Verbum Patris excipit	Caused a unique action
Dum deludit rationem	When he violated reason
Dum naturam decipit	And tricked nature.
Casualum dictionem	The noun received
Substantivum recipit	The use of cases
Actioque passionem	And the active voice of the verb
In hoc verbo concipit	contained the passive.
[Refrain]	*[Refrain]*
In hac Verbi copula	In the copula of this verb
Stupet omni regula	All the rules are stupefied
Verbum caro factum est	The Word was made flesh.
2. Logica	Dialectic
Inter locos locum nescit	An argument drawn from contraries
Locus a contrariis	Is not among the arguments.
Suum locum obtupescit	Its voice is mute.
Exceptum ab aliis	Excluded from all the others,
Fit elinguis, obmutescit	Dialectic falls silent.
Fallitur in propriis	It is false in its properties
Et de suis erubescit	And it blushes
Logical fallaciis	for its error.
[Refrain]	*[Refrain]*

3. Rhetorica	Rhetoric
Peregrinat a natura	The subject wanders
Nominis positio	From its natural position
Cum in Dei transit iura	When the human condition
Hominis conditio	Passes under divine law.
Novus tropus in figura	A new trope in the figure
Nova fit constructio	A new construction
Novus color in iunctura	A new color in the joining
Nova fit translatio	A new metaphor is born.
[Refrain]	*[Refrain]*
4. Arithmetica	Arithmetic
Dum ab uno non recedit	Even if it is not separated from the One
Alteratur unitas	Unity is split
Dum in unum se concedit	Separation is unified.
Unitur alteritas	Even if it recognizes the One
In diversum idem cedit	The same becomes the other
In idem diversitas	The other same,
Suum tamen non excedit	Whereas the simple substance
Limitem simplicitas	Does not exceed its limit.
[Refrain]	*[Refrain]*
5. Musica	Music
Dum factoris et facture	When a miraculous harmony
Mira fit coniunctio	Unites Creator to Nature
Quis sid modus lingature	What can be the mode of joining?
Quis ordo, quae ratio	Order, reason
Quae sint vincla, quae iuncturae	Scales, chords
Qui gompho, quae unio	Rhythm, notes
Stupet sui fracto iure	Musical proportion is stupefied,
Musica proportio	Its rules broken.
[Refrain]	*[Refrain]*
6. Geometria	Geometry
Sue artis in censura	Geometry errs
Geometra fallitur	In the judgment of its art
Dum immensis sub mensura	When the immeasurable is

Terrenorum sisitur	Placed under terrestrial measure.
In directum curvatura	The arc of the circle is
Circuli convertitur	Changed to a straight line
Spheram claudit quadratura	And the square is enclosed in a sphere
Et sub ipsa clauditur	And collapses under its own weight.
[Refrain]	*[Refrain]*
7. Astronomia	Astronomy
Solis lumen nube tectum	The light of the sun, covered by clouds
Nubis sub velamine	Clouded by a veil
Nostrae nubis fert obiectum	Strikes the objection to our darkness
Nec hebet in lumine	It is not blinded by light.
Nostrum vergit in defectum	A sun born of a virgin
Sol ortus de Virgine	Consents to bear our defects
In effectum dans effectum	A dark light
Lumen in caligine	Giving strength to our weakness
[Refrain]	*[Refrain]*

By declaring that the seven liberal arts cannot explain the miracle of the Incarnation, Alain places the *Rhythmus de incarnatione Christi* in direct opposition to *The Marriage of Mercury and Philology.* The latter totalizes knowledge through letter and number, whereas the former silences all the rules of human knowledge and remains entirely out of its domain: "In the miracle, one must not seek reason" *[in miraculo non est quarrenda ratio]* (*De fide,* col. 362). Grammar cannot grasp Christ incarnate; he is both divine subject and complement of the human object. Dialectic is reversed by the union of contraries represented by a God made man. In rhetoric's vast storehouse there is no new trope for the unprecedented metaphor of the Incarnation. This has produced a new noun (a modern, or Christian, word) that has its place neither in the proper nor in the figured because it is both at the same time. *Peregrinatio,* "peregrination," a rhetorical term that originally designated a metaphorical transfer, becomes a homonym when applied to theology. For Alain of Lille, it indicates a metaphorical shifting unique to biblical style; it thus comes from a sacred rhetoric, the *rhetorica sacra.* Certain words in the Bible "wander from their proper meanings and create a new meaning."[4] These meanings are always to be understood in relation to the theocentric signified.[5]

As for arithmetic, it cannot explain the dual unity of Christ. The harmony of the Creator *(Factor)* and the creature *(factura)* is beyond the reach of music. Geometry cannot comprehend an immeasurable divine being reduced to the measure of man. Nor can it describe the "squaring of the circle" that changed the eternal cycle (and thus an encyclopedia such as Martianus's) into linear time and vice versa. Finally, the Christic sun wears the Incarnation's veil of flesh. The Incarnation homonymizes the concept of the veil *(velamen),* which for the pagans means the layers of a simulacrum. Christian discourse accords a new status to the *velamen,* the figure, the metaphor, and the representation in general. As Alain states in the stanza on rhetoric, the veil now designates the body of Christ. It is a reality, clothing the Christian in a real mystery, just as Tertullian would have wanted it.

The *Rhythmus de incarnatione Christi* resembles a profession of the faith of unreason. It is important that we understand it as something else. One must first accept the mystery as such before the rational, human aspect of the Incarnation comes forward. Alain then takes up his refrain, which emphasizes the powerlessness of all rational rules *("stupet omni regula")* before the miracle; hence, the title of one of his most important treatises, the *Theologicae regulae.* As Marie-Dominique Chenu and Etienne Gilson have pointed out, this treatise joins the theology of mystery *(scientia caelestis)* to the theology of creation *(theologia naturalis).*[6] Alain combines the two doctrines through an axiomatic mathematics, using a method borrowed from Euclid as he appears in Boethius. Then, like Abelard, Alain adds an eighth science to the *septennium* of the liberal arts, a knowledge that is at once their origin, goal, and peak.[7]

After doing the necessary obeisance to the mystery, Alain then wants to develop the rational science that accounts for it. This calls for rewriting the ideas of the *Rhythmus de incarnatione Christi* in a "scientific" project. Reflected in this way, the *regulae* undergo a series of shifts in meaning, a peregrination that is in no way metaphorical. From grammar and poetry, where the rules are incapable of seizing the Incarnation, the *regulae* shift to the fields of theology, philosophy, and Euclidean mathematics. Once there, they take on an increasingly rational meaning. The mystery now becomes the impossible paradigm of a unified science of the letter, and the Incarnation plays the role of empirical knowledge *(experimentum).*

But what is a science, and how does it correspond with the "supercelestial" science (theology)? Alain's first sentence in the *Theologicae regulae* turns to an Aristotelian way of thinking and states that each science "is founded by the rules that are its proper foundations" *[omnis scientia suis nititur regulis propriis fundamentis]*.[8] There are principles proper to each domain of knowledge; unlike grammatical rules, these principles cannot be modified according to man's will. Specialization and independence characterize these ways of knowing, since the principles of one field are not shared by another. Each knowledge is relative. The ideal of a unified science does not appear in these opening lines, and Alain seems to reintroduce the Aristotelian impasse as his provisional starting point.[9]

Theology intervenes, however. It does not

> err in its rules, for they are the most worthy, preeminent over all others, in their obscurity and subtlety. . . . The necessity of the rules of theology is absolute and unbreakable, since they form the basis of faith and they cannot be changed either by deed or by nature (*Theologicae regulae,* col. 621).

The supercelestial science's profession of faith in no way hinders knowledge (unless one were to confuse an axiom for an arbitrary imposition of meaning). Rather, faith is the starting point for a rational effort.

To begin, theology, the eighth science, gives meaning to the *septennium.* It is the "well-spring," the "mother's breast" of all rules, "the most general maxim." For this reason, "it embraces in its generality, all the maxims, no matter what their particular capacity." The rules belonging to each of the disciplines of the liberal arts are rooted in something indemonstrable. According to Gilson's excellent formula, the sciences other than theology "are founded on what is only the habitual course of nature, which is a regularity and not a necessity."[10] Necessity is based on an immediately self-evident proposition *(communis animis conceptio)* from which all others derive. For Alain, this proposition belongs only to theology, and so the first rule of his axiomatic system is "The monad is that through which any given thing [and also a discipline of knowledge] is one" (*Theologicae regulae,* col. 621).

However, to unify knowledge is not to totalize it. God, as the unnamable and inconceivable object of all knowledge, is he who renders every science incapable of totalization, *and he thus makes it true.* To admit that humans cannot account for the mystery is not to renounce reason (as is typically done in this situation). It is *the very condition of rationality.* The mystery is the demand for incompleteness that makes

Alain's theology the prolegomenon of modern science. A posteriori, it is possible to point out that what Alain explicitly rejects in his formula is still present in the work: the totality of knowledge and the unity of science. The first is a sign of his unconscious demand for an ultimate proposition, for the desire for an All—in essence a religious demand. The second, in contrast, responds adequately to all the criteria of modern science.

The *Theologicae regulae,* wishing to develop a science of theology, were on the right track, that of linguistic and philosophical realism. We must make a detour into another text here. In the *Distinctiones,* Alain takes up the particular problem posed by the Bible's metaphors and by its figurative style in general:

> According to Aristotle's explicit authority, those who are unaware of the power of words *[virtutum nominum]* rapidly fall into fallacy [or sophistry]. It is thus dangerous to be unaware of the power of theological terms while commenting on the Gospels *[pagina sacra],* where seeking something is perilous and finding it difficult, where the words of those of whom we speak are unknown to us, where the words *[sermo]* do not tell us of the thing *[res]* as it is, where the terms wander from their proper meanings and seem surprised by novelty. (*Distinctiones,* col. 687)

Although Aristotle's authority is invoked, it is obvious that the "virtues" of the biblical names cannot be understood within a pagan system of knowledge. How, then, is one to found a correct reading of the inspired words of the Bible?

To this end, the thirtieth axiom of the *Theologicae regulae* poses a distinction between "abstract" and "concrete" names:

> Rule 30: *Every essential term is meant either mathematically or abstractly.* According to Aristotle, all mathematical terms designate the thing mathematically, which means abstractly, without consideration for any manifestation in a substance. For example: "whiteness" and "blackness." Concrete or arbitrary terms, on the other hand, mean, concretely, the properties inherent in substances, such as "white" or "black." In theology, we use mathematical terms that indicate the deity without any consideration of the person's mode of being. For example: "deity," "divinity," "nature," *"ousia"* [being], "essence," or "substance." Concrete terms indicate his nature to the extent that is appropriate. For example: "Lord," "just," and "merciful." (*Theologicae regulae,* cols. 635–36)

The terminology itself indicates a radical innovation over the classical distinction. It is no fluke that Alain calls the abstract "mathematical."

> Rule 31: *When speaking of God, mathematical terms are less inappropriate than concrete ones.* Mathematical terms, in fact, tend toward the simple. The more simple something is, the more that thing has the manner pertaining to God. For God, as was stated above, is simple in every part. (*Theologicae regulae,* cols. 635–36)

Alain evokes the dizzying possibility of quantifying the Real (God), far surpassing the founding thinkers of Christian knowledge whom I have already analyzed. Mathematical terms are more proper names for this "scientific" God. This is a key step. Even if "mathematical terms" remain metaphorical, the signifiers of a metaphysics, they open the possibility of reattaching the symbolic to a matheme. Alain anticipates the concept of modern science by unifying the fields of experience and ideas under the banner of mathematics, a unification made possible by his fidelity to the Christian epistemological break.

Nature, speaking to the narrator of *The Plaint of Nature,* perfectly formulates the innovative relation between the philosophy of mystery *(philosophia caelestis)* and the philosophy of creation *(philosophia naturalis)* that is already implicated in the concept of the Incarnation.[11] At the same time, she asserts the incompleteness of "natural" reason before the mysteries of theology and its fundamental accord with them:

> Nor is it surprising that in these matters [man's rebirth in baptism and faith] theology shows no close kinship with me since in many instances our paths to knowledge, though not opposite, are different *[nel adversa, sed diversa sentimus].* I establish the truths of faith by reason, she establishes reason by the truths of faith. I know in order to believe, she believes in order to know. (*The Plaint of Nature,* 125)

It is a historical irony that this attempt did not continue. It was not until the Galilean revolution that the entire universe was considered a single field offered to the investigation of knowledge, and even then, Galileo was not aware of his great predecessor, who for a long time had been covered by a veil of Scholasticism. Thomism, under Aristotle's influence, had intervened in the meantime, radically separating theology from philosophy, and this became official church doctrine. The unity of science could not exist for Saint Thomas Aquinas or for his disciples.

Their work thus anachronistically continues pagan thought despite its success in the realm of reason, because they fail to think through all the consequences of the concept of God incarnate.[12]

Even though his work did not resonate with his contemporaries, and as a result was completely forgotten, Alain of Lille is the only thinker to have seen (almost) all the consequences of the Incarnation, and well before the scientific revolution of the seventeenth century.

TERMS: THEIR COMPATIBILITY

The doctrinal correctness of mathematical terms also points to rhetoric. Let us turn to one of Alain's observations on the use of tropes in the Bible. For him, as for everyone in the Middle Ages, what was written in the Bible was absolutely true. This brings about a problem because the New Testament is full of metaphors, parables, and allegories. Alain writes, "One must sustain the tropes, not extend them" *[tropi sunt sustinendi, non extinendi]*.[13] For him, this is a rule. To sustain the metaphor means to relate it continually to its truth-effect. To not extend it is to unroll it continually. This use of the image opposes the poetic practice of amplification. As I pointed out in the discussion of Quintilian, the amplificatory practice of *extendere verba* is one of the privileges extended to poetic license.[14] A biblical model now justifies the spectacular and figurative, the fiction of language. This establishes a Real at the center of the rhetorical. In apparent opposition to this sustaining of the metaphor that he proposes, Alain writes in a baroque style, especially in *The Plaint of Nature* and *Anticlaudianus*. However, the Bible, with its varied styles, also legitimates his use of the plethora of rhetorical figures.

The demand for the unity of thought is thus satisfied, no matter how diverse thought appears. Alain's collected works resist being pigeonholed into ethical, speculative, and poetic genres. There is a dominating principle of unity holding their diversity together. Even more so, grammar is controlled by the *ad placitum,* the arbitrary whim, and so cannot be considered a science. In opposition, rhetoric is scientific, and the topoi are its yardstick. He now approaches the complete fulfillment of what was begun by Tertullian (see chapter 2): the homonymy of rhetoric. Because pagan thought was rhetorical, and thus vacuous, it destroyed itself. Rhetoric, though, was reborn as a thought having a relation to the Thing and the Real. Imagined as a scientific discipline, it transforms the

Asiatic style of poetic treatises into the integrating function of their rational project (this is how one must read the *Rhythmus de incarnatione Christi,* commented upon above) and vice versa. The metaphors used in theoretical and abstract works are never *only* metaphors. They are in contact, at some point, with the Real.

Here again, Alain appears as the precursor genius. In the structure of knowledge that he unfolds, rhetoric, a science ruled by commonplaces, is an asymmetrical counterpart to mathematical terms. The necessity of the letter is at work in the signifier. Poetic and axiomatic language, the sciences of nature and speculative philosophy, are directed henceforth not in opposite but in diverse manners *(non adversa sed diversa)* in pursuit of this same Real.

THE REAL OF THE BOOK

Alain's thought, as I have demonstrated, winds up in an antithetical poetics.[15] In *The Plaint of Nature,* he explicitly formulates this aesthetic. On the one hand, there is narcissistic writing (the hermaphroditic, sodomitic writing of a *falsigraphia,* to use Alain's term), proposing itself as its own goal, joining the same (sex) with the same. Alain explicitly relates such writing to the "insanity of Manichaeus" and the "lies of Arius" (*The Plaint of Nature,* 140–41). Rhetorical thought and heretical ideology both give rise to a "sophistic pseudographer," a *sophista falsigraphus* (*The Plaint of Nature,* 134). Heresy and the literature of the same reawaken the nothing, the "dead mother," the vain cult of the idols—a dead cult with a phantom structure that makes it even more powerful, as Nature says to the narrator: "Note well that some of the daughters of Idolatry of old, which was once thoroughly uprooted, are at the present moment trying to restore their mother's dominion and, by certain conjuring incantations, to raise her from the dead for a new life" (*The Plaint of Nature,* 170).

Poetic heresy is the literary exception to a correctly written book of the world. Mimetic writing *(orthographia)* repeats the creative move in its representations without ever assuming the privilege. It celebrates Nature and points to the one Creator, thought of as the supreme artist/maker/artisan/writer of all things *(summus artifex omnium rerum, Auctorem omnium, eternus Auctor, summus Auctor).*[16] Orthography is the creator of the book of the world:

All the world's creatures
are a book, a painting for us,
a mirror
. . . .
The rose shows our state
It is a gloss *[glosa]*
It is a commentary *[lectio]* on our life.[17]

This analogy's metaphorical status is shown in the second line cited above. Alain is mining a known lode of commonplaces, which I have shown to be equally important for Augustine (see chapter 3). The metaphor of the book is not applicable only to creation; it also covers, in descending steps, human experience and then human awareness:

> In effect, there is a threefold book in which man is obliged to contemplate his nature: the book of science, the book of experience, and that of conscience. The book of science is written in a codex [that is, consigned equally to the two Testaments and to the book of nature]. That of experience is written on the body, and that of conscience on the heart. The book of science is written in letters of gold; that of experience, in lead; and that of conscience, in horrible letters. The book of science is the sacred writing in which man deciphers his nature; the book of experience is the human body, where he understands his misery; the book of conscience is the cauterized spirit in which man recognizes his guilt. The book of science teaches the theory of human life; that of experience, the practice; and that of conscience, the abuse.[18]

The book of Revelation is the source of this image,[19] and Christ, as the model book, the "book of life," strengthens it.[20] This metaphor carries over to other medieval works. Saint Bernard uses the image of the medieval copyist to explain the book of consciousness that must be compared to the example *(exemplar)* of the book of life. If our books are poorly copied and in need of correction, it must be done with the utmost urgency, before the final collation of texts on judgment day.[21]

Alain, however, is very innovative in his use of the traditional commonplaces because it is important for him to uncover the rational grounds of orthography. This foundation not only lies beneath correct human writing but is also the basis of a true knowledge, a break with pseudography. The Creator's real production repeats itself continually in the active procreation of nature. By comparison, human activity is artificial and limited. However, it is no less concrete, for if man is made in God's image, then his activity is also the image of his Creator's. As in Isidore of Seville, man can produce truth:

> Those artificial things [*artificialia:* objects, liberal arts, language as a whole] that take their being from man's work can be neither said, nor created, nor procreated; rather, they are produced *[feri].* In effect, fabrication *[factura]* applies to artificial things, generation to bodies, and creation to spirits. For this reason, one can say that the human artisan *[humanus artifex]* is a fabricator *[factor].*[22]

For the sake of Christians, Alain must produce a topos of *bienfacture* ("good production"), both distanced from and analogous to divine production and having nothing in common with the idolatrous fiction of *falsigraphia.* His innovation, which goes beyond Tertullian's and Augustine's assaults on the gnoses, is to found his attack rationally on a *theologia naturalis* and not on the mystery of faith.

HERESY AND LITERATURE

Sometime between 1185 and 1200, Alain, who is called the "knight of theology,"[23] goes into battle against the hydra of heresy and writes *De fide catholica, contra hereticos, valdenses, iudaeos, et paganos. De fide* is an instruction manual meant for the ecclesiastics who might be sent to debate in a public forum against heretics. For this reason, the majority of the treatise is devoted to the Cathars, and it can be seen as a fairly accurate source on Cathar Docetism. Alain must present the Provençal theses objectively, and only rarely does he yield to the polemical slander that fills other, numerous and implausible, refutations of Docetism. On the other hand, even though he takes his inspiration from Augustine's anti-Manichaean debates, Alain does not merely repeat those old arguments, which by his time have become rhetorical tropes.[24] To be effective, the treatise must present the opposing doctrine as it is.

Using the problem of evil, the Cathars reject free will and repeat, almost line by line, the Manichaean hypothesis of the dualism of creation: An unchanging god could not create a nature that undergoes perpetual change and that thus is bad, so Lucifer, the principle of change and instability, is thus the origin of the visible world. Furthermore, he is the creator of the spirit that is in the world: "Lucifer was the creator *[auctor]* not only of corporeal things but also of spiritual things" (*De fide,* col. 313).[25]

The devil is thus the First Cause, and so man is absolved from all original sin, since all he does is imitate the "prince of the world" and the "father of men." Mimesis ceases to be the "imitation of nature in its modes of operation" and becomes the mechanical repetition of evil. As Alain writes, "Imitation does not come from the evil of the world and of its creator, but from human free will, which imitates Lucifer in his perverse works *[per prava opera]*" (*De fide,* col. 310).

In heresy, the "spirit that always says no" becomes the catchall description of human activity in this world, as it is ascribed to the prince of darkness. The Albigensian doctrine of the First Cause *(auctor)* is laid out in scriptural terms. The devil is, above all, a writer, the patron of the literary evil of men.

If Lucifer is the First Cause, then what role is left for God? For the Cathars, he is completely impotent and in no way participates in the creation of the world; otherwise, he would participate in evil. Instead, he produces fictional simulacra having no relation to terrestrial life. Good divine action, although essentially limited to poetic production, opposes real, but evil, creation. God writes fiction. The docetic thinkers that Tertullian combated also thought that the greatest fiction of all is the Word made flesh: "Certain heretics even say that the Son of God showed men a shadow of human nature, and not the truth" (*De fide,* cols. 321–22).[26]

As is always the case with gnoses, flesh is evil by definition and so must be fictionalized. For the church fathers, the theory of Christ's *adumbratio* ("shadowing") means the Incarnation. In classical rhetoric, and particularly for Cicero, *adumbratio* connotes both an outline and also the fictional as false. It is in this sense that the term is used by Marcion, the third-century Gnostic who quotes several passages from the Gospels in his defense. Heresy homonymizes the *adumbratio,* changing the Incarnation into a phantasm (*phantasma,* as Guibert of Nogent writes).[27] This move also implicates every scriptural authority that uses the word. Falling back on rhetoric and Gnosticism, the Cathars try to homonymize the notion of Incarnation as it is understood canonically (and this is what distinguishes them). Guibert reports this opinion of John, count of Soissons, as typical of the heretics: "[A pious cleric] once explained to John of Soissons how the Lord has suffered and how he was resurrected. Then the count, with a mocking tone, said, 'That is just a fable, just wind'" *[Ecce fabula, ecce ventus]*.[28] This disincarnation obviously has the same consequences for doctrine as did third-century Docetism, which held that Christ did not suffer the Passion and that his body, a pure representation, was impassive, just like the bodies of Greek gods: "Hilaire says that Christ suffered no pain, no Passion. . . . For this same reason they say that he neither ate nor drank, nor was he crucified and truly raised from the dead. Certain heretics even say that he was not born of a virgin, and that he was not conceived" *(De fide)*.

The miracles are theatrical representations with no real force. Similarly, the Eucharist, and all other sacraments with it, are devoid of substance. The doctrine of the putative flesh of Christ strikes not only at the heart of dogma but also at the institution that sustains and perpetuates dogma through time.[29] As did many sects, Catharism questions whether the church is the intermediary between God and man.

Heresy uses a palimpsest to disincarnate the body of Christ. Because the body is essentially a deceitful metaphor and simulacrum, it is outside of the heretical canon. The fruitful concept versus history dialectic of the Gospels is entirely obliterated.[30]

The Cathars in this context show just how far they distrust the propriety of language. The Gnostics of the third century could not have despised it more (see chapter 2). The denial of the Incarnation leads the Cathars logically to a radical Pyrrhonian skepticism. One need only cite the examples assembled by Jean Duvernoy:

> I found a man [the inquisitor writes] sewing sleeves and shoes. When I saw him I said, "Is this a tailor?" The man answered, "Thus we are, or so we think." And, looking out a window toward the gardens that we could see from that place, he said to me, "Look, we think that pigs have damaged these gardens."[31]

Or again, this passage from Eberhard of Bethune:

> You hold nothing to be true, even that there is a God, but you all act as if you are full of doubt, saying, "As we think, as we imagine, it seems that, if this is so, if such and such turns out to be." Here is how you speak, and you are not liars. Yet you fall into heresy.[32]

To invert and contest Catholic dogma also requires a return to the linguistics of impropriety. It is not surprising, then, that in the thirteenth century, Etienne of Bourbon called the Cathars the descendants of rhetors and sophists. This is very malicious, since if this is so, then the Scholastic doctors of the Sorbonne are beaten on their own turf: "They who seemed to be simple peasants used their sophisms and double meanings to twist the words of the men who were the greatest sophists of Paris and the greatest clerics and who did not know of their falseness."[33]

As we can now see, Tertullian and Augustine did not succeed in their accusations of the Gnostics. The Cathars are one more manifestation of these deceitful sophists.

The sophistic tendency is the starting point of a series of falsely "natural" arguments employed by the Cathars against the canon. The Incarnation, the virgin birth, and the miracles are all fables, they hold, because there is nothing in nature to substantiate them: "That which contradicts nature does not belong to Creation."[34] This refutation is commonsensical and empirical, deriving from the sensualism that Alain of Lille accuses the heretics of employing (*De fide,* col. 307). However, it would be a mistake to read such sensualism as a prophetic sign of the modern scientific spirit. Such a position confuses the critical spirit with Pyrrhonian skepticism. On the one hand, the Cathars' sensualist argument contradicts their conception of the Real as an apparition and an evil simulacrum. On the other hand, thinking in this way leads directly to the death certificate of empirical science. A thinking of appearance and be-seeming *(parêtre),* Catharism takes things for what they appear to be, denies all propriety to language, conceives of nature as an evil work, and is thus a dead end for all investigation and all progress in the material world. The Albingensian heresy relies on a structure of knowledge that, in essence, is metaphoric. Common sense leads directly to the imaginary or to literature. The accusation of "fable" that the heretics level against the Gospels turns against them.

In his dedicatory prologue to William VIII of Montpellier, Alain of Lille repeatedly insists on the fictional character of Cathar doctrine:

> In their bacchic delirium *[debacchantes],* they are swept along into ancient and recent heresies. Given to philosophical speculation, but in fact devoted to the mirror of the senses, they produce fictions *[confingunt]* out of whole cloth, creating monstrosities according to their desire and their free will without regard to human or divine reason. . . . Starting with the diverse heresies, they assemble [*compingunt,* "they jerry-rig,

> they slap together"] a universal heresy. They create one idol from many, one monster from many, as if they were making a homogeneous poison from several venomous plants. (*De fide,* cols. 307–8)

The Cathar is the negative model of the writer of fiction, combining the rejection of reason, an idolatrous narcissism, the privileging of the senses, a magical pharmaceutics of varying elements, and a passion for the signifier without the corrective of the letter. In his refutation of their thought, not only does Alain propose a doctrinal corrective for the benefit of the faithful, but he also becomes the inspiration for numerous medieval texts of literary fiction. He produces the pejorative model for a negative Luciferian aesthetics, and ironically, he supplies the model for the idolatrous pursuit of literary desire.

8

The Counterfeit: The *Roman de Renart*

THE (NO)THING

The relation of the title character of the *Roman de Renart* to the art of writing is visible in the first lines of the first branch. The amphibology of the term *rien* (*rem,* "thing" or "nothing") refers to the Real and/or the nothing in Old French:

> Perroz, qui son engin ess'art
> Mist en vers faire de Renart. (1–2)[1]

> Perrot, who devoted his cunning art to putting into verse the deeds of Renart.

Alain of Lille's denunciation of the literature of the same echoes in branch 14, *Renart's Confession.* This episode exposes the essential relation between this art and the forms that heresy assumes. The protagonist himself announces his own heretical nature:

> Sire, dist Renart volentiers;
> J'ai bien este .IX. anz entiers
> Parjures escomeniez,
> Mais ce n'est mie grant pechiez:
> Ja par esconmenacion
> N'avra m'ame dannacion;

Si ai este popelicanz
Et renoiez plus de .VII. anz
Et si ai este soudomites
Et encor sui ge fims erites. (14,484–92)

For [nine] whole [years] I have been a perjurer and excommunicated; but that is not a very serious offence: my soul will never be damned because I am refused communion. [I have been a Publican and denied God for seven years.] I've been a sodomite sir, and a perfect heretic.

Denial, sodomy, heresy: It is as if Alain of Lille's treatise were lying open before the branch's copyist. Renart's art of writing finds its origin in the same negativity that marks heretical and literary idolatry. This kinship goes beyond a similarity in the contents. The structure of confessional speech, as the writing frames it in its portrayal, transgresses the accepted dogma of confession. Renart's devilish truth can only reveal itself by placing itself at odds with the canon: The fox disobeys the obligation of silence that the secrecy of confession imposes. The narrator/writer underlines the theme of this transgression by the simple act of putting it in writing. The narrator's protestations of Christian morality are intended to appease the reader, who will soon encounter an entire list of crimes and sins, and to excuse the author who relates them.[2] These words hide a profound identity between the narrator's art and that of Renart.

Hubert the Kite, the confessor in this episode, is in no way the spokesman of the religious domination of crime, unless it is through a radical inversion of his values. In fact, he states,

Mais cil qui assez ont fait mal
Li foi menti, li desloial,
Les parjures et les erites
Cil sont des paines d'enfer quites. (14,475–8)

[Those who have done great evil,] Disloyal rogues, traitors, renegades: those are the ones exempt from the torments of Hell.

Faced with such a priest as this, Renart eagerly and quickly runs through the catalog of his sins. These become virtues in Hubert's inverted system. The law of inversion expounded by Renart dominates all the discourse in the branch, and especially the narrator's virtuous introduction.

—Sire, j'ai mout este parvers
S'ai mainte foiz fait a envers. (14,733–44)

"Sir, I've been very wicked and done many things that I shouldn't have done."

The narrator, the confessor, and implicitly the artist *en abyme* all produce the devil's *prava opera* ("perverted works") that Alain of Lille denounces. So close scrutiny of the structure of Renardic enunciation is important and will reveal what is ultimately at stake in its representations. The narrator opens branch 14 with a group of ancient rhetorical recipes. He deprecates the other Renardic writers, and he proclaims that he is the only one who possesses the truth:

Tot vos ont de Renart fable,
Mais g'en dirai la verite
En ceste branche en une aloigne;
On nel tenez mie a manconge. (14,349–52)

There have been many tales told of Renart; but in this branch I shall tell the truth without beating around the bush, so don't imagine I'm telling lies!

The supplement *(aloigne)* that carries the image of the branch also contains the truth of the *Roman.* The trunk from which, metaphorically, this branch grows is absent. The *Roman de Renart* plays with the scriptural sense of the word *"branche."* To my knowledge, this makes it the first vernacular text to take explicit notice of this term, although Geoffrey of Vinsauf formulated a theory of the branch in Latin in the *Poetria nova.* There, he speaks of the opposition between the natural (linear) order of discourse and eight types of artificial order. As is always the case for Geoffrey, the artificial receives a positive connotation, in exact opposition to Alain of Lille: "The latter is sterile, but the former fertile, from its marvelous source sending out more branches from the parent trunk, changing one branch into many, a single into several, one into eight. . . . From their trunk it arises like a shoot."[3]

Renardic truth derives from the logic of the supplement, of the continuation, of the graft. It dismisses the origin (the first, authentic text or manuscript) and writes a never-ending accumulation of branches. The trunk that would be the host for these grafts does not exist. Thus, there is no reference point that binds them together. The *Roman de Renart* negates the unity of its form. The repeated production of branches recalls the Augustinian "thorns of the passions." For Alain of Lille, this is hermaphroditic writing, and thus it needs to be exorcised. The speaker, according to Alain, should let himself be guided by the prescriptive harmony of the natural order.[4] Any other discourse occurs as an addition to nature and so is perverse. Beginning in the first branch, Renardy asserts its diabolic irrationality. The word *rain* ("branch," a near anagram of *rien*) refers both to the branch it introduces and to lust, which, according to medieval physiology, originated in the kidneys *(reins)*.[5]

> [Renart] n'est pas chose resnable,
> Einz est un rain de vis doiable. (2249–50)

> He was no proper creature, but a limb of the living devil.

The romance radically inverts the constellation of ideas established by Alain, which links aesthetics, rhetoric, logic, and the erotic. This action begins in the oldest branches. Lucifer also has a secondary origin. By setting theology on its head and reversing its values, the *Roman* identifies itself with this origin. In the branch of the confession, Renart is "led by his devil" (14,213). An "illness in his flanks" (14,496) having given him the urge to speak, Renart reveals what his inverted religion holds most sacred: the sex of the she-wolf Hersent. This is the thing (using his own terms) he desires most. Of course, it has nothing to do with the Thing of the Incarnation. The adulterous sex is a *pertuis,* the gateway to the pleasures of Eden. It also echoes the name of Renart's castle/den, Maupertuis, which means "bad hole":

> Pertuis? El mont n'a si grant chose,
> Mout est hardis qui nomer l'ose
> Que por seulement que m'an membre,
> Me fremisent trestuit li membre
> Et herice toute la char.
> Par mon chief ce n'est mie eschar:
> Ce est or li plus nobles nons
> Qui soit en cest siecle que cons,
> C'est mervoille, quant on le nome,
> C'est la riens qui plus destraint home.
> . . . .
> Et lui done plus en .I. jor

De bien de joie et d'amor
Que boche d'ome ne puet dire.
Cons est li plus soverains sires
C'om puist encontre amor prover. (14,561–79)

Cranny? I'm wrong, for it is a great thing, which you have to be very bold to mention. For just to remember it, I tremble all over and I get goose-pimples; and I swear I'm not joking. For there's no nobler word in the world. Yet, amazingly, just to pronounce it is the biggest disgrace for a man and the most responsible for his downfall. Yet when he wants to put it to use, there's no question that it brings him more joy, satisfaction, and honour in one day than the mouth of man could utter. That is the best doctor to be found for love.

Unnamable and yet named, thing and nothing together—this is how theology has defined God, the "sovereign lord," and precisely how Renart has defined the vagina. In this move, he founds a paradoxically ecclesiastical order in which he holds the preeminent position:

Ne cuidez pas que ce soit fables:
Je ne vodroie mie estre abes,
Se Hersent n'estoit abeesse
Ou clereiere ou prioresse,
Ou ele estoit en tel leu mise
Qu'ele feust fors de justise;
Qu'eusse de lui toz mes buens
Et els de moi toz les suens;
Qar mout est l'ordre bone et bele
Qui est de malle et de fumelle. (14,587–97)

Don't think I'm spinning you a yarn: I wouldn't want to be an abbot unless Hersent were an abbess or a cellarer or prioress, or that she was put in a place beyond their authority, so that I could enjoy myself with her and she with me. For it's a splendid order that includes males and females.

The confessor intervenes to upset the order of Renardic writing. Although at first he seemed to be in perfect accord with the penitent, the kite systematically destroys the idol/thing of the religion of lust by painting an "inverse portrait." (Another famous example of this inversion comes from the *Jeu de la feuillee* by Adam de la Halle.) The kite demonstrates that Renart does not have a desire that he addresses outward to the Other; rather, he is being held captive by his imagination. Hubert is thus clearly identified with the narrator, who, in the opening lines to the branch, denounces the folly of believing his own thought.[6] One could well believe that his confrontation with a "reality" has annihilated the imaginary image and replaced it with the "truth." However, like Adam de la Halle, Hubert sets about constructing a phantasm of negative values.[7] He draws on all the resources of medieval misogyny, starting with Tertullian's rhetorical tropes. Hersent is old, ugly, fickle, and forgetful. Sexually insatiable to the point that no penis can satisfy her, she is also the figure of an inexhaustible desire to write. If Renart were entirely reduced to a penis by synecdoche, he still could not completely fill Hersent, *nondum satiata* ("never satisfied"):

> Se tu estois coille et vit,
> si seroit ce assez petit. (14,689–90)

> If you were but nuts and a cock, you still would be too small.[8]

The wound she bears can never heal. She is a devil, properly speaking (14,608), even "the gate to Hell" *(diaboli ianua),* just as in Tertullian's *On the Apparel of Women:*

> Ce est li gorz de Satenie
> Que quant que il ateint s'i nie. (629–630)[9]

> It is the pit of Satan, and all that penetrates there, drowns.

Note the dexterity of the play between the rhyme and its echoes. The text reads, "all that penetrates there, drowns," but it also reads, "is negated." Her sex is a form of *Satanie,* "Satan, [who] negates." This negation also takes in the stability of masculine desire:

> Mais il ne trueve si grant tente,
> Puis qu'ele est enz, que ja la sente,
> Ne que ce s'estoit un neanz. (14,639–41)

> Never will he find such a large sounding probe that when it is in her, she will feel it any more than it were nothing.[10]

The metaphors for writing multiply in this passage, in terms taken directly from Alain of Lille. Hersent's vagina is the anvil/page/plowland

(Hersent: *la herse,* "furrow") that annihilates the penis, the hammer/pen/plow, by yielding to it.[11] Their action, however, is repetitive and never complete. So Renart's writing can never be whole either, because it submits to their perverse law. Hubert's extended curse puts all these aspects of the desire to write into play:

> Ele a plus cous de coille euz
> Que n'a de *foille* en .II. seuz
> En este qant les foille sont. (14,661–63; emphasis added)

> She has had more balls hit her than there are leaves on the elderberry tree in summer.[12]

> Hersant poile et Hersant tont,
> Hersent escorche, Hersent *plume.* (14,668–69; emphasis added)

> Hersent skins and Hersent shaves,
> Hersent peels, Hersent plucks.[13]

And Dufournet's version:

> Hersent escorce, Hersent *plume.*
> Maldite soit tote *anclume.*
> Qu'ele a plus cops de coille ous
> Qu'il n'a *foilles* en cent sous
> En este quant les foilles sont. (553–57; emphasis added)

> Hersent peels and Hersent plucks. Curses on every anvil. She has been struck by more balls than there are leaves on a hundred elderberry trees in the summer.

This radical condemnation of femininity on the part of Renart's confessor asks a double question of the fox. How can he defend the image of his desire against the misogyny that upsets and negates it? Or, in other terms clearly implied in the text, what writing might he use to oppose Hubert's disparagement of writing? Alain of Lille will not serve this purpose. Renart cannot turn to a rational writing that refers to a transcendent Real because he has just omitted the divine from his inverted religion. There are, then, two conflicting discourses that cannot be regulated with reference to a third term outside them. To preserve himself from annihilation in this *logomachia,* Renart chooses the only alternative left to him: to eliminate the terms of the imaginary Other and leave his own as the only option. Renart, certainly, will convert Hubert to his heresy:

> Je vos ferai en mon Dieu croire. (14,717)

> I'll make you believe in my God!

This conversion, however, occurs with the destruction not only of the opposing discourse but also of the one who spoke it. The nothingness of Renardic speech literally consumes the confessor. Using the pretext of giving the kite a kiss that would bind them as lord and vassal (this is feudal etiquette's homage of the *osculum*), Renart devours him. Thus the "beak" (line 14,837) that supported the imaginary opposition disappears in the fox's maw. Once more, Renart's mouth is the instrument that imposes his desire on the Other.

Renart's desire to *fere la chose* (either "make the thing" or "make love") is to image/imagine the thing.[14] He cuts it off from its (theo-logical, rational) reference and makes it inconsistent by submitting it to the imaginary; he causes rhetoric to control it and thereby introduces a fundamental instability into the text. The first branch recounts the wanderings of the object of desire through its changes in signification.

In another episode, a vat of dye becomes the emblem and the means of rhetorical ornamentation. At the beginning of *Renart the Dyer* (as the branch is traditionally known), the fox flees a group of pursuers who want to execute him for his never ending criminality. He escapes to a tanner's hut and dives into a vat of gold dye, changing his color from the usual red, signifying deceit, to gold, a symbol of rhetorical ornament, of gilding. The protagonists can no longer see Renart's false nature. For the reader outside the text, this permutation of signifiers is all the more obvious. Renart has transformed himself into a rhetorical figure that symbolizes the very rhetoric he uses to trick his enemies.

Furthermore, Renart takes on the metaphorical role of a textile/text, a blank space that receives all decoration. He is now a reflection of what he always was, a visible figure for the page that supports a fiction:

> *Mout se regarde, et se remire,*
> De joie commença a rire. (2324–25; emphasis added)[15]

> He looks himself carefully up and down and bursts into happy laughter.

Underlining and accompanying this change in appearance is a change in language. To complete his disguise, the fox abandons his "Breton" French, the supreme language of Arthurian fiction. He begins to speak a composite language that combines elements from a scattering of dialects and regions. He thus is an (un)worthy heir of the maker of the *Sequence of Saint Eulalia,* who, as we saw, also draws on multiple traditions. Renart, both in his appearance and in his speech, reveals the open secret of vernacular poetry. The only thing missing to make the metamorphosis complete is the one essential element of the oral tradition: music.

Ysengrin the Wolf, Renart's mortal enemy, soon provides for this need. Unable to recognize the fox under the layers of rhetorical ornament that now cover him, Ysengrin leads his nemesis to a villager's hut. There he shows him a hurdy-gurdy *(vitelle)* that hangs on the wall. The villager's hut is an explicit figure for hell. A dog that recalls the mythical Cerberus stands guard at the door, and there are devils inside (line 2579). Poetry, in its musicality, is closely linked to Lucifer. Furthermore, because music is not verbal, it stands outside and in excess to poetry. If the body (of the saint or of the deceitful fox) is a figure for the language of poetry, then its music has associations with waste and excrement. For the narrator of the first branch, "villagers are made of a devil's shit" (line 513). By entering the hut, Renart places himself in a fundamental relation with "villainy," even though he is a feudal lord. To conceal this relation, he tries to change the trappings of peasant status into literature.[16] The hurdy-gurdy leads to a wealth of associations. Hanging *(pendant)* from a nail, it also symbolizes the penis (the *pendant,* line 926). Because it can be detached, it is also a sign for the symbolic castration shared by both sides of the sexual division. The *vitelle* is at once a cock *(vit)* and female *(elle).* The hurdy-gurdy also acts as a metonymy for the fox himself. Renart constantly risks being hanged *(pendu)* from a branch that cannot be any other than that of the *Roman.*[17] In the end, when Renart succeeds in stealing the instrument, he hangs it from his neck. This completes the circle of the metaphor and brings all its instances together (line 2542). The hurdy-gurdy is thus the thing itself (and not the signifier) of poetic fiction, the secret of the music of literature. Renardy is a letter/literature that arises at once from excrement, castration, diabolism, and villainy.

To steal the hurdy-gurdy is a twofold action. On the one hand, Renart takes possession of the secret of poetry. On the other, he completes his own false, fictional identity. Wanting what is not his, Renart reveals the hurdy-gurdy to be the substratum of desire. In order to achieve his ends, he must overcome the barrier that stands in the way of this desire. The transgression can only occur in paying the highest possible price: The economy of musical writing can only lead Renart to a disfiguring mutilation at the hands of the villager. The fox's entire strategy aims at escaping this danger and then forcing someone else to settle the account.[18] He imprisons Ysengrin in the villager's hell and makes off with the hurdy-gurdy. Now that Renart is absent, the wolf is left in his place to pay the bill for his writing. Castrated by this Cerberus, Ysengrin has sacrificed his "thing" to the economy of literature.

> Mout fu dolanz, mout se demente,
> Por ce qu'il a perdu la chose.

> Grief-stricken, he is full of anguish for the loss of [his thing].

The loss of the penis combines with the loss of the colors of rhetoric. When Ysengrin is emasculated, deprived of the *ornatus facilis* ("figures of speech"), he immediately turns pale. His value decreases sharply. The she-wolf then establishes the relation of the thing to rhetoric. Hersent, Ysengrin's wife, complaining of her loss, parodies the troubadour formula that designates the lady the object *(rien)* of desire, the source of *joie.*

> Or ai ge perdu toute joie
> Et la riens que je plus aimoit;
> . . . .
> Dolante, lasse, que ferai?
> Quant j'ai receu tel anui,
> Que ai ge a faire plus de lui?
> Mais aut ermites devenir,
> En un bouchage Dieu servir:
> Qui de tel chose est mahaigniez
> Joie en pert tout, ce sachiez,
> Et hardement, force et color;
> Perdu a tote sa valor. (2761–72)

> I've lost all joy and the thing I most loved! . . . I've never known such trouble: what use is he to me at present? Anyone would be stupid to lie with him now, for he's worth no more than a tree-stump. I don't want to sleep with

him anymore as he's not to be touched. Since he can't make love, what use is he to me? Let him go and become a hermit, serving God in a wood. [Whoever is deprived of such a thing loses all joy, you must know, and strength and force and color; he has lost all of his value.]

Renart's goal is to perform the impossible task of elevating the letter/thing/garbage to the level of a signifier. The wolf's mediation is necessary to do this, and it is the wolf who pays the price for the transfer. Nevertheless, all of rhetoric's colors are given to the fox, who does not undergo a castration. Instead, he finally masters the musical essence of literature:

Tant fis Renart qu'en .XV. dis
Fu bien de la vïele apris:
Saiges fu et bien esprovez,
Onques tiex bers ne fu trovez. (2809–12)

In a fortnight he managed to play [the hurdy-gurdy] so well that he had completely mastered it. [He was wise and well-learned, and never was a nobleman found like him.]

Renart's mastery, however, is utterly fictional. It is the wolf who involuntarily has the experience of literature, at the price of his color. His castration represents his complete loss of all rhetoric. Odysseus, chained to the mast of his ship to escape musical death at the hands of the Sirens, is a precursor to Renart. If literature is the play of signifiers, then, in Saint Paul's terms, its writing creates a body without a soul, essentially a dead thing. Renart and Odysseus can only gain literary power by avoiding its key event: the experience of death. Always and everywhere, Renart refuses the crucial test. By offering the Other as a sacrificial victim, he makes his literature into a pure rhetoric that has no plot consistency; it is an enormous scam.

Ysengrin, therefore, is the only true author. His encounter with the Other has reduced him to the loss of rhetoric, to castration, and to silence. However, the text reveals its own authorship here in a reflection necessary to its writing. Renart and Ysengrin cannot do without each other. The text (literature) can only be written *between* the fox and the wolf. It arises in the paradoxical opening that divides the mortal experience of the siren song (of hell, filth, castration—of the letter) from the survival of the signifier necessary for the text's living speech. The text is produced in the thread running from Renart's red fur, which identifies him as the one to be hanged, and the playful gilding that allows him to sing of his death. This is why the fox wants to establish the greatest distance possible between his two identities. He does not want to "resemble himself" at any price. As the "troubadour" with a fresh coat of dye says to Ysengrin,

> Pour tout l'avoir que Diex aver
> Ne voroie lui resambler. (2487–88)

> For all the gold God's got, me wouldn't want to be like him.

THE SAUSAGE RELIGION

In the first branch, the thing submits to dispersion and metaphor. The "thing" but also "nothing," "hangings" *(pendants),* and "sausage" name and displace the sexual secret of writing. Sausage, with all it connotes, is the key to branch 15.[19] Renart and Tibert the Cat, driven by hunger, find a sausage:

> Mes par mervilleuse aventure
> Une grant andouille ont trovee
> Les le chemin, en une aree. (104–6)

> By an amazing chance they came across a great [sausage] in a ploughed field beside the road.

The fox seizes it and in so doing repeats a series of motifs that mark Renardic textuality. I have already discussed these:

> Quant [Tibert] vit que el ne pot estre
> Renart fut de l'andoille mestre;
> Par le milieu aus dens la prent
> Que de chascune part li pent. (121–24)

> Tibert [saw] there was nothing else for it. Renart was master of the [sausage] with his teeth gripping it in the middle so that it hung down at both sides.

A group of signifiers take shape in the animal's gullet. First, Renart is sexualized in his possession of the imaginary phallus, a fantasy of mastery through the deflection of castration. He also achieves supremacy over the perpetual threat of death by hanging. Even more explicitly, he masters being itself with the rhyme *estre/mestre.* An abundance of meanings has suddenly come forward. This in no way stops Renart from speaking to interpret them, to give them his own meaning. From the beginning of his meeting with the cat, his speech has relied on the forms of good faith, of truth, of loyalty, and of belief. The rhetoric of the sermon dominates his discourse here, which changes the character of its object, the sausage:

> Avoi, Tibert! Ce dist Renart,
> Ne fuiez pas, n'aies esgart!
> Arrestes, si parles a moi!
> Souviegne vous de vostre foy!
> Que cuidiez vous que je vous face?
> Ne cuidiez pas (je Dieu ne place!)
> Que ja nul jour ma foy vous mente. (17–23)

> "Hey, Tibert!" said Renart. "Don't run away! Don't be scared, but stop and talk to me! Remember your promise! What do you suppose I'll do to you? Don't imagine that I'll ever break faith with you, please God! I wouldn't have taken this path today unless I'd expected to find you, because I want to keep my word to you. Aren't you very anxious to keep yours, Sir Tibert?"

Tibert turns the rhetoric of truth against itself and seizes the sausage from the fox. This transfer contains more than the comic trope of the deceiver deceived. Renart's rhetoric does get used against him in a denial of the imaginary possession of the phallus, but a blasphemy also takes place. Tibert, in order to keep the having/being of the sausage to himself, climbs a Christic symbol, a cross. Renart is unable to follow him, underlining once again his diabolic nature. Tibert perches atop one of the cross's arms and paradoxically treats the sausage as if it were the Eucharist:

> Vous deussiez molt bien savoir
> Que ceste andouille doit valoir.
> Que ceste chose saintifiee,
> Si ne doit pas estre mengiee
> Se sus crois non ou sus moustier:
> Moult la doit l'en bien exauchier. (203–8)

> "You should well know how precious this [sausage] is: it's a sanctified thing that should only be eaten on a cross or on top of a church. It must be treated with great reverence."

An ironic trap now ensnares the sausage, which only a moment before had been a sign of being and mastery/measure. It is taken up in a discourse that produces it as a relic *(chose saintifiee)* or even the body of Christ. Tibert and Renart both speak the same language. As the spokesmen of a literary discourse, they mimic Christian discourse and thus undermine its thingism. Christian speech now appears on the level of a fiction. A new sausage religion comes into being with Tibert as its highest and its only priest, and this allows him to turn an accusation of heresy against Renart. The same move also hides the fact that Tibert is a heretic who is accusing another of heresy. To share the discourse of the relic is in effect to cause the sausage to lose its supreme status as a holy thing:

> Pires estes que uns herites
> Qui me rouves chose geter
> Que l'en ne doit deshonnourer.
> Par fot, ja n'aure tant beu
> Que je a terre la vous ru.
> Ce est saintisme chose en loy:
> Andouille a nom, bien le saves,
> Nommer l'aves oy asses. (226–33)

> You're worse than a heretic to ask me to throw something that should not be dishonoured. By faith I'd never get so tipsy as to chuck it to the ground for you! That would go against my beliefs. There is one very sacred thing in religion, and, as you well know, its name is [sausage]: you've heard it so called often enough.

Branch 15 leads to the logical conclusion of any discourse of or on the thing in literature. Having been brought about by a rhetoric, the thing fictively founds an inverted religion. The otherness that originally marked it disappears in favor of a desiring game of signifiers. Drawing on the very forms of Christian discourse, the two animals systematically invert its conceptual and linguistic thingism. They produce, instead, a Eucharist and an Incarnation that, although indivisible, are profoundly perverse. The letter designating the thing has become a rhetorical signifier.

The *Roman de Renart* creates a synonymy among the *thing/res* of desire, of writing, and of the theology that it inverts. The goal is to upset the careful "differences" that Alain of Lille established in the "res" article of *Distinctiones:*

> Thing is sometimes taken in the wider sense, so that the three persons of the trinity are called one "thing." . . . It sometimes has the narrower sense of the Church in its real body; for this reason, Donatius can say nouns indicate either things or bodies. At times it means the incorporeal realities because we can have true notions [*notitia:* concrete notations, writing] of the incorporeal things; this is why the bodies of things are called "things"; this is why the reason that understands corporeal bodies is called reason. . . . The thing is taken to mean the truth because we say: "This is not a thing for us to discuss [a subject]," or "things are not like that." It can be taken to mean sexual congress, since we say: "he did the thing with her." It is taken to mean an advantage *[utilitas]*. . . . It is also taken to mean a proposition. (cols. 925–26)

Alain of Lille establishes a discursive grouping of terms under the form of a catalog of homonyms. There can be no relation between the Trinity, truth, and concept, on the one hand, and the sexual thing, on the other. He synthetically outlines the realism of difference at the very basis of his entire enterprise. But what if the thing that designates God and the Incarnation were synonymous with the cause of desire? In the case of the sausage, the *Roman de Renart* responds that this could be the case. It is the very point of its affront, through which it demonstrates the profound identity between literature and Alain's conception of heresy.

FERE LA CHOSE

In branch 13 *(How Renart Perfected the Twat)*[20] Renart, Ysengrin, Brichemer the Deer, and Chanticler the Rooster come together to plow and sow a wheat field. Before they are done, they will push the rhetorical logic of the signifier as the basis of the thing to its ultimate consequences. The story begins with a group of standard metaphors for writing. It is easy to read the images of plowing, of sowing, and of harvesting as erotic emblems as well as emblems for writing. The field is the page/womb, the plow the pen/penis, and the wheat the book/child.[21] Here, we have "labor" in all of its meanings: till, work, and give birth.[22]

Renart leaves to hunt in the woods, and in his absence his companions eat the harvest. Renart brings them to court, and to resolve the lawsuit, the four protagonists decide to accept the judgment of King Connin—a meaningful name. The text presents him as Renart's double:

Li rois ne tint mie peresce,
Contre Renart mout tost se dresce,
Si l'a dejoste lui asis,
Car il estoit moult ses amis. (13,774–77)

The king waited no longer, but stood to face Renart, and sat him at his side, for he was his very good friend.

The erotic-scriptural metaphors that I mentioned above now assume their full meanings. In effect, the king makes vaginas:

Li rois une beche tenoit
De d'autre mestier ne servoit
Que de cons feire seulement. (13,779–81)

The king held a spade that served no other purpose than to make twats.

A hoe artificially produces the Other (sex), just as the pen produces writing. By using a farm implement, the king has shown once again that alterity's origin lies in a production that depends entirely on the artificiality belonging to writing. The vagina is a furrow (*roie,* lines 13,516, 13,880), at one and the same time a trace and a line in a field, a page and a body.[23] The "origin of the world" has its absolute origin in the text's secondary status:

—Sainte Marie, sont si lait
Tuit li autre comme cist est?
—Oil, se Diex santé me prest,
Car tuit sont en un coing feru
Et de cest beche fandu. (13,802–6)

"By Saint Mary, are they all as ugly as this one?"
"Yes, and God give me health, because they have all been hit in the crotch, and split with this spade."

Just as we saw in the kite's speech, the vagina is overdetermined as Luciferian. It is *diaboli ianua,* a bottomless pit that devours everything:

C'est li goufres de satenie
Qui tout englout et tout recoit. (13,900–1)

It is Satan's pit that swallows all and takes all.

The text then complicates the open space of writing that it just produced by weaving together its metaphors. The king's fictional work remains incomplete:

Mais nais fesoit ne bel ne gent,
Que, qant la ploie avoit fandue
De la beche grant et molue,
Si remanoit hideuse et grant,
Ne ja ne reclousit nul tens
Que demi aune a grant mesure
Ne parut bien la fandeure. (13,782–88)

These were neither pretty nor noble, for when he made the wound with the large, rounded spade, it would never close up, but the gash seemed to be about half a yard in length.

The organs of excrement and of procreation and pleasure are still joined together in the king's writing/creation. A difference must be drawn between them, and the devouring horror of the vagina covered by a rhetorical *vestitio* that beautifies it, masks it, and refers to it. Renart asks to be allowed to finish what the king has begun and to complete its artificiality. He uses Brichemer's neck as a peritoneum to separate the anus and the vagina; Chanticler's crest then forms the vulvae, and Ysengrin's beard, the pubic hairs. Renart's actions displace the necessary castration from his own body onto the bodies of his opponents, while he remains whole. He thereby creates a new space for writing, where desire is entirely on the side of the woman and the rhetoric that produces and hides it is on the masculine side. Renart's mastery of the situation sets him in the place of the king, who recognizes the fox's wisdom and agrees with his advice. Moreover, Renart assumes a godlike role. His writing on the feminine body creates a new world, which only differs from the true in its secondary origin. Finally, Renart's/God's mastery in the text is circular. He unifies the story, its actions, and its object. It is he who produces the tale *(conte),* which can be read as a combination of two words: *con,* "twat," and *te,* "you." The branch's narrator draws attention to this anagram in the conclusion to the text:

Sanz plus en mestre et riens oster
Ici plus ge bien oposter
Et laisser dou conte dou con.

Nus n'en doit dire se bien ou non,
Qu'el monde n'a si douce rien
Com est li cons, ce set l'en bien
Ici parfine la chancon
Come Renart parfist le con. (14,159–66, emphasis added)

Without adding or taking anything away, here is where I leave off *the* [twaddle] *of the twat.* Let nobody speak ill of it, for in the world there is nothing so sweet as a twat, as is well known. So here ends the song of how Renart made twats.

The writing of fiction creates everything that used to be attributed to God. Renardy's absolute artificiality places all of nature, including divine creation, in question by mimicking it. The episode eliminates the alterity of the thing and reduces it to the result of the signifier's effects. The double meaning of the word *rien* perfectly designates this operation with its simultaneous reference to both the thing and the nothing.

THE FEIGNED ORIGIN

The passion for origins arrives late in the *Roman de Renart.* As the branches are added onto and compiled, it becomes more and more necessary to discover a starting point. This movement has an analogue in the tradition of the chansons de geste (*Enfances Guillaume, Enfances Vivien,* and others). The first texts of the Renart cycle seem to have appeared at the end of the twelfth century. *Renart's Childhood,* which describes Adam and Eve's apocryphal creation of the animals, is from the first half of the thirteenth century. Another text devoted to the question of origins, *Renart the Magician* (branch 23) dates from this period as well. *Renart the Counterfeit,* the immense compilation that tells of the origin of Renardy, dates from the fourteenth century. The logic of the postscript dominates this writing, which reveals its own origins, so this logic needs to be explored if we are to understand how the Renardic project attempts to make sense of itself.

The fox is once again on trial for his crimes at the beginning of *Renart the Magician.*[24] The branch opens with an intertextual assembly of several preceding episodes as Renart's deeds/texts are enumerated before the judge, Noble the Lion. At the end of the trial, the fox is condemned to death by hanging. This produces a rhyme between *art* and *hart,* "hanging."

Li rois a apele Renart,
Si li a livre par la hart. (951–52)

The king called Renart and gave him over to be hanged.

To escape his punishment, Renart makes up on the spot an imaginary land of milk and honey. Yvoris, the king of this imaginary country, has just one heir, his daughter, whom, according to Renart, he wishes to marry to Noble. The latter falls under the spell of Renardic rhetoric and the fictional country that it creates from whole cloth. He decides to suspend the sentence and to send Renart as his ambassador to Yvoris's court. What intrigues Noble the most is the power of metamorphosis that Renart ascribes to the king's daughter:

N'est beste tant con terre dure
Dont ne puist prendre la figure:
Molt par se set transmuer,
Quant ele se veut remuer. (989–92)

There is no animal living on earth whose form she cannot take. She is very capable of transmutation when she wants to change.

The ambassador has a problem. He must confirm the imaginary fiction that he has created. He brought forth a pure seductive sophistry designed to save him from death, and now he has to bring the princess before his king. The narrator emphasizes the impossibility of the task by underlining Renart's lie:

Renart Meismes nu savoit
Mais le roi amuse avoit:
Tel chose li faisoit acroire
Qui ne pooit pas estre voire;
Mes si le voloit enivrer
Qu'il se peust delivrer. (1059–64)

Renart himself knew nothing of it, but he had amused the king. He had made him believe things that cannot be true. But he had besotted him so he could be free.

Renart's goal is also that of the "realist" writer. He has to make others believe his rhetorical fiction. A legal argument and a poetical figure must be shown to copy the truth. The *Roman de Renart*'s "realism" can only have this one meaning. This excludes the commonplace of medieval criticism that sees a "realist" depiction of the epoch in this text, as it also does in the *fabliaux*. "Realist" art uses the most obvious sleight of hand. For confirmation, it refers to its own fictitious simulacrum. Hermeline, the fox's wife, tells him to go to Toledo to escape the trap that his own imagination has set for him:

> Loe li a que s'esience
> Velt aprendre de nigromance:
> "Jusqu'en Espaigne vos lassez.
> A Tolete en set on assez;
> Ce est un ars de tel maniere
> Que, qui bien en set la maniere,
> Tot fait a son commandement
> Que ce est l'art d'enchantement.
> Se de cel art apris avez
> Et de l'enchantement savez
> Par vostre enchant le roi ferez
> Quanque fere li deverez." (1169–80)

> She praised her whose wit desires to learn magic. "You must go to Spain. These things are well known in Toledo. This is such an art that he who knows its ways does all that he wishes, this is the art of enchantment. If you have leaned this art, and know enchantment, through your spell you will make the king do everything you wish."

In the tradition that begins with the prologue to the *Lais* of Marie de France, the essence of poetic speech is the science *(escience)* of making the dead speak. The entire passage cited above links art (that of realist writing) to the *pharmakon,* a magic tied to necromancy (etymologically, the art of making the dead speak). Branch 23 reveals this to be Renardy's basic nature. It is a magical and lying art, yet a powerful one, since its goal is nothing less than to gain absolute mastery over life, death, and political power.

In Toledo, Renart learns the fine points of the necromancy of writing. One must sacrifice a rooster or a black cat, being careful not to invoke the cross or to make its sign on one's body (line 1356), and then utter an incantation:

> Apres die sanz autre fable:
> "Oiez d'enfer tuit li deable!

> De ceste oevre soiez seignor
> Et si soit fet en vostre honor!" (1361–64)

> After this, say without hesitation: "Listen, all you devils in Hell! You are the lords of this work, and it is done in your honor."

One can no longer doubt the diabolical origin of the text/*oevre.*

Having mastered the craft of necromancy, Renart hurries back to Noble's court in the Forest of Broceliande, in the privileged space of Breton fiction (line 1405). Upon his arrival, he conjures up an inverted court of monstrous beasts, pure plausible phantasms who have no part in divine creation:

> Par enchant a fet maintes bestes,
> De tex i a qui ont vint testes.
> . . . .
> *Bestes a fait qu'ainz Dex ne cria*
> Et molt de diverse maniere,
> Et aussi con devant derriere. (1489ff; emphasis added)

> "He made many animals with his enchantment, some with twenty heads. . . . *He made such beasts as God never created,* and in many different forms, and some even faced backwards."

Renart gains control over the king's desires by creating Fiere, imaginary King Yvoris's imaginary daughter, who will become Noble's wife. The lion certainly shows the signs of power, but Renart secretly reigns in his place. Rutebeuf attempted to show this, and the branch entitled *The Coronation of Renart* makes it completely explicit.

At the wedding feast for the king and queen, Noble challenges the inverted court to a contest of minstrelsy. The devils win the contest in a burlesque of courtly manners and so reveal the truth of the royal court, where good does not exist. This scene, with its games of fictional and diabolical immateriality, also reveals the essence of the very move that presides over the writing of the *Roman de Renart* (and even over all literature). The writers of the various branches, experts in necromancy, produce talking animals that "God never created." The narrator of *Renart's Childhood* has already confronted this problem. He justifies the existence of talking animals by appealing to the biblical precedent of Balaam's ass. Religious authority is obviously made to cover for the transgressions of literature, since talking animals can only result from a divine miracle.[25] Every heresy has assigned the power of the Creator to worldly activity. The Luciferian writer of the *Roman de Renart,* through the themes of necromancy and talking beasts, once again unseats the divine in favor of the profane.

Renart/Lucifer becomes the origin of the world and its creatures, in a repetition of the cosmological scenario of the Cathar heresy et alia. He is the maker of fictions condemned by Tertullian, the producer of an antinature marked with the seal of evil. The animals that he creates have no body, exactly like the devil of orthodoxy, the Gnostic Christ. These are simulacra capable of assuming any shape; they are pure images that can do without food:

> Deable n'a de manger cure. (1706)

> The devil has no need to eat.

Branch 23 allows us to deduce a metaphysics of writing. It repeats the Gnostic heresies point by point, in the inversion of the Christian conception of creation. Renart, a new Pygmalion, shapes the idol of art, creates a cosmos, or a *chaosmos,* with an infinity of permutations: He creates literature. Literary discourse contests the Incarnation by specifically negating it. Its emblem in the text is Fiere, Noble's wife, who can take on all shapes because she has no being or identity of her own. She and literature are a diabolical nothing.

THE COUNTERFEIT

Renart the Counterfeit is the final medieval avatar of the *Roman de Renart.*[26] It was written at the beginning of the fourteenth century by a "cleric of Troyes," of whom we know nothing. In the tradition of Martianus Capella and Isidore of Seville, this cleric produced a compilation of texts. A true summary, *Renart the Counterfeit* draws on and rewrites numerous preceding branches of Renardy, but it also incorporates the *Roman d'Athis et Porphyrius,* the so-called ancient romances (*Eneas* and the *Roman de Thebes*), hagiography, the Bible, mythology, the *lai Laustic* and *Bisclavret* by Marie de France, and episodes from Arthurian romance. It also contains a universal prose history from the reign of Augustus to the year 1328, told by Renart to King Noble. *Renart the Counterfeit* anticipates Guillaume de Machaut's *Le Voir Dit,* written some forty years later. They both show a sweeping ambition that appears to rewrite the whole of medieval textuality.

Just as we have seen with Martianus Capella and Isidore of Seville, the problem in compilatory writing is always to locate what organizes the whole. The principal task of this writing is to produce a coherence from the heterogeneous collage of discourses that it refers to. To clarify the major points of this branch's compilatory principle, we need to follow the trail left for us by the "cleric of Troyes" who openly explains himself. Having fallen into the sin of acedia (which is the *acedia mortifera,* the well-known melancholia of medieval monks), he has also fallen into sloth, its consequence.[27] He writes to cure himself. However, no book of penitence, no medical treatise, recommends the composition of *Renart the Counterfeit.* This is not a curative drug. It plunges the author into a world where Renart rules as the absolute master, a world melancholically charged with every vice. The text explicitly notes the identity between writing and acedia, with its attendant sloth. The text prolongs these vices, rather than interrupting them, and it causes them to "branch" into a monstrous growth, arising like a pustule on the trunk of sins:

> Dame oyseuze a moult de branches,
> Malvaisez, perileuses, franches. (39–40)

> Lady Idleness has many branches, evil, perilous, and free.

And further along:

> Pour ce est d'oizeuze la branche
> Dure, pesme, courtoise et franche.
> En tel oizeuze, c'est prouvé,
> Chelui qui cest livre a rimé
> L'an mil trois cens dix et noeuf
> Commenca ce livre tout noeuf. (97–102)

> This is why idleness's branch is hard, foul, courtly, and free. In such idleness, as we know, is the man who rhymed this book, in the year 1319, started this new book.

On the other hand, in opposition to Martianus and Alain of Lille, who assigned the lordship over the *septennium* of liberal arts respectively to Harmonia and Dame Theology, our cleric gives the crown to the discipline of Renardy:

A brief parler, tous les sept ars
Sont tous enclins a celles pars,
Ne nul des sept ars, s'il [n]'y touce,
N'est si fonde que il ne loche,
Car sans lui doibvent bien locher.
Certes si font ilz tous clochier;
Car sans lui sont tout d'onnour monde
Selon la chevance du monde.
Et qui est cil qui n'a beance
De science avoir et chevance?
Combien que des ars assez sache,
Tant q'un chascun peut s'I atache.
Se tout aprent et tout detient,
Se de cellui art ne retient,
—Si me garde Dieu d'avoir la fievre!—
Adont sera tenu pour chievre:
On dira a jung qu'il est yvres,
Ou que c'est un sac plain de livres.
Sache loi ou dialecticque
Riens ne scet, s'il ne scet practique;
Mais s'il scet de ceste maistrie
De Renart qui tous ars maistrie,
Apregne tant comme il voudra;
Sans cel art, petit lui vauldra. (309–32)

To be brief, all the seven arts tend to this, nor is any of the seven arts so well-founded that it won't shake if it is touched by it, because without it, they all must shake. They all limp along, because without it, all honor goes as go worldly fortunes. And who is he that does not desire to have knowledge and good fortune? He knows of these arts as anyone who can acquire them. If one learns all, and retains all, but knows nothing of this art—and God keep me from the fever!—he will be called a goat. They will tell children that he is drunk, or that he is a book bag. To know law or dialectic without the practical, is to know nothing. But if he knows what Renart, who has mastered all, knows, he will learn as much as he wants. Without this art, it is worth little.

Renart the Counterfeit's hidden yet foundational art of Renardy, like all medieval writing, attempts to insinuate itself into the *septennium.*

Renardy brings meaning to these seven arts by practicing them in the world. However, these ancient studies are applied not to support the revealed truths of religion but to subvert them. Although the practice of Renardy is negative, it serves the seven liberal arts. Without a worldly application, they would remain a collection of hollow sentences without reference to anything but themselves.

The fox comes very close to Geoffrey of Vinsauf's poetic of the *rejuvenatio.* Renart's art, which renews the ancient or ruins the new, "makes the old new and the new old" (line 282). The novelty here obviously has nothing to do with the announcement of the good news of the Gospels, yet the narrator associates himself with it when he continually claims to be writing a new book (lines 18, 102, 380). Here is the first clue that Renart could very well be the narrator, and vice versa. Like any compiler, the narrator of this branch does not pretend that he is inventing anything with regard to the contents of his work; these come quite explicitly from other sources. The novelty is the previously neglected meaning that these contents receive from the framework that organizes them. *Renart* is not a pre-text, an original manuscript, a first sense. He has no being of his own, and so he is a "cipher," a thing that is (not). His writing is characterized by its supplementarity: It adds a branch to a trunk that does not exist. As a whole, *Renart the Counterfeit* is a gloss on the primary text. The narrator thus gives us this meaning of counterfeit:

> C'est le Contrefait de Regnart,
> Car sur Regnart poeult on gloser,
> Penser, estudier, muser
> Plus que sur toute rien qui soit.
> *Le texte layt, prende la glose.* (104–8, emphasis added)

> This is Renart's counterfeit. For one can comment on Renart, think about, study, and muse on him more than on all that is. Leave the text, take up the commentary.

As the following citation makes clear, the need for a gloss is a matter of life and death. Virgil, the legendary model of all poets, dies at the end of the fourth branch of *Renart the Counterfeit.* The cause of his demise is his inability to let go of the text and take hold of the gloss:

> Se sa teste gardee eust,
> Ja si trestot mort [Virgille] ne fust.

Mais il s'en passa simplement,
Et print le texte seulement,
Combien de gloser bien sceust,
Tresmal advis par lui prins fust. (29,645–50)

If he had kept his head, Virgil would not have died so soon. But he tried to do without it, and took the text alone, even though he knew how to gloss, he made a very bad decision.

Renardy limits itself to the deviant, secondary quality of commentary. One must avoid all primary, original, or authentic texts/meanings and limit oneself to the deviant secondarity of the commentary. The moralized blackness of lying signs stains the whiteness of the unmarked page, where the art of the gloss entirely obliterates the preceding meaning:

C'est l'art qui fait du blanc le noir
De la mensonge fait le voir. (279–80)[28]

It is the art that makes white into black and makes truth of lies.

This is a line that must be reread in its secondary meaning. Certainly Renart turns everything on its head, but Renardy also, and in every case actively, alters its lie or the absence of primary truth and gives literature its reference to truth. Renart is the one who always finishes by revealing and producing a truth (for example, by demonstrating the truth of heresy or of the structure of desire). He has this power, even though he starts with a fabulous, allegorical, mythological, or even factual covering, that is to say, with a sophistic rhetoric fundamentally indifferent to the true and the false:

Et Regnart nous dit et enseigne
Que bon est que homme se tiegne
De dire mencogne ne voir,
S'amours de pluseurs voeult avoir. (113–16)

And Renart tells us and teaches that it is good for us to keep from telling the truth or lies, if we want the love of many.

The cleric of Troyes is implicated in this process:

Cil clerc plusieurs fois s'en faint,
Sa langue maniere constraint,

Et mist ce derriere devant.
Pour ce commence cest rommant
Pour dire par escipt couvert
Ce qu'il n'osoit dire en appert
Et jetter lui convenoit foeur
De la cheminee du coeur. (117–24)

This cleric lies several times, and constrains his language, and puts first what is last. He started this book so he could say in concealed writing what he dared not say in the open, and so throw it far from the hearth of his heart.

The challenge is to "find the truth *against* the lie" (line 76; emphasis added). Not only does the *contreoeve* (lines 34,789, 40,550)—an act of writing, the counterfeiting of the romance—fabricate unbelievable fictions, but it also produces truthful representations. Otherwise, it would be impossible to distinguish fiction from the truth without equivocating with the false. Julius Caesar's horse is an ideal paradigm for this operation mingling the false and the true. The animal is a unicorn, and so it is stamped with the mark of fable. However, a positive *counterfeit* of it does exist. The author refers to it in the fiction by placing it in the temple of Venus:

Puis fu che cheval contrefais
De droit marbre bien a devis,
Et ou palaix de Romme mis. (21,514–16)

Then was this horse manufactured and well-formed from pure marble, and placed in the palace in Rome.

Renart is the model of Romanesque writing. Associated with every form and force of negativity, he is the master of a "science" that produces vernacular texts. The cleric of Troyes declares that he himself is Renart's equal and that he intends to transmit his science to his readers:

Ains voeul que tous soit sceu
Une science qu'aprins ay
De grant auctorite, et scay
Que plusieurs y prendront grant bien,
S'ilz le veulent entendre bien. (224–28)

So I want everyone to know this science that I have learned from a great authority, and I know that many will find great good there if they are willing to listen well.

The writer perches on the branch of sloth and *controeuve* (line 57). He is a liar who "effaces good natures and counterfeits good people" (lines 60–61). Yet he is also an inventor/creator in the language that makes the false into a sign of the truth by showing its untruth.[29] The "blunder" *(bourde)*—that is, the Romanic language and its literature—takes on a positive ring:

Maintes bourdes sont graciezes,
Et sans nuire, et si sont joyeuses;
Mieulx vallent, qui bien les scet dire,
Que ne fait ung grant voir plein d'ire,
Car plusieurs voirs sont si pervers,
De hayne et de mal couvers.
Pour ce vault bourde gracieuze
Myeulx que verite ennuyeuze. (29,953–60)

Many blunders are graceful, and without harm, and are even joyful. They are more worthy to those who can speak them, than a great hateful truth, for many truths are perverse, and cloaked in hatred and evil. This is why a graceful blunder is worth more than an annoying truth.

In the carnivalesque reversal that writes serious literature as a farce, all values are transmuted. Alain of Lille emphasizes the diabolism of perversity, for example. From now on, perversity will be on the side of truth, and so fiction changes signs.

The counterfeit is the inversion of Christian discourse. The signs of this *Umwertung dem Werte,* the devaluing of values, are everywhere in the branch. First of all, the narrator is not a true cleric, no matter what he says. He does not wear the tonsure, having broken his vow of chastity. Excluded from the ecclesiastical community, he is one of those "bigamous" clerics (married to a woman rather than to the church) whom Adam de la Halle denounced in the *Jeu de la feuillee* in the preceding century. The first branch of *Renart the Counterfeit* ends with this admission:

Et pour ce en feray une histoire
Nouvel escripte et nouvel fait
Que cil clerc a encores fait;
Clerc, non, car couronne n'ot point:
Par femme perdy il ce point.
Le grant deable ayt de celuy l'ame

Qui premier estably bigame!
Or m'en tais, n'en puis aultrement,
Ce poise moi certainement. (3190–98)

This is why I will tell a newer story more newly recorded than the one made by that cleric. Cleric? No, his head's not shaved. A woman lost him that title. May the great devil take the soul of the inventor of bigamy. Now I will shut up, and I can do nothing else, for this weighs heavily on me.

At a deeper level, the origin of the Renardic science (which is also the writer's) is entirely Luciferian. In the second branch, Noble again wants to hang the fox, who has been condemned by the royal court. Once again, Renart escapes by charming the king with his speech. This time, he takes the place of the narrator and produces *Renart the Counterfeit.* It is pure invention, but it suffices to acquit him of all of the charges:

Son ire passa en l'oyant
Delyt prend en lui escoutant
A parler moult Renart prisa
Et Renart en parlant prins l'a. (5961–64)

His anger passed as he listened, and he took delight in listening; Renart prized speaking, and through speaking, Renart took him in.

The king, taken in by the ornament of science that the speaker uses, asks about his origins. Renart responds in this surprising manner.

—Sire mon corps fu nez n'a guerres
Et assez prez est mes repaires.
Mais mon sens et mes ars est fais
Long temps avant qu'Adam fut fais
Et avant que le monde fust
Ne que cha aval riens eust. (5983–88)

"Sir, my body was born not long ago, and my den is near here. But my wisdom and my art were made a long time before Adam and before the world, and before there was anything here below."

Renardic cosmology creates a world before Genesis. Renart does a heretical rewrite of the biblical pre-text. This frightens Noble, who reminds the fox, in very Christian terms, of orthodox dogma, in whose name he commands the speaker to silence. In particular, and not without contradiction with his own nature, the king cannot agree with a cosmology where the bestiality of desire precedes human reason:

Car comment porroit ce estre?
Depuis que Dieu, Le Roy celestre,
Eust fait ciel et terre et mer,
Fist il bestes, ne nul parler
Ne doit qu'elles fussent devant,
Ne qu'en terre fussent pessant.
C'estoit abisme et obcurté,
N'y avoit veue ni clairté,
Ne nulle [r]ien n'y habitoit;
De tout ce qu'on voit riens n'estoit.
Doncques ne t'en creray ja mye;
Tayz toy, ne diz plus tel folye! (5993–6004)

How can this be? After God, the celestial king, made heaven and earth, he made animals, and no speech came before them, nor was it present on the earth. There was darkness and emptiness, there was no light or sight, and nothing lived here. Nothing of what we see existed. Thus, I will believe you no longer; shut up, and speak no more foolishness.

Renart responds that his apocryphal genesis has nothing to do with matter and the body (nature). The soul lies at the base of his discourse. Renart's reading of the biblical text is heterodox and has a great deal in common with Gnosticism. It allows Renart to affirm his spiritual priority over the First Cause, and it lends coherence to his Romanesque cosmology in an inversion of the chronology of Creation. (In Genesis, soul and body result from a quasi-simultaneous creation.) The angels who fell from Paradise engender Renardy in a capital, because spiritual, fornication, as Saint Augustine would say:

Car je vous tesmoigne pour voir:
Devant tout, ce est mon savoir,
Au moins de ce bien me creez
Qu'avant que monde fut creez,
Furent fais anges beaux at gens:
Bien poez scavoir se je mens.
—Quels anges?—Ceux qui s'orguillyrent
Qui tantost en enfer cheyrent. (6007–14)

But I am telling you truly that my knowledge comes before all, at least believe me in this, that before the world was created, beautiful and sweet angels were created. You can easily tell whether I am lying. "What angels?" "Those who became proud and then fell into hell."

Renart pushes the rewriting of Genesis, begun in the branch of *Renart's Childhood,* to its ultimate conclusion. He turns the originary text against itself. Divine creation was little more than a clumsy repair job. Its goal was to fill the seats of Paradise with human souls, now that their first occupants had been evicted:

Mais pour ces sieges recouvrer
Vault Dieu le monde faire ouvrer,
Faire homme qui naturelement
Par sa semence durement
Remplesit les sieges vuidies.
. . . .
Fait fut le monde, et [Dieu] homme y mist
Et por ce povrement le fist. (6047–56)

But to refill these seats, God needed to make the world, to make man, who naturally, through his seed, quickly refilled the empty seats. . . . The world was made, and God put man there, and this is why he made him poorly.

Just as in Marcionism, Manichaeism, and Catharism, matter (nature) is held to be bad in essence. The spiritual art of negativity and of evil (Renardy) has the privelege of the pre-text. In the same move, this negativity gains the status of absolute truth, but this "truth" is only a pale rhetorical imitation of truth:

Par Nature n'est pas mon art
Ne par Nature n'est Renart.
Mon corps a bien Nature fait,
Mais mon art a des lors attrait.
Par mon art s'orguillirent anges,
Par mon art sont du ciel estranges,
Car se mon art n'eussent tenu,
Ja du ciel ne fussent cheu. (6021–28)

My art is not from nature, and neither is Renart. Nature has shaped my body, of course, but my art has come to me since. Through my art the

> angels became proud, and by my art they are foreign to heaven, for if they had not adhered to my art, they never would have fallen from heaven.

The art of compilation emphasizes the quasi identity of this cosmology with the dualism of the Manichaeans. Renart clearly mentions heresy while he unrolls the prose fable of universal history for the king. Manes's *engin,* "ingenuity, ruse," twins him with Renart, who is *de moult grant engin,* "very clever":

> En cellui tempz, fut ung herese en Perce qui fut de moult grant engin, qui avoit nom Manes. Il fut le commencement des Manicees, qui mettent deux dieux, ung bon et ung malvais. Le bon fist toutes les choses non visibles, comme les anglez et les ames humaines. Le malvais dieu fist toutes les choses corporelles que l'on peut veoir. Et ainsi selon leur oppinion, l'homme est composé de deux choses, dont l'une est bonne, et ce est l'ame et l'autre est malvaise, et ce est le corps.[30]

> In this time, there was a heretic in Persia who was very clever, and his name was Manes. This was the beginning of the Manichaeans, who have two gods, one good and one evil. The good one made all the invisible things like angels and human souls. The evil god made all corporeal things that we can see. And so, according to them, man is made of two things: one good, which is the soul, and the other bad, and that is the body.

However, he does not need to refer to Manes. Confirming the identity of heresy and literature, the text mentions two articles of the Cathar faith.[31] Alain of Lille refuted these in the *Contra haereticos* (they are the beliefs in the void of heaven, and the two principles of creation).

In heresy, negation is the source of all that is. This is especially true of *Renart the Counterfeit.* It represents the rebirth of the entirety of medieval textuality over which it reigns. (The fox's name is sometimes spelled *Regnart* in the manuscript.) *Renart*'s radical, originary, and absolute evil hides behind a concealing sense of the good and is its latent truth. The activity of the compiler appears anodyne and innocent, but it purposefully invokes and demonstrates the origin of every text in Renardy. The compilation's result is anti-Catholic. The text makes clear, as we have seen with Martianus Capella and Isidore of Seville, that compilation is never a disinterested gesture of juxtaposition. The encyclopedist's intention, whether good or bad, always becomes apparent in the gaps that lie between his quotations and borrowings. To illustrate my point, I need only turn to the story of the Incarnation as it appears in *Renart the Counterfeit.*[32] Renart himself retells this story, but in his own way. Of course, there is no question of drawing a Christian lesson from the story of Christ as it appears here. The event of Jesus' birth demonstrates the truth of astrology, a science formally condemned by Saint Augustine in the *Confessions.* It also confirms the prophecies of the inspired pagans who had predicted the Incarnation. This historical event becomes a pawn in Renardy's game. As such, it moves from the letter to the signifier.

One problem remains unsolved here. It has profound implications not only for the "publication" of *Renart the Counterfeit* (that is, its being written out), but also for the "publication" of every other branch of Renardy. The cleric of Troyes announces at the start of his compilation that the law of dissimulation controls his writing (lines 121–22), so he must now use all the resources of rhetorical *vestitio* to tell the truth to and of his century. He will disguise it with the masks of fable, *controeve,* allegory, and even history. The text itself, however, explicitly gives the lie to this strategy. The rhetorical veil is too thin; it never covers the naked truth. The narrator is constantly threatened with exposure, and is being attacked from all sides:

> Car trestout son volloir ouvry
> Et a aucuns se descouvry
> Qui faignoit ses amis estre.
> Mais depuis, si fu mue l'estre,
> Qui le mirent en bas degre
> Quant ilz eulrent sceu son secre. (22,451–56)

> And soon he worked his will and revealed himself to all those who claimed to be his friends. But since then, those who know his secret have remained silent when they have seen him in such low station.

To write *Renart the Counterfeit* is not to hide. The text lays bare a sincerity that says all, or says the All:

> Mais ay aprins a dire tout
> Quancques je peanse tout au bout. (22,549–50)

> But I have learned to say all that I think, from end to end.

This law of truthful speech formally contradicts its main character, the great master of all veils:

> Regnard, qui bien son penser couevre
> Sans cryer et sans monstrer s'oeuvre. (22,643–44)

> Renart, who knows how to cover his thoughts without shouting and without showing the work.

The very enunciation of the counterfeit is taken up in a duplicitous structure that continually inverts and destroys it. The dissimulation is given the lie by the written publication of the ruses that expose its mechanisms, its aims, and its strategies as visible to all except to the blinded protagonists. The "sophic" (sophistic) path of Renart is not one, since it forms the prize of the reader's pleasure through the unveiling of all of its formulae.

This hiding/showing problematic is fundamental to all the branches. The cleric of Troyes here asks a question that cuts to the heart of the structural integrity of the Renardic text. The ruse (including that of language) is a false ruse, for the simple reason that the writer makes it public.

Furthermore, Romanic rhetoric fails by succeeding. Renart masters his textual space only by avoiding every risk (castration, hanging, death, and so on), putting the wolf in his place. He thus reveals the emptiness of the means used to stop him, as well as his mastery's deceitful nature. The fox is nothing without Ysengrin to receive every blow. Renart delegates the mortal risks of writing to Ysengrin. In his absence, the fox can do nothing, not even take part in his own text. The whole of the *Roman de Renart* thus runs into the dead end of literary negativity. In destroying the Incarnation, it is in constant danger of reconfirming its positivity. The text cannot be read outside the dogma that it denies, and so the *Roman* must resay all the words of that dogma with more force than ever. There is only one step from deriding to being derided, and the writing seems to propose only two possible outcomes to the reader: laughter or resentment.

PARADIS(COURS)E

Renart the Counterfeit is caught in a dead end by proposing the antithesis to Christian discourse and, through inverting it, reproducing it.[33] However, a previous branch, *The Well (Le puits),* escapes this trap.[34] The branch begins with a famine in Renart's home country. So, gnawed by hunger and thirst, he goes to seek sustenance in foreign lands:

> L'autrier estoit venuz conquere
> Sa garison an autre terre (3291–92)

> One day he had gone to another district in search of provisions.

The local fauna is alien to Renart the outcast:

> Mais n'i voit rien de sa pasture. (45)[35]

> [There was] nothing to see of his sort of food.

Then he comes across an abbey inhabited by white monks. Next to it is a well and a barn whose strangeness is also emphasized:

> Mot par estoit grande la grange,
> Mais a aucuns est mout estrange. (3335–36)

> It was an excellent farm, though not known to many people.

In the *Poetria nova,* Geoffrey of Vinsauf assembles the same rhetorical tropes found in this topography under the name of *peregrinatio.* The tropes are easy to spot. Lambs represent words. (Their role is taken here by the grouses and capons that Renart covets.) They go out to pasture in foreign fields in the migrations of a metaphor.[36] The abbey is thus a poetic text, filled with words that the fox intends to swallow into his devouring gullet. As for Renart, his hungry approach to the abbey is the very movement of metaphor.[37] His wandering migration is that of words, obliterating propriety and replacing it with the creation of a new meaning. Just as with the villager's hurdy-gurdy, the appropriation here comes at a price that must be paid before one can enter into metaphor:

> Or est Renart en grant balance,
> Que, s'il puent aparcevoir
> Que il les voille decevoir,
> Li moine retendront son gag
> Ou li meimes en ostages,
> Car felon sont a demesure. (3356–61)

> Now Renart is in a risky situation, because if the monks catch sight of him trying to dupe them, they will take some forfeit from him or take his person as hostage, very cruel people that they are.

The moat also has a place in the textual topography of the scene. At first, it is a metaphor for femininity. Like the dyer's vat, it also contains *eve,* "water," in Old French. This clearly refers to the mother of humanity. Branch 3 *(Renart's Childhood)* portrays her as having an unmasterable, desiring, and savage femininity.[38] In *The Well* as well, femininity remains out of Renart's grasp:

Mais il ne pot a l'eve ateindre. (3403)

But he could not reach the water.

However, the water soon becomes a deceitful mirror. Its surface hides the masculine same and only seems to show Renart the alterity of the woman:

Dedanz conmence a regarder
Et son anbre a aboester
Quide que ce soit Hermeline,
Sa fame, qu'aime d'amor fine,
Qui herbergie fust leenz. (3413–17)

He turns his eyes down and glimpses his reflection. He supposed it was his wife Hermeline, his true love, who had found a place down there.

Renart calls out to Hermeline in the well and hears his own echo. This confirms for him that the annihilating shadow and the narcissistic image are what they appear to be. He thus decides to dive in and rejoin his wife, and the well becomes hell:

Maufe l'ont mis en cele trape. (3432)

Devils have sprung that trap on him!

The Lady is no longer an inaccessible symbol of alterity. Now she is the courtly poet's projected image, which he wears himself out chasing. He only ends up embracing the nothing of his own shadow, and so the poetic of *fin'amor* (the courtly love of the troubadours and trouvères), which has dominated the passage to this point, shifts to the account of a narcissistic fantasy.[39] Referring also to the *puys* (a gathering where authors would present their literary productions in competition), the well *(puits)* is the space of a mirror poetics. One image refers to another, and on to infinity with no destination in alterity, thing, or truth.

Ysengrin then happens along, and he is also attracted to the abbey.

He also finds the well and sees his reflection in it. Not only is his image reflected, but his actions reflect those of Renart. Thus, he confirms the endless play of the poetics of the mirror.

Dedanz commence a esgarder
Et son ambre a aboester.
Com plus i fu, plus esgarda,
Tot ensint con Renart entra;
Quida que fust dame Hersant
Qui herbergiee fust leanz
Et que Renart fust avec lui. (3461–67)

He leaned over the well; and there he caught a glimpse of his own reflection. The more he saw, the more he gazed at it, just as Renart had done. He supposed it was Lady Hersent who was taking cover in there, and Renart with her.

Once set into motion, the transfer and shifting of images cannot stop. In this game of reflections, Renart holds the transgressive position of the adulterer, which is also that of the courtly poet. Ysengrin, on the other hand, takes on the role of the jealous husband, the law that stands between poet and lady. Looking into the well, Ysengrin mistakes his shadow for the she-wolf, his lawful wife. The effect of the textual mirror thus not only projects desire onto its narcissistic shadow but also produces the law as a reflection without consistency or depth. In this way, its effect is one of a surface or a signifier. In the literary text, the law (husband) is an image for the Law. This occurs in a play of diacritical differences that are brought about by the signifier but do not transcend it.

Renart is once again trapped in the mortal snares of an alterity conceived of as the same (for the well is at once death, woman, and hell). Ysengrin, once more, will provide him the means of escaping his fate. Renart begins his manipulations by pretending to have already succumbed to the trap:

Mais l'en m'apele feu Renart
Qui tout savoit d'angin et d'art. (3495–96)

But I'm known as the late Renart, who was so clever and cunning.

Through this fictional death, the fox reveals the status of what he is (not). In the tension between the *Roman de Renart*'s lie and its pretense to the truth, he exists as an image: the pure voice of a bodiless story that never stops producing echoes out of echoes. The echolalic basis of literature becomes a theme a century later in *Renart the Counterfeit.* In this inspired rewriting of the episode of the well, Renart asks Ysengrin to confront his reflection, the false Hersent. Thus, the wolf is tricked into believing what the fox has been saying about the well:

> "Or le [Hersent] huche, se je d'y voir."
> Lors huche le loup se voir dit,
> Et la voix lui respond "Voir dist." (28,010–12)

> "Now ask Hersent if I am telling the truth." So the wolf asks if this is true, and the voice responds, "This is true."

Such is truth in literature. It hangs from the echoes of rhymes, forming itself in the desiring reply of a voice whose source is lost in repetition.

But let us return to the second branch, *The Well.* To deceive the wolf, Renart strings together the commonplaces of a religious *doxa* with the purpose of convincing his listener that he is dead:

> Nus hom ne s'en doit merveiller
> Se je suis morz, que tuit morront
> Trestuit cil qui en vie sont:
> Par mi la mort les convandra
> Passer au jor que Dieu plaira. (3500–04)[40]

> No one should be surprised if I am dead: all those now living will also die. They will have to pass away on the day God pleases.

Having studied his ancient rhetoric carefully, he portrays the well as a paradise. He fills it with empty signs that appeal to Ysengrin's desire. In Renart's rhetoric, Paradise ceases to be a (Christian) space where beatitude makes all desire obsolete. Heaven is now a place where earthly desires can be appeased with infinite pleasure:

> Conpere, j'ai ce que je voil:
> Je n'oi onques cure d'orgoill;
> Se tu ies ou resne terrestre,
> Je suis en paradis celestre.
> Caienz sont les gaaigneries,
> Li bois, li plain, les praieries:

Ceenz a riche pecunaille,
Ceenz puez veoir mainte aumaille,
Et bues et vaches et moutons,
Espreviers, ostors et faucons. (3521–30)

Companion, I have all I desire. I never was bothered with pride. Whereas you're in the earthly kingdom, I am in heavenly Paradise. Here are the farmsteads, the woods, the meadows; here are the great riches; and there's a great quantity of cattle to be seen here, many ewes and goats, and you can see an abundance of hares, bullocks, cows, and sheep, sparrowhawks, goshawks, and falcons.

In the final trope of Renardy/rhetoric, the two buckets in the well become the scales of justice:

Renart set bien som sen despandre,
Que por voir li a fait entendre
Poises sont de bien et de mal:
"Par Dieu le pere esperital,
Diex si par est issi puisenz
Que, quant li biens est si pesanz,
Si s'en avale ca dejus
Et touz li maus reva lassus." (3555–62)

Renart astutely gives Isengrin to understand that it is the balance for weighing good and evil: "by God the divine Father, his great power is such that when the good weighs heavy enough, it drops down here and all the evil [returns] up there."

Ysengrin can no longer resist the accumulation of these multiple seductions, and so he leaps into the bucket. Having inverted every Christian value and hierarchy, the text seems to reestablish them in this one rising/falling movement of the buckets:

Isengrin l'a araisone:
"Renart, biau frere, ou va tu?"
Et Renart li a respandu:
"N'en faites ja chiere ne frume:
Bien vos en dirai la costume:
Quant li uns va, li autres vient,
C'est la costume qui avient." (3602–8)

> Isengrin questioned Renart: "Good friend, why are you coming up?" To this Renart replied: "Don't pull a long or sorry face: I'll tell you just what the custom is. When one comes down, the other comes up; that's the normal procedure."

In classical rhetoric, the tropes of commutation never simply invert or repeat what they change.[41] An inversion always creates a new meaning. The same is the case in the *Roman de Renart.* In the movement of the buckets in the well, the drama and fiction of the text make this explicit. In the first place, the well-mirror returns to its canonical status as hell. In the same movement, Renart's rise toward the earth changes it into a heterodox paradise. The troping of values creates an anti-Christian excess:

> Ge vois en paradis laisus,
> Tu vas ou puis d'enfer lajus;
> De deaubles sui eschapez
> Et tu t'en revas a maufez:
> Par Dieu le pere esperitable,
> Ici conversent li doiable. (3609–13)

> I'm going up to paradise, and you're going down into hell. I've escaped from the devils: you, for your part, are bound for the demons. . . . By god the divine Father, down there is the abode of devils.

In Renart's words, heaven is in no way a transcendent beyond those beatitudes one earns in the "vale of tears." One fulfills one's desires in the *hic et nunc,* the "here and now," of a completely earthly enjoyment. Earth *reflected by hell* is Heaven. The music of language and its play of assonance, originating in the diabolic hurdy-gurdy, dominate all speech about the hereafter. The twisted speech of fiction and Renardic rhetoric links itself indissolubly to paradis(cours)e. Just as for Martianus Capella or Guillaume de Machaut, the permutation of values in writing is a para-discourse, a para-bolique discourse, that twists all correct speech into its fictional curving.

The "moral" of the second branch *(The Well)* pushes non-Christian discourse on the Incarnation past heresy to its greatest limit: atheism or the death of God. The material, the incarnate is all there is, and a transcendent heaven no longer exists. The entire world is empirical and concrete. It has no depth other than that of the desire it evokes. There is no more need of a beyond to legitimate the here and now. Furthermore, this world of desire without penitence and without salvation arises entirely in the back-and-forth of a writing that makes values and meanings come and go like buckets. "The well" is thus clearly distinct from the Cathar heresy. In Gnosticism, there always exists a transcendence in whose name the world and matter are devalued. In *Renart the Counterfeit*, the fox exists entirely in the here below; his discourse is that of (im)pure presence, where all transcendence gives way to sensual experience, to the enjoyment of an absolute now:

> Car le monde prent a sa part
> Le fait et la ligne Regnart,
> Et lait Raison, dont tout bien vient,
> Et a l'oeuvre Regnart se tient,
> Qui ne pense ne estudie
> Fors qu'a ceste presente vie:
> Au present tent, le present tent,
> A nulle aultrefin il ne tent. (39,241–48)

> Renart's line is to take the world as his own, and to forget reason, from whom all good comes, so Renart keeps to the created, and neither thinks nor studies anything except this present life. To the present time, the present time, and to no other end does he work.

The branches *The Well* and *Renart the Counterfeit* can be seen as the fictional outlining of the heresy of the Free Spirit, which had a certain success in the thirteenth and fourteenth centuries. For its adherents, there was no heaven or hell; everything happened in the *hic et nunc* of human life. For them, it was possible to unite with God, to be Christ, without having to observe the liturgy. Whoever achieved this unity could pursue his carnal desires with no fear of retribution. If need be, he could change roles and unite with one or the other sex, and if possible, this would be done on the consecrated altar. It was forbidden to believe in the Incarnation or the Resurrection. Work was considered useless, for one must, above all, enjoy life completely.[42] This radical denial of transcendence, this elevation of material enjoyment, goes beyond Gnosticism. It corresponds point by point to the Renardic paradise and to its ideology glorifying the parasitic feudal lord (or the Hegelian master), who consumes—that is, destroys—the fruits of servile labor.

Through the labor of its writing, the text produces an institution (or counterinstitution, Tertullian's *ecclesi diaboli*). The Renardic text thus circles back on itself. Its speech creates a religion of the pure present, a material (sausage) religion that it practices in its own creation. *The Coronation of Renart* describes this fiction-religion and promotes the triumph of the fox over the whole world.

By the twelfth century, Saint Bernard had already compared the heretics who infiltrated the church to a *"Renart tapi dans son taniere"* (fox hiding in his den).[43] After him, Gautier of Coincy, in his *Life of Saint Leocade,* compares healthy mendicants to the fox.[44] Thus, from the very beginning of the appearance of the cycle, Renart was used in edifying texts as an example of a heretic. The question arises: Can literature be anything but a heresy, a denial of dogma, yet deceitful because it always finishes by confirming dogma?

Curiously, although Renart restates the heretical thesis, the treatises on heresy and the manuals of the Inquisition never mention his literature. The inquisitorial practice distinguishes clearly between those it pursues and those mentioned in the Bernardian metaphor cited above. Because it works its fictions independently of dogma, Renardic textuality escapes the law, the eye of the Grand Inquisitor. Renart does not confirm the law; rather, he is its exception. He has no value to be condemned and burned in the auto-da-fé. The bodies of the heresiarchs, on the other hand, were too real and too easily thrown onto the fire. From anonymy to pseudonymy, from branch to supplement to gloss, meanings circulate in the Renardic practice of writing. Their active and insatiable negativity can never be pinned down. Simply put, Renardy does not oppose the logic of the Incarnation; rather, it plays on its limits, in every sense of the word. *Oportet haereses esse* ("We need heretics"): After having been expelled from the social body, the heretics take refuge in literature, under the mask of disincarnate and thus unburnable "authors."

9

Disincarnation: Guillaume de Machaut

ORDENANCE

The *Voir Dit,* most notable for the virtuosity of its style and rhetoric, is also Guillaume de Machaut's poetic masterpiece. Within this poem, every genre is handled with the utmost grace. A brilliant use of intertextuality holds together what is at once a poem, an epistolary tale, a verse narration, and an autobiography. The *Voir Dit* evokes an entire library and an entire way of knowing, by referring to or containing elements of courtly poetry, mythology, the Bible, and Arthurian romance, seemingly without limit. It is as if Guillaume de Machaut had complete control over the writing of fiction, both in the use of its elements and in its language.

Machaut's use of one word crystallizes his virtuosity and his confidence: *ordenance,* the law of speech, the order of fiction. This word connotes mastery, and at the beginning of manuscript number 1584 of the Bibliothèque Nationale de France in Paris, it establishes Machaut as the authority over his work: "Vecy l'ordenance que mestre Guillaume de Machaut veut en son premier livre" [Here is the order that master Guillaume de Machaut wants for his first book] [trans. D. L.].

What then follows is a catalog of the author's complete works in chronological order. To my knowledge, this is the first list of complete works to be assembled in medieval literature. Most striking is the fact that it proceeds from a proper name, with the will and control attributed to that name, and not to the good or bad intentions of a copyist. (The copyist retains his own particular power, since the manuscript is not signed, in the modern sense of the word. This alone would authenticate the corpus.) Machaut gives his writing the ability to define his fictional identity.

The equivocation in the word *ordenance* constantly maintains this power over writing as a force in the text. Machaut at first appears to cede power to the Lady, the recipient of the *Voir Dit* and the letters and poems it "reproduces":

Eins sera tout a lordenance
De celle en qui gist mesperance. (506–7)

Instead everything will accord with the wish
Of the woman in whom my hope lies.[1]

The power of the Lady extends beyond the book to the life and death of the poet, to his very being:

> Ma mort et ma vie, Mon deduit * et ma ioie *[2] Ma douleur et ma sante gist en voz mains et en vostre ordenance * et en poez ordener comme de ce qui est vostre sans riens retenir. (L 35)

> My death and my life, my pleasure and my joy, my suffering and my good health all lie in your hands and under your control, and you can direct me like the man that is yours with nothing held back.

And elsewhere: "Si met mame, mon cuer, ma vie et quanque iay en vostre ordenance" [So I consign my soul, my heart, my life, and whatever is mine to your guidance] (L 11).

Machaut's privilege as the master of arts, his lordship over the book, seems denied to him in the very text his mastery produces (and in contrast to the implicit attribution in the table of contents). The ontological domination of his own *bios* also appears to be weakened. The Lady does not have to submit to his mastery, in a metaphorical reproduction of feudal relations. Instead, a parity of positions must be worked out. This is indicated by the pet names they use, *ami* and *amie:*

> Et ma treschiere dame ie vous suppli que se iamais vous me escrisiez aucune chose que vous ne mappellez pas signeur; quar qui de son serf fait

son signeur ses annemis monteplie; Et par dieu, cest trop plus biaus nons damy ou damie; Quar quant signourie saute en place amour se fuit. (L 2)

And my most dear lady, I beg that if ever you write me you do not call me sir, for whoever makes a lord from his slave multiplies his enemies. And by God the title "darling" or "friend" is a much more beautiful name, for when lordship leaps ahead love takes flight.

The text's own production, as a theme in the text, is closely linked to the questions and problems of power. What Machaut denies to himself in this quote is nothing other than the very "lordship" of the *Voir Dit.* He does not need it because the Lady writes perfectly (Letter 36) and thus is the mirror image of the author. She is the equal of her supposed lord, and like him, she is a poetic master (lines 3962–75). She has the power to correct *(ordener)* the text and to enclose her signature within it using her own *enseigne* (monogram) or her signet.

According to a law of symmetry and reversibility in the positions of the two correspondents, this mistress of poetic space in her turn humbles herself before Machaut:

Sil vous plaist vous les maprenez a mieus faire et dire [bons dis et bons chansons]. Car ien aprenoie plus de vous en un jour que je ne feroie dun autre en un an. (L 3)

Please show me how to write [excellent poems and songs] better because I would learn more from you in one day than I would from someone else in a year.

The *Voir Dit* appears to have difficulty articulating the name of its "author"; all the speakers are engaged in a merciless rivalry. A law of parity dominates them under the sign of brotherhood or sisterhood,[3] and thus they are fighting for the attention of the reader. The only difference between the competitors is the letter *e,* which is the only means of distinguishing between the names "dami et dami<u>e</u>." Machaut's secretary/copyist reminds him of this in a speech where paternity or maternity (of the text) is caught in a swirling vortex of parental and feudal relations:

Et que diroit vostres bons freres
Qui vous est fils sires et peres
Qui si doucement vous norrit
Que chascuns bons de ioie en rit. (6709–12)

And then what would your brother say,
Who to you is son, father, and lord,
Who takes care of you so kindly
Every good man smiles from joy?

Thus, in the *Voir Dit,* "la souvereinneté se taist et unite parole" [sovereignty is silent while our words are the same] (Letter 11). The spinning top of enunciative mastery, like Fortune's wheel, continually turns back upon itself. In a letter to the Lady in which he criticizes two of her poems, Machaut seems to reestablish surreptitiously the position of the master and lord of poetry:

> Les .ij. choses que vous mavez envoies sont tresbien faites a mon gre * Mais se ie'estoie un iour avec vous ie vous diroie et apenroie ce que je napris onques a creature * Par quoy vous les feries mieux. (L 6)
>
> The two works that you have sent me are very well composed according to my taste, but if I could spend one day with you, I would instruct you, teaching you what I have never taught anyone; and in this way you would compose even better.

The writer thus seems to be in possession of a secret *you* that grants a surplus of poetic virtuosity that the Lady does not have. What, then, is this key to literature? Upon first reading, one will respond, tautologically—and thus insufficiently, but the text must be read literally—that the power of the fiction is that which perfects the work and places it *hors pair,* out of reach of the confraternal jealousy of other poets:

> Car ores vient le fort et les beles et subtives fictions dont ie le pense a parfaire * par quoy vous et li autre le vees volentiers * et quil en soit bon memoire a tous iours mais. (L 35)
>
> Now it's time for the difficult, the beautiful, and the subtle fictions with which I intend to perfect it, and because of these you and others will willingly look at it, and may it attain a worthy reputation for all days to come.

THE TRUTH OF THE FICTION

The *"beles et subtives"* [beautiful and subtle] fictions make the book perfect, and in the same action give it an atheological eternity close to Saint Augustine's blank language. These fictions also designate a speech that creates its own truth within its poetic structure and without reference to anything true. One immediately thinks of the mythological parables that proliferate throughout the book. But not only this—for the promise to tell the truth, which gives its name to the entire text (*voir* means "true")[4] and supports its fictional framework, is always drawn toward a polysemia whose moments it is necessary to spell out here.

The true is hidden, secret:

Dont iay mainte pensee eu
Que chascuns na mie sceu. (526–27)

And I've had many thoughts
No man has recognized at all.

It is a hypothesis, not an assertion:

Bien porroie estre voir disans. (284)

I could well be telling the truth.[5]

In opposition, it is an aporia that does not depend on any authority other than its own assertion that it is a treatise on poetry or love:

Le voir dit weil ie quon appelle
Ce traitie que ie fais pour elle
Pour ce que ia ni mentiray. (518–20)

I would like this work that I am composing for her
To be called *The True Poem*
Because in it I'll not lie.

Drawing its truth from fiction, the activity of writing is thus necessarily associated with the counterfeit. Here, Machaut reveals himself as the worthy heir of Master Renart:

Car cils qui wet tel chose faire
Penser li faut ou contrefaire. (528–29)

But anyone who attempts writing such poetry
Must either think such thoughts or feign them.

For Machaut, as for Lacan, truth is not everything; it is impossible to speak it completely, which authorizes the writer to return to the resources of fiction when true speech does not suffice:

Mais ce nest pas neccessite
Que quan quon dit soit verite
Nen ce quon dit na pas le quart
De verite se diex me gart. (8052–55)

But it isn't necessary
That everything one says be the truth
—Not even a quarter of the truth
Need to be spoken, so God preserve me!

What literature sets out is only "a quarter of the truth," a proportion that raises the question of the remaining three quarters. To reduce them to a lying counterfeit—too simple a concept for literary fiction—is not sufficient, since the author swears to us that the discourse we are reading in the *Voir Dit* is truthful as a whole. Let us suppose, then, that the poet uses a masterful trick to tell the truth. What, then, is the status of his discourse?[6]

We will respond to the question by rereading a mythical parable that the story tells *en abyme.* Believing the denunciation of obscure *losangiers* (gossips) who describe the Lady as unfaithful,[7] Machaut has locked away her portrait inside two trunks. One night the image comes to him in a dream and, in a parable, tells him he must not give the slanders of the jealous any credit. Pagan fiction comes to the aid of the *Voir Dit* in the form of two *exempla* taken from mythology.

In the first, a crow, who as an innocent messenger, "jadis plume blanche/avoit plus que noif sur branche" [at one time . . . had feathers / Whiter than snow on the branch] (7792–93), sees Coronis, Phoebus's lover, committing adultery. This is elevated to the level of a secret truth.[8] As an emblem of he who sees the truth and transmits it without thinking, the crow wants to denounce the lovers to Phoebus, his master. In flight, he meets the raven and tells him the story. The raven attempts to dissuade him from being the spokesman of the truth, quoting, in support of his advice, the portrait of the Lady; he thus destroys the boundaries between true speech and mythology by blending one with the other. He says, "Tout voire ne sont pas bon a dire" [Not all truths are worthy to be spoken] (7852).[9]

A second *mise en abyme* teaches us that the raven has paid for his knowledge. For in his turn, having surprised Erichtonios, he was fired from his job as Pallas's messenger. As the *Voir Dit* tells it, this mystery is nothing other than a vast metaphor for the births of fiction. Erichtonios was born of the Earth and the sperm of Vulcan, who had become aroused in the pursuit of Pallas. In a way, he is Onan's son, and furthermore, he has two mothers, because Pallas adopted him; everything here points to a diabolical origin:

Li ennnemis et li mauffez
Fu une fois si eschaufez
Que son germe en terre espandi
La terre souvri et fendi
Et de ce la terre concut
Un enfant que pallas recut. (7902–7)

This enemy and devil
Was one time so hot
He spilled his seed on the ground.
The earth opened up and split,
And from this ground was conceived
A child that Pallas took.

The top of Erichtonios's body is human, but the bottom half is a serpent.[10] He is thus a figure for the diabolical genealogies of fiction, which once again demonstrates its monstrously equivocal nature. Pallas quickly places this monster in a trunk (to hide the monstrosity of its origin by neutralizing it), but one day, when the trunk's guards open it, the raven sees inside. He hurries to spread the truth, and as payment for his services, he is quickly fired from his job as messenger and replaced by the owl. This latter springs from a tainted lineage, in contrast to the raven:

Et si coucha avec son pere
Et maintenant Pallas sen pere. (7978–79)

And she sleeps with her own father.
Now Pallas has taken her up.

The goddess thus adorns *(pere)* herself with the incestuous bird. The echo of the rhyme itself displays writing's monstrous plumage. Fatherhood and generations are confused, and the language of transmission, symbolized by the messenger, is made the "peer" of originary language.

However, the parable does not have the intended effect on the crow, who immediately carries on with what he sees as his mission. On the level of the framing fiction, that of the relation of Machaut to the Lady, the *exemplum* also works against its intended effect by suggesting the existence of deceit and adultery.

But let us return to the second narrative trunk. When Phoebus learns of Coronis's deceit, he kills her and has her embalmed. Coronis, it turns out, was pregnant, and she is thus delivered from her labors.

Mais il la fist ouvrir et fendre
Avant tout ouevre et lenfant prendre. (8098–99)

But he had her split and opened
Before all this was done and the child removed.

In this way, Aesculapius comes into the world from the womb of his dead mother (idolatry?). The scenario of his birth mirrors, by homology, that of Erichtonios, once again supplying a metaphor for the impure origins of fiction. Furthermore, the use of the word *"oeuvre"* links his origins to the *pharmakon* of writing, giving to the text a power of magical resurrection that directly opposes Catholic dogma:

Esculapius ot a non
Et si sceut plus de surgerie
Que nul homme qui fust en vie
Car il faisoit les mors revivre
Si com je le truis en mon livre. (8101–5)

Aesculapius was his name,
And he knew more about surgery
Than any man then living,
For he made the dead come back to life,
So I find in my book.

The crow, a white page, finds himself blackened with writing through his wish to proclaim this perverse genealogy of the text. This is the payment he receives from the sun god for having the audacity to transmit the truth:

Et dist en signe de memoire
Sera ta blanche plume noire
Et tuit li corbel qui lont blanche
Laront plus noir que nest anche
A tousiours perpetuelement. (8110–14)

Saying: "In remembrance of this
Your white feathers will henceforth be black.
And all the crows who have white feathers
Will have them blacker than ink
Forever in perpetuity."

This is the secret, "blacker than ink," in which the writer dips his pen, and which Machaut describes elsewhere: "Car tousdis leur fis du blanc noir" [For he forever changed them from white to black].[11]

The Renardy of fiction thus once again mimicks Augustine's blank writing. The poet thus slaps ink on the gaping spaces of an originary language, pretending to cover it over with a multiplicity of signs. This is the secret that guarantees Machaut a peerless authority over his poetic contemporaries, or, as he narcissistically has his Lady say,

> Les .ij. balades que vous mavez envoies sont si bonnes que on ni saroit trouver que redire * Mais ce nest pas comparison * car ce que vous faites me plaist trop mieux a mon gre que ce que li autres font. (L 38)

> The two ballads that you have sent me are so good that no one could find a way to reword them. Yet there is no comparison between the two, for what you have composed pleases me much more than what others have written.

HORROR

It remains to be seen whether the mastery of this secret, this enigma without the signs of power over language and its codes, is not inverted, whether the writer is not, in the final analysis, mastered by the order of the secret. For as the crow and the raven show us, the truth exacts a price from those who tell it. The secret deprives them not only of their innocence (of their belief in the transparency of communication), but also of their position of power over the gods. He who dips his pen in something blacker than ink cannot have prestige of any sort.

Blank language escapes all transcription. Beyond the range of the sign, it imitates, in the fornication of poetic writing, those biblical *exempla* that Guillaume de Machaut affirms to be "impossible":

Par exemples te vueil prouver
Qui sont contenu en la Bible
Et qui sont a nous impossible.[12]

On the other hand, the Lady, as a mirror image of the figures of mastery, is also the keeper of a secret that governs her writing, that comes before her and persists after the last word is written. She is in no way a stable signifier; her symbolic figure is always taken up in an equivocating logic:

Et si avez double visage
Tout einsi comme avoit limage
De fortune * dont li uns pleure
Et li autres rit a toute heure. (8793–96)

And you also have two faces,
Just like the image
Of Fortune, one that cries
And the other that laughs continuously.

Her duplicity, the very one of the image of writing, becomes obvious in its double effect on the narrator. On the one hand, the Lady saves him from melancholy and death by her "Lazarus, come out," which is an example not of biblical resurrection but of Aesculapius's powers:

En moy ou elle ouvra iadis
Trop plus que sains de paradis
Car iestoie dou tout perdus
Maz * desconfis et esperdus
Mais .ij. fois ma ressuscite. (1576–80)

In me when she assailed me in the past,
Better than the saints of paradise could have done
Because I was completely lost,
Beaten down and she revived me.

On the other hand, she is the sign of something that reduces the author to impotence, that petrifies him, that silences his work:

Mon tresdous cuer et ma treschiere amour iay grant doubtance que vous ne tenez meins de my de ce que quant ie sui en vostre presence * ie nay scens * maniere * ne avis * et sui comme uns homs perdus. (L 16)

My very sweet heart and my very dear love, I fear very much that you think less of me because when I am in your presence, I have no sense, no demeanor, or wit, and am like a man who's lost.

When presence "arrives," makes an appearance, the narrator remains immobile under Amour's threat of death:

La vi ge damour la maistrie
Car iestoie comme une souche
Dalez ma dame en ceste couche
Ne ne mosoie remuer
Nient plus quon me vosist tuer. (3796–3800)

There the power of love was apparent to me,
For I lay just like a log
Beside my lady on this bed.
And I didn't stir any more than I'd have done
Had someone been threatening to kill me.

The Lady is a figure for a petrifying mother, gifted with the simultaneous power of death and resurrection, and running throughout all of the signs of mastery like one who has forever deprived them of power and of speech. A sign of the horror that changed Lot's wife to a pillar of salt (5636–62),[13] the Lady is also identified with the Gorgon's head:

Quame ce chief ne resgardoit
Qui en pierre ne fust muee
Tant fust soutive ne desree
Ovides le dit en ses fables
En moralitez veritables. (5676–80)

For no soul could look upon this head
And not be changed to stone,
However wise or crafty he might be.
Ovid says so in his *Fables,*
In his true "morals."

Machaut's lover is a source both of horror and of comfort.[14] Faced with these, the *Voir Dit* is written in the alternation of denial and fascination. At the same time, the text desires with all its might the carnal conjunction of the narrator and the Lady and is equally horrified by a paralyzing presence. This becomes clear at the very opening of the work. The Lady is smitten with the poet, not because she has seen him but because she has read his work and heard others speak of his fame as a poet. She thus approaches him through the intermediary of a rondel that Guillaume de Machaut's secretary reads to him:

Car pour les biens que de vous dit
Tous li mondes communement
Conquise lavez bonnement
Celle qui onques ne vous vit
Et qui vous aimme loiaument,
De tout son cuer vous fait present. (210–15)

But because of the good that
All the world in unison says of you,
You have with virtue conquered her,
The woman who has never seen you
And who loves you faithfully
With all her heart makes you this present.

In parallel, Machaut falls in love not with the Lady but with the rondel:

Ie tieng se dieux me doint ioie
Que le rondel quelle menvoie,
Et son cuer quelle me presente
Soit en bonne et en vraie entente. (274–77)

That I believe, so God give me joy,
It was with virtuous and true intent
She sent me the rondel
While also offering me her heart.

A little later, he writes of his love for the Lady:

Car son renon et sa vaillance
La grant biaute dont elle est pleinne
Sa fine douceur souvereinne
Et la bonte qui an li maint
Me font esperer quelle maint. (303–7)

For her renown and her worthiness,
The great beauty she abundantly possesses,
Her refined, sovereign sweetness.
And the virtue that makes its home in her
—All make me hopeful she loves me.

Literature, and not presence (even fictional presence), lies at the origin of their love. Letters and poems become substitutes and fetishes embellishing the bodies of the lovers. In the *Voir Dit*, love is the desire for the signifier insofar as it is separate from vision and the body. Machaut emphasizes this again, in a ballad:

Onques ne vi le corps gent
Cointe et legier
De celle qui liement
Me tient et ioliement
En son dangier
Ne il moy. (977–82)

I have never laid eyes on the gentle form,
Attractive and lithe,
Of the woman who merrily
And happily holds me prisoner
Under her haughtiness;
Nor it me.

Desire originates in the textual signifier, and it condenses and dissolves there as well. After the lovers meet for the first time, the Lady sends her portrait to Machaut. The image immediately replaces vision and presence in a distancing that is the source of the life and certainly the very writing of the text:

Je verroie le dous visage
Le dous oueil et le cointe atour
Et le gentil corps fait a tour
Dont iay lymage bele et cointe
Qui de pais et de ioie macointe
Qui me rent toute ma vigour
Par son amoureuse rigour
Et qui me fait parler et vivre
Et faire pour samour ce livre. (1673–81)

I would look upon the sweet face,
The tender eyes, the lovely demeanor,
And the beautiful figure, shaped just right,
Whose lovely and alluring image I possessed,
Which has made me a friend to peace and joy,

Given me back all my strength and power,
Making me speak and live,
As well as compose this book out of love for her.

Absence is the life of desire and of writing:

Car vous me faites vivre en pais et en ioie long de vous * Et se ie estoie en vostre presence ie porroie bien querir ce que ie ne vorroie mie avoir. (L 6)

You make me live in peace and joy far from you. And were I to come into your presence, I might well be looking for what I would not like to have.

When it is a case of presence, of taking possesion of the body as a physical whole, Machaut equivocates. When the Lady offers him her "treasure,"[15] the poet refuses it with an ambiguous no that, however, avoids saying an absolute no.

De mon tresor que tant prisiez
Qui ne porroit estre prisiez
Amis ie vous abandoing
Prenez le tout ie le vous doing
        lamant
Et ie li respondi tantost:
Qui tout me donne tout me tolt. (2839–44)

"My treasure, which you value so highly
That no price could be set on it,
Darling, I give over to you.
Take everything. I make you this gift."
        The Lover
And I answered her at once:
"Who gives me everything, takes everything."

Refusal of the poisonous and total gift of the Other is what gives the gift its value. Accepting it causes a radical deprivation of its presence, and so its arrival must then be suspended, infinitely deferred by writing. The text accumulates obstacles that hinder presence. Pseudohistorical referents are useful in guaranteeing that a meeting will not take place; the Hundred Years' War, with its pillage, disorder, and epidemics, is a constant theme in the text. For this reason, mediated forms of communication become enormously important. Letters, messengers, poems, portraits, and fetish objects appear one after the other, deflecting the meeting of the lovers into writing. The episode of the first kiss, the first carnal contact between the two lovers, is the paradigm for this logic of absence. It takes place during one of Machaut's *neuvaines,* an exercise of piety that lasts nine days. The temporal framework of the first amorous contact is thus sanctified, or the inverse, *de*sanctified, according to a logic to which we will return. The kiss is only possible when Machaut's secretary, the mediator of the desire who communicated the Lady's rondel to him, places a leaf between the lovers' lips, an obvious metaphor for the parchment page. The page neutralizes the horror of the body and makes amorous and carnal communication possible by submitting it to a second textuality:

Mes secretaires qui fu la
Se mis en estant et ala
Cueillir une verde fueillette
Et la mis dessus sa bouchette
Et me dist baisiez ceste fueille. (2517–21)

My secretary, who was present,
Stood up and walked over
To pick a small green leaf
He put on her tiny mouth,
Telling me: "Kiss the leaf."

This logic of disincarnation is very close to a Gnostic loathing of the flesh. The coitus scene is its culminating point, at which a miraculous cloud descends, concealing both narrator and reader while revealing the character of the truth as fiction. The cloud is a metaphor for the page decorated with writing. It covers the emptiness that structures the (fictional) amorous conjunction:

Si queinsi de la nue obcure
Eusmes ciel et couverture
Et tous .ij. en fumes couvert
Si quil ni ot rien descouvert. (4124–27)

Now in this way from the dark cloud
We had both sky and covering,
And were so completely hidden
Nothing was left to view.

We know nothing more. The narrator and the reader, like Polyphemus in the legend that appears later (6885–7220),[16] are stupefied by the writing that veils what is happening in the fiction it produces.

The central scene of (non)possession lasts the time it takes to compose a ballad. A poem is superimposed on and confused with the carnal union, sublimating it and substituting for it:

Et si dura longuettement
Tant que ieus fait presentement
Eins que venus sen fust alee
Ceste chanson quest baladee. (4130–33)

This lasted long enough,
That I composed on the spot,
And before Venus departed,
The following song in ballad form.

Reading and writing dominate pleasure and desire to the exclusion of everything else. These two acts are self-sufficient and thus reduce the presence of the event taking place to a supplement.[17] Where blank language, horror, and castration continually threaten the wholeness of fiction with a silence, Machaut has the stroke of genius to place his art in a necessary relation to them. His writing, and even the title of his book, admit to the presence of what they lack. The truth of the *Voir Dit,* obviously having nothing to do with autobiographical sincerity, is a syncopation that interrupts the very even, elegant flow of the rhetoric—even if the sounds of the words "silence" or "break" immediately appear in the textual space to cover it over:

Et . . . il li couvient recouper
Ses paroles de sincoper
Par souspirs puisiez en parfont (*Le Remede de fortune,* 1760–62)

And . . . he . . . must cut up his halting words with sighs drawn from the depths.

Inevitably, the paradox is that writing only breaks off or falls silent by producing more signs, even if they are the ones that admit its failure. The *Voir Dit* uses the marks of the break it creates (Letter 32 is burnt; Letter 35, missing; Letter 42, defective; and so on) as fictional signs of lack, incorporating them into the literary space. In opposition, linearity—a continuity that does not dissolve—shows that the book is necessarily "in pieces" (Letter 10), made up of smooth fragments torn from a nameless horror. This occurs in spite, or because of, the book's marvelous harmony.

DESANCTIFICATION

Guillaume de Machaut is one of the very few medieval writers whose name appears in extratextual archives. Because he was the canon of the chapter of Reims, we can be certain that this master of the arts knew perfectly what he was doing when he spoke of theology. In spite of this, I will continue to follow the internal clues contained in the *Voir Dit* as I take up the question of the relation of his fictional writing to the canon.

References to God, to the Catholic liturgy, and to the Bible abound in the text. To begin my discussion, and to illustrate the problem, I will give precedence to the portrait of the Lady, which plays a fundamental role in the very structure of desire (and of writing). This portrait makes its first appearance in an easily recognizable hierarchy of creation:

> Et certes se ie avoie vostre douce ymage * apres dieu et vous ie lameroie * serviroie * et oubeiroie. (L 4)

> And surely if I possessed your sweet likeness, after God and you yourself I would love, serve, and be obedient to it.

There is nothing here that is not canonical. These lines faithfully evoke the order of creation just as Alain of Lille developed it in *The Plaint of Nature.* God is the Creator, Nature's *artifex* (who produced the Lady), and the image is an "ape [or sign] of Nature," a third-order representation, distanced from the thing but referring to it in faithful mimesis.

This very canonical view of representation is soon upset. The image becomes a relic. Furthermore, the poet elevates it to an idol, the object of a cult in which he elides the distinction between creature and Creator. Beauty represents a totality, as the baptismal name of the portrait indicates:

> Et quant ie la vi si tresbele
> Je li mis a non toute bele
> Car tantost li fis sacrefice
> Nompas de tor ne de genice
> Einsois li fis loyal hommage
> De mains, * de bouche * et de corage
> A genous et a iointes mains. (1560–66)

And seeing how very beautiful she was,
I gave her the name All-Beautiful,
At once making a sacrifice to her,
But not one of bull or calf;
Instead I performed a true act of homage
With my hands, mouth, and heart,
On my knees, my palms together.

Machaut does away with pagan and Hebrew forms of religious sacrifice and substitutes a confused ritual combining feudal homage and a Christian prayer to the portrait. This substitution represents a fundamental perversion of the formulas of the Catholic liturgy. An adoration addressed to the idol directly contradicts religious devotion by mimicking it and assuming the form of its ritual:

Eins sera de moy aouree,
Servie amee * et honnouree
Comme ma souvereinne deesse
Qui garist tout quamour blesse
En moy ou elle ouvra iadis
Trop plus que sains de paradis. (1572–77)

Rather by me she will be adored,
Served, loved, and honored
As my sovereign goddess,
Who has healed all that Love wounded
In me when she assailed me in the past,
Better than the saints in paradise could have done.

The use of hyperbole is extremely important in this passage, describing Toute-Belle, "All-Beautiful," as superior to a Catholic saint. Surpassing the canon while shamelessly applying the figures of desire to it is one of Machaut's favorite strategies.

Symmetrically, Toute-Belle's lover gives her a rosary *(paternostres).* It carries the name of Christianity's most sacred prayer, the one that Christ taught his disciples. It is not, as it should be, an aid to help her in her devotions. Instead, she wears it upon her person as a relic of the body of the Other, turning it away from its religious function and placing it in the service of the metonymic circulation of desire. She then sends the poet a little locket, a perverse narrative frame and shrine, to enclose her own image/idol, and so the trunk containing the image becomes in its turn a "holy body."

> Mon tresdous cuer je vous envoie ce que vous mavez mande et vos paternostres * et vous promet loiaument que ie les ay portees tout en lestat que ie les vous envoie .ij. nuis et .iij. iours sans oster dentour moy * Et de puis que li fremailles fu fais * ay ie tous iours porte les paternostres en ycelle maniere que je le vous envoie * Si vous pri que vous les weilliez porter et ie vous envoie unes autres petites et .i. petit fremaillet pour vostre ymage * et les ay einsi portees longuement en lenviron de mon bras. (L 28)

> My very sweet heart, I am sending what you requested and your beads as well, and I promise faithfully that I have worn these things, in the condition I am sending them for two nights and three days without removing them from me. And as soon as the chain was made, I wore your beads just as I send them to you. And I ask you to please wear them, and I am sending another one along with a chain for your image, and these I have worn a long time around my arm.

From this point on, everything the lovers exchange, including, of course, the poems and letters, becomes immediately in the text what it always was, a fetish object of desire and of writing, a false relic of the absent body that permits one to mimic the cult of the saints. This is apparent in the Lady's inaugural rondel:

> Si me bailla un rondelet
> Qui nestoit pas rude ne let
> Nil nestoit mie contrefais
> Einsois estoit si bien fais
> Et en tous cas si bien servoit
> Que nuls amender ni savoit
> Et le pris a grant reverence
> Et si le baisay sans doubtance
> Plus de cent fois ou environ
> Et puis iostay mon chaperon
> Et devant lui magenouillay
> Ne de moy pas ne leslongnay. (183–94)

> Then she handed me a rondel
> That was hardly amateurish or ugly;

Nor was it a work at all badly done,
But rather quite ably composed
Because it read so well in every way
No one could have improved it.
And I accepted it with great reverence,
Kissing the poem unabashedly
More than a hundred times or thereabouts;
And afterward I doffed my cap
And got down on my knees in front of it.
Nor did I let this writing get far from me.

Or, in an even more explicit twisting of the cult of relics, his lover's letters are adored, this time *for themselves:*

Or avez vous oy comment
Celle qui ma en son comment
Menvoia lettres et iouiaus
Et reliques et dis nouviaus
Et certes ie les aouroie
Et si richement les tenoie
Comme ce fust mon dieu terrien. (5133–39)

Now you have heard how
She who rules me
Sent a letter and a keepsake
As well as relics and new poems
And surely these I worshipped
And guarded quite reverently,
Just like my earthly god.

This is not the only time the text twists Christianity around. Further along in the story, the lovers meet in a church to hear mass. The liturgy then becomes the frame for their desire:

La belle gracieuse et douce
Qui mes mauls amoureus adouce
Oy la messe tout entiere
Et ie lescoutay par derriere
Mais trop richement me chei
Que quant on dist agnus dei
Foi que ie doy a saint crapais

Doucement me donna la pais
Entre .ij. piliers du moustier. (2943–51)

The beautiful lady, sweet and gracious,
who assuages my lovesickness,
heard the whole mass,
While I listened from in back.
But a very happy chance befell me
When the "Agnus Dei" was being said:
By the faith I owe St. Caprais,
She sweetly gave me the kiss of peace
Between two pillars of the church.

The kiss of desire is completely assimilated to that of the *pax Dei,* the one given by the faithful to the paten containing the Eucharist at the moment of the elevation—that is, literally and canonically, to the very body of the Incarnation. Rather than sanctifying love by the presence of the *corpus Domini,* the sacramental host, the analogy perverts the liturgy of high mass from top to bottom. The *Voir Dit* emphasizes this perversion. Desire itself is the object of devotion, and not the Eucharist or transcendence:

Ie repris ma devotion
Mais plus estoit mentention
A penser a ma vrauelette
Cest a dire a ma damelette
Quelle nestoit na saint na sainte. (2969–73)

I took up my devotions again,
but my mind was more on
Thoughts of the darling woman,
That is, my little lady,
Than on any saint, woman or man.

DISINCARNATION

To take full measure of literature's profanation of theology, in play from the very first line of the text, one must return once again to the text's primal scene. In this passage, a sexual union overcomes the horror of presence that is intimately linked to the perversion of the Incarnation.

A prayer to Venus, the pagan goddess of love, or rather to her idol, opens the scene, repeating the twisting of Christian devotion:

Je magelongnay sans atendre
Et encommensay ma priere
A venus par ceste maniere
Venus ie tay tous iours servi
Depuis que ton ymage vi. (4039–43)

I got down on my knees at once
And began my prayer
To Venus as follows:
Venus I have always served you
Since looking upon your image.

The object of the prayer is obviously completely profane. Machaut asks the goddess to help him overcome his fear of the body and of the other (4055–89), and Venus grants his wish. She descends from the empyrean "couverte dune obscure nue" [covered in a dark cloud] (4097), which she spreads over the lovers. Thus, the union is described in Christian terms; desire/writing places the economy of the miracle at their service:

Et la fist miracles ouvertes
Si clerement et si apertes
Que de ioie fu raemplis
Et mes desirs fu acomplis. (4100–3)

Then she worked an open miracle,
One so clear and manifest
That I was filled with joy
And my desire was satisfied.

Venus's *velamen,* an emblem for all the subtle veils of fiction and of writing, plays a crucial role in the scene. Thanks to it, the carnal union is entirely concealed from view. These concealed bodies are entirely disincarnated (and characterized) by the mantle of fiction, and thus desire and union come not from the body but from the literary signifier. Furthermore, in its role as an *adumbratio,* Venus's cloud refers to the Cathar conception of the Incarnation as a phantasm.[18]

One could object to this reading of the body *en abyme* as the reference to truth in literature. The poet, like Saint Thomas at the foot of the cross, has in fact touched the body of desire that functions here according to the traditional topos of nudity/truth. However, the Lady's twin sister (her double) lies next to her. The narrator assures us that in spite of this, it is the unique and individual body of the Lady that he touches, even though he sees nothing, just as in the scene of the fictional coitus:

> Car nulle goute ni veoie
> Mais certeinnement bien savoie
> Que ce nestoit pas sa compaigne. (3811–13)

> Now I couldn't see a thing
> But knew quite well
> This was not her companion.

The threat of confusion is all the greater because of the implicit incest with his lover's sister. Nothing confirms his certainty of the Lady's bodily individuality (her identity) except for the words that state it, paradoxically dismissing the threat of a doubled and substituted object of desire.

Several pages later, another scene replays the logic of referential concealment. Machaut contemplates the naked/true body of Toute-Belle:

> Mais la belle ne dormoit mie
> Einsois par sa grant courtoisie
> Par devers moy se retourna
> Nelle pris autre atour na
> Fors que les oeuvres de nature:
> Tant belle quonques creature
> Ne pot estre a li conparee
> Tant en fu richement paree. (4018–25)

> But that beautiful woman was not sleeping at all;
> Instead through her great courtesy,
> She turned my way.
> And she had put on no attire
> Except what nature had provided
> And was so beautiful no woman
> Could have compared to her,
> So richly was she endowed.

The naked body is, first of all, a cloak *(parure),* an adornment of words that come from a codified rhetoric of description that Machaut uses several lines later to speak of his Lady. The body disappears under the cover of a topical language, a trope that is marvelously symbolized by the turning movement the Lady performs to present herself, naked, to the gaze of her lover.

The strategy of profanation and disincarnation culminates in the miracles that Toute-Belle performs for her lover.

The *Voir Dit* opens in dispossession, impotence, and the absence of poetic inspiration, all covered with a rhetorical profusion:

> Si que parfondement pensoie
> Par quel maniere ie feroie
> Aucune chose de nouvel
> Pour tenir mon cuer en revel
> Mais ie navoie vraiement
> Scens matiere * ne sentement
> De quoy commencier le sceusse. (57–63)

> And then I gave deep thought
> To how I might compose
> Some kind of new work
> That would keep my spirits high.
> But, truly, I did not have
> The theme, material, or inspiration
> With which I could begin one.

Thus, in the beginning is the impossibility of beginning the book. Suffering from melancholy *(acedia mortifera),* the narrator is deprived of *sentement,* which is the very motive for writing in Machaut's poetics. *Sentement* (in Old French, simultaneously "sentiment" and "sensation") is what guarantees the truth of writing: "Qui de son sentement ne fait son dit et son chant contrefait" [He who from his sentiment does not make his poem and his song, is [faking it]] (l. 8).[19]

Toute-Belle sends Machaut a love poem that simultaneously gives him the necessary *sentement.* This authenticates the work in an obviously fictional gesture (since all literature does its part to counterfeit), yet it is still the necessary principle of his writing: "Car vous mavez ressucite et donne mercy qui est souffissance * et rendu mon sentement que iavoie tout perdu" [For you have revived me and granted me the mercy that is satisfaction, given me back the sensibility I had lost completely] (L 6). As a consequence, Machaut's "resurrection" is none other than that of his musical and poetic performance. "Car iamais par moy ne fust fais chans ne lais se vous ne fussiez" [For I never would have composed a lay or a song had it not been for you] (L 6).

A sulphurous equivocation marks the Lady's textual origins. Far from being analogous to a saint or a miraculous virgin, the Lady prefigures Aesculapius, "who made the dead come back to life," and thus mirrors him. The resurrection of the dead does not give birth to fiction. Rather, the source of fiction is a reincarnation in which the textual signifier dominates the body in a hyperbole that surpasses the miracles of the saints:

> Car [vos douces courtoises et aimables escriptures] font et ont fait plus grant miracles a ma personne * que ie ne vi onques faire a saint ne a sainte qui soit en paradis. (L 2)

> Because [your sweet, couteous, and loving writings] have accomplished—and still do—great miracles for me, such as I have never seen accomplished by any saint, either man or woman, who is in paradise.

In a repetition, the portrait also brings about a pseudoresurrection. In the *Voir Dit,* the image has the status of a saint's body, to adore,

> comme mon dieu terrien * et comme la plus precieuse et glorieuse relique que ie veisse onques en lieu ou ie fusse . . . si tost que ie vi vostre douce ymage, je fui garis et hors de merencolie. (L 10)

> as my earthly god and as the most precious and glorious relic I have laid eyes upon in any place I've been . . . as soon as I laid eyes upon your sweet image, I felt healed and passed beyond my melancholic thoughts.

The poet has twice been revived in a scenario that exceeds the biblical miracle. On the one hand, his resurrection mirrors that of the Bible. On the other, the "miracle" is produced by a literary or pictorial simulacrum, a substitute/fetish of the body of desire, and not a relic in the Christian sense of the term.

Reflexively, Machaut returns the favor to his Lady. As she admits at the end of the story when he is reconciled with her, he has also worked a resurrection, himself assuming a rank of literary "sainthood":

Si vous plaise savoir que iay bien oy et entendu tout ce que li porterres de ces lettres ma dit de par vous par unes lettres de creance * Et se ma ressuscite mon cuer * ma joie * mon esprit * Et moy donne tel estat * quil nest ioie en ce monde qui ne soit tristece encontre la parfaite ioie que iay * de ce que dieus amours et venus ma deesse qui a oy mes priers * mes complaintes et mes lamentations ont remis vostre cuer ou il doit estre * et en voie de verite. (L 46)

It may please you to know that I heard and listened to all that the bearer of this letter told me on your behalf as per that testimonial letter. And this has revived my heart, my joy, my spirit, putting me in such a state there is no joy in this world that would not be sadness compared to the perfect joy I possess, to wit, that God, Love, and Venus, my goddess, who has heard my prayers, my complaints, and my lamentations, has returned your heart to where it should be, and on the path of truth.

This letter is obviously heterodox. Placing God, the allegorical figure of Love, and the pagan goddess on the same level, assimilating the (Augustinian) *gaudium* and the joy of love, quoting the text of the Gospels by twisting it ("I am the way the truth and the life"), the Lady's letter is a confession of faith, but of a wholly literary faith. The *Voir Dit* derives from a literature that works miracles, and it tries to surpass and exceed, in every way, the evangelical text and the Catholic liturgy:

Car onques mais ie ne vi certes
Faire miracles si apertes
Com elle fit a ma personne
Et ce si bon renom li donne
Quon dit quant elle finera
Quen paradis sainte sera
Quar bien puis dire en verite
Que .ij. fois ma ressuscite. (818–25)

Because surely never before had I seen
Any miracle performed so manifestly
As the one she worked on me.
And this affords her such renown
That when the woman dies, they say,
She'll become a saint in paradise,
For in truth I can very well say
She has [revived] me on two occasions.

Further along, Machaut comes back to this point. In the name of the amorous experience of literature, he ironically contests canonical saintliness and its miracles:

Ne sont ce pas belles miracles
Or querez un saint qui ce face
Et quen leure une fievre efface
Il puelent moult * bien lay creu
Mais encore ne lay pas veu
Quonques nul miracle ne vi
Si grant * com dun amant ravi. (927–33)

Now aren't these fine miracles?
Go and find a saint who accomplishes the same,
And who can within the hour bring down a fever.
These holy men can do much; such has been my firm belief.
But I have never yet witnessed
Or seen any miracle as impressive
As that of a lover enraptured.

Nothing in the *Voir Dit* escapes profanation. Its literary space surrounds even the most venerable symbols of the church and rewrites them according to its own heterodox desire. This also happens to the Trinity. At the very beginning of the book, Love, the poet, and Toute-Belle assume the places of, respectively, the Holy Spirit, God the Father, and the Incarnate Son:

Or faisons une trinite
Et une amiable unite
Que ce soit uns corps et une ame
Damours * de moy * et de ma dame. (316–19)

Now let's compose a trinity
And a loving union.
That Love, and I, and my lady
Might exist as one body and one soul.

The end of the work repeats the beginning almost point by point in what appears to be an eternal circular structure. The trajectory of the romance seems to carry it toward an inevitable rupture between the two lovers. From the moment of the mock carnal union under Venus's dark cloud, everything works to keep the lovers apart: difficulties in communication and travel, the black death, the poet's job, brigands, and jealous gossips. The story uses every means at its disposal to restore an infinite and reassuring distance between the bodies and to put an end to the unbearable horror of presence, inscribing itself in what Machaut calls the "perverse thought" of desire and the love of literature.[20] However, when it seems that the break can no longer be avoided, Machaut's secretary, replaying his own role in the affair, intervenes one last time as the mediator of communication. The secretary is Machaut's double. The writer, himself a secretary to princes (in the *Fontaine amoureuse,* he is a stenographer/copyist to Jean de Berry), gives the secretary the role of mediator in the opening of the *Voir Dit,* when he transmits Toute-Belle's first letter to the poet.

> Mais vous serez mon secretaire
> Pour parler apoint et pour taire. (362–63)

> Thus you'll be my secretary,
> Speaking when appropriate and keeping silent.

The secretary's function is not only to copy an original text or to transcribe the poet's dictation. Having been given the power of speaking *or* of keeping silent, the secretary exercises a decisive influence on what happens in the story. Machaut also confers upon him the title of *escrivain,* and justly so, because he enters the game of the correspondence. Furthermore, when Toute-Belle throws the original text into the fire in a fit of pique,[21] the secretary's copies remain the sole repository of their writings; everything in the *Voir Dit* is secondary. This role, placing Machaut's power of *ordenance* and writing in parentheses, culminates at the end of the story. The poet wants to put an end to his amorous relation with the Lady, but the secretary comes to him to dissuade him from this act. The double is now also a monk and a master of arts:

> Un mien ami qui estoit prestres
> Et en lart de logique mestres
> Vint a moy et me salua
> Et moult sagement margua. (8593–96)

> A friend of mine who was a priest,
> A master in the field of logic,
> Came by and greeted me;
> He spoke to me with great wisdom.

The friend's argument is not based on scholastic dialectics or on theology. He brings into play an allegory of Fortune, whose pagan origin is explicitly noted in the text (8691–8890); he will only be able to persuade Machaut by breaking the confidence of the confession the Lady has made to him (8600–8616), and which she forswore later (Letter 44). Thus Machaut's *belief* (8641) in the lover's message and the messenger is established through a break in the theological pedestal of truth, carried out by a compromised Catholic priest. Perfect harmony can only come to the story ("Et quant a vostre livre il sera parfais" [And concerning your book, it will be completed], [Letter 45]) in a final transgression of the imperatives of Christian discourse. This is the secret that the secretary could not keep.

The "paradise" to which the *Voir Dit* so often alludes thus has nothing to do with the Eden of the Bible. Just as for Martianus Capella and in the Renart cycle, it is a paradis(cours)e *(para-dis),* a parabolic phrase that counters the "straight" discourse of the thing, of the Incarnation, and of difference and that replaces everything, and certainly the whole of theological discourse, with a twisted literary speech.

THE LITERARY OBJECT

The atheological logic of writing in the *Voir Dit* places the semantics of the words "experience" and "thing" into question. The narrator alludes to their status in a letter to his Lady:

> Car vous saves quil nest si iuste ne si vraie chose comme experience * Et vous poez assez savoir et veoir par experience que toutes mes choses ont este faites de vostre sentement * et pour vous especiaument de puis que vous menvoyastes *Celle qui onques ne vous vit * et qui vous aimme loiaument * Car elles sont toutes de ceste matere * et par ihesucrist ie ne fis onques puis riens qui ne fust pour vous. (L 8)

> For you know that nothing is as true or indisputable as experience. And you can see and realize enough by experience that all my works have been composed from the emotions I feel for you, especially since you sent me "The Woman Who Has Never Seen You and Who Loves You Faithfully," for all my poems are on such themes. And, by Jesus Christ, I have composed nothing since that was not for you.

Despite the reference to the Cause/Object of the Incarnation ("by Jesus Christ"), the poet's primary experience is literary. A poem was sent to the poet by Toute-Belle on the faith of his renown as a poet. The words "see," "know," "experience," and "true" receive a paradoxical status in the letter. Always assumed in the obliqueness of a literary sign, in the equivocal nets of fiction, they cannot refer to anything like a commonsensical experience. The evidence for this is everywhere: For Machaut, the Thing is the origin, and experience and truth the event, of writing, without which there is no desire.

To the exclusion of everything else, and even at the price of forgetting God, Toute-Belle writes,

> Si ne cuide mie quil ne pest avenir chose par quoy ie ne vous peusse oublier * car il nest riens de quoy il me souveingne tant, *nes dieu prier.* (165, emphasis added)

> And so I do not think anything could happen that could make me forget you, for nothing is so much in my memory *except praying to God.*

This interpretation leaves one last question unanswered. Why, given his discourse's radical heresy, did Machaut not wind up on the fire like the Albigensians who came before him? Why did he die in melancholy, but still a canon of Reims, covered with honor, benefits, and prebends? Several explanations are possible here. One is historical: The patronage of the powerful (Jean of Bohemia, Jean de Berry) may have sheltered him. The other is historico-philosophical: If one accepts Jacqueline Cerquiglini's thesis of a general crisis of truth in the fourteenth century, the *Voir Dit*'s transgression would not be an isolated case. But the text perhaps provides the response itself, explicitly using horror to create the Thing as literature, in opposition to any First Cause and all Incarnation. This is the risk all literature runs when it is written outside the discourse of the incarnate reference. One could read the *Voir Dit* in a derisory and neutralizing manner by returning it to a pure play on and of language, without effect on any Real, Thing, or reference. This reading can only happen if horror, the Real of the text, is placed in parentheses. This is a precaution no doubt calculated by Guillaume de Machaut, for example, when he repeatedly takes his text apart and demonstrates the fictional mechanisms of his enunciation. The *Voir Dit* can only be a fable without the weight of truth, in the tradition of Augustine or Isidore of Seville. This interpretive possibility would have placed its canon-author out of reach of ecclesiastical censure.

Coda

Sains Julians!
Con vauc torban!
Soi serrazis o crestians?
Qals est ma leis?
Non sai.

Saint Julian! How befuddled I am! Am I a Saracen or a Christian? What is my belief? I do not know.[1]

Raimbaut d'Orange wrote these words at the end of the twelfth century, torn between a language that is full of the Incarnation and one that is vague and uncertain, that of idolatry, heresy, and impiety (these are all possible readings of the word *serrazis*): the language of literature.

One goal of the present book is to demonstrate that it is impossible to make a definitive distinction between the Christian letter and the literary signifier; a gnossology must recognize that such a conclusion is necessarily impossible because of the nature of its improbable object. Literature's difficulty is also precisely its greatest resource. Or, in the terms of the Provençal troubadour, the *torbar,* "trouble," metamorphoses into its mirror image, the *trobar,* "poetic discovery." The literary exception neither undoes nor establishes the laws of enunciation; without them, it could not delimit its own uniqueness.

Furthermore, if modernity is truly "medieval" (as Mallarmé claimed in *Catholicisme*), then this book written by a medievalist would have to carry over into a second volume. Its project would be far more than that of adding to the necessarily incomplete catalog of disincarnations that occurred before 1500. Among its gnossological projects, it would bind a series of later moments to the light of the Incarnation: the Racine of the so-called religious plays; the Balzacian Christ of paternity; Thomas and J.'s resurrections in the work of Maurice Blanchot; and Pierre Klossowski's perverse Eucharist. This book is necessarily truncated, and in more than one way; I cannot conclude it. The fecundity of an idea, however, is measured not only by its results but also by the unthought that it cannot master.

Notes

INTRODUCTION

1. René Girard, *Things Hidden since the Foundation of the World* (Stanford: Stanford University Press, 1987); and *The Scapegoat* (Baltimore: The Johns Hopkins University Press, 1986).

2. Alexandre Kojève, "L'Origine chrétienne de la science moderne," in *Mélanges offerts à Alexandre Koyré,* bk. 2 (Paris: Hermann, 1964), 295–306.

3. Ibid., 302. All uncredited English translations are those of the translator of the current volume.

4. Ibid., 303. This is why I thought it necessary to keep the notion of God the Creator, even though I, like Kojève, am centering my study on the Incarnation. This allows us to see a rational, and therefore explainable, design in nature. I make this statement to explain the attention I have paid to the idea of creation in Tertullian, Saint Augustine, Isidore of Seville, and Alain of Lille. The idea of the God-man is incomprehensible without this concept. I quote Pierre Duhem: "In the name of Christian doctrine, the church fathers struck down the pagan philosophies on points that we, today, would consider more metaphysical than physical. These points, however, are the cornerstones of ancient physics. Such a theory is the idea of eternal matter, or the belief that the stars rule earthly affairs, or the continual rhythm of the Great Year. Using these attacks to ruin the cosmologies of Peripetism, Stoicism, and Neo-Platonism, the church fathers make way for modern science"; *System du monde,* bk. 2 (Paris: Hermann, 1914), 408 [trans. D. L.].

5. For example, see Alexandre Koyré, "Les Origines de la science moderne," in *Etudes d'histoire de la pensée scientifique* (Paris: Gallimard, 1985), 61–68.

6. This raises a legitimate question: Why Rome and not Byzantium? To answer would require the writing of another book. Let me point out, however, that from 1453 onward, the Orthodox Church is no longer in a central position. Also, and this may be more fundamental, its doctrine is more one of Platonic contemplation than one of objective explanations of physical phenomena. Maximus the Confessor makes the contemplation of nature *(physike theoria)* more a mystical offering to God than an epistemological enquiry.

7. Jean-Claude Milner's decisive article "Lacan and the Ideal of Science," in *Lacan and the Human Sciences,* ed. A. Leupin (Lincoln: University of Nebraska Press, 1991), 27–42.

8. We see now why the thinkers of the Incarnation (the church fathers) and later the scientific epistemologists (Karl Popper, Kojève, and Koyré, among others) all line up on the side of a philosophical and linguistic realism against nominalism.

9. Boethius, *A Treatise against Eutyches and Nestorius,* trans. H. F. Stewart and E. K. Rand (Cambridge, Mass.: Harvard University Press, 1953), 119. See the brief but illuminating commentary by Alain de Libera, *La Philosophie médiévale* (Paris: Presses Universitaires de France, 1989), 70–71.

10. Boethius, *A Treatise,* 95.

11. Ibid., 95–97.

12. On this point, see Pierre Duhem, *Sauver les phénomènes* (Paris: Hermann, 1908), chap. 7. Duhem shows that in Galileo's trial, the church merely demanded that the new theory be brought into accord with the rules of scientific rigor then in force; failing this, it was to be taught as nothing more than hypothesis. Paul Feyerabend returns to this idea in the thirteenth chapter of *Against Method* (London and New York: Verso, 1988), 129–38. What can be said of "pure" science can also be said of technology. Lynn White, in his works, has shown that the Middle Ages were an epoch that experienced remarkable technological progress, and that these advances were due to the Christian spirit: "History, far from being cyclical as it is in most religions, in Christianity is unique and unilinear; it is accelerating toward a spiritual goal; there is no time to lose; therefore, work, including manual work, is an essential and pressing form of worship. Moreover, matter was created for a spiritual purpose and it is neither to be transcended nor despised; the dogmas of the incarnation and of the resurrection of the flesh vouch for this"; *Medieval Religion and Technology* (Berkeley and Los Angeles: University of California Press, 1978), 236. Also see B. Stock, "Rationality, Tradition, and the Scientific Outlook: Reflection on Max Weber and the Middle Ages," *Annals of the New York Academy of Science* 441 (1985): 7–19.

13. In particular, see Leo Steinberg's admirable work, *The Sexuality of Christ in Renaissance Art and in Modern Oblivion,* 2nd ed. (Chicago: University of Chicago Press, 1996).

14. Jacques Lacan, *Séminaire XX, encore* (Paris: Seuil, 1975), 22–38. See also Milner's commentary in "Lacan and the Ideal of Science," 36–41.

15. Jacques Lacan, *Ecrits* (Paris: Seuil, 1966), 819.

16. It was into this trap that Erich Auerbach fell, despite his erudition and intelligence. He presupposed that the Western tradition was moving to more and more realist representations. I will not make an issue of the excellence of particular textual analyses. On the topic of stylistic mutation, see Auerbach, *Mimesis* (Paris: Gallimard, 1968), 51–60.

17. This deliberate coinage is based on the Greek roots *idios,* "unique, individual," and *gramma,* "writing." [Translator's note.]

18. I take this word from Fernando Vidal's observations.

19. Here I am following the principles laid out by François Regnault in "Lacan and Experience," in *Lacan and the Human Sciences,* ed. Leupin. What Regnault says of the patient in analysis can also be transposed onto literary texts: "Lacan . . . gives a rule that can be thus quoted: 'Never consider the case [literary text] as such.' Or better still: 'In a case [text], look for what contradicts it.' Such an attitude consists in playing with the twofold meaning of the word 'case' (*Fall* in German): 'it is but a case [text],' which means that because of its conformity to the species it belongs to, it can be treated or cured [or interpreted] as such; and 'It's a case [text],' which means that it cannot be understood because of its singularity"; 47.

20. A *mise en abyme* is a figure in a work of literature that reflects the creation of the text in which it occurs; as defined by L. Dällenbach, *Le Récit spéculaire* (Paris: Seuil, 1977). [Translator's note.]

21. For more details, see my study in *Barbarolexis: Medieval Literature and Sexuality* (Cambridge, Mass.: Harvard University Press, 1989), chap. 1.

22. Geoffrey of Vinsauf, *Poetria nova,* trans. Ernest Gallo (The Hague: Mouton Press, 1971), 57.

23. Ibid., 53.

24. With regard to theology and philosophy (and these remarks can be extended to all of the cultural activities of the Middle Ages): "If the fifteen centuries in question were undeniably Christian, then Christianity had a long way to go to work its way into all of the domains of culture. Without a doubt, theology and morality (if not law) in a certain measure were all rapidly Christianized (the Christianization of theology, strikingly, was in no way total). But if one wishes to see it in the first artistic style that was specifically Christian (because it willingly ran counter to the 'nature' of wood and rock), one has to wait more than ten centuries. As for philosophy, the enormous effort put out by the entire Middle Ages had, if not as its goal, at least as its result, the rediscovery of a more or less authentic (and thus pagan) Plato and Aristotle"; Kojève, "L'Origine chrétienne," 300.

25. "The church. Jesus was not mad when he said that he was God. He thus created a sect that held him to be the true God, and this sect became a church, that is, a real world in which man *lives*"; Alexandre Kojève, *Introduction à la lecture de Hegel* (Paris: Gallimard, 1947), 258.

26. Ibid.

27. Geoffrey of Vinsauf, *Poetria nova,* 75.

28. His mistake, in my eyes, was in wanting to demonstrate the *historical* relation between Catharism and troubadour poetry, a relation that is difficult to document positively and that does not ask the question of conceptual affinity, which is concrete.

29. Geoffrey of Vinsauf, *Poetria nova,* 91.

1. THE BE-SEEMING

1. See Florence Dupont's article "Cicéron sophiste romain," *Langages* 65 (1982): 23–46.

2. Rhetoric lasted until the middle of the nineteenth century. The influence of postromanticism caused it to lose all official status in pedagogy. However, rhetoric still survives, and very vigorously, in all of the "persuasive arts": not only in literature, but also in advertising, marketing, political campaigns, the media, and the like.

3. Cicero, *De optimo genere oratorum,* book V, para. 14.

4. Cicero, *De oratore,* trans. E. W. Sutton and H. Rackham (Cambridge, Mass.: Harvard University Press, 1948). All quotations from *De oratore* are taken from this edition.

5. To show this would require a lengthy discussion. For my purposes, it is necessary to note that if one agrees with Gorgias's statement that all positive knowledge is impossible, then knowledge must all be rhetorical in essence. It is not necessary that a statement be true; rather, it must be convincing at the proper *(kairos)* moment before a given audience. For further discussion, see Eugène Dupréel, *Les Sophistes: Protagoras, Gorgias, Prodicus, Hippias* (Neuchâtel: Le Griffon, 1948), 62–74; Léon Robin, *Les Origines de l'esprit scientific* (Paris: Albin Michel, 1963), 177; Barbara Cassin, "Du faux ou du mensonge à la fiction (de 'pseudos' à 'plasma')," in *Le Plaisir de parler,* ed. Barbara Cassin (Paris: Minuit, 1986). For Gorgias's return in the Ciceronian text, see below.

6. See Alain Michel's discussion of this in his article "Cicéron" in *Encyclopaedie Universalis* (Paris, 1985).

7. I refer to two passages from Friedrich Nietzsche's 1874 course on Aristotle's *Rhetoric:* "It is not difficult to show that what is called 'rhetoric' as a conscious work of artistry was already at work in the becoming of language as unconscious artifice, that rhetoric is a continuation in the clear light of the understanding of an artifice that is *already in language*"; quoted in Bernard Pautrat, *Versions du soleil: Figures et systèmes de Nietzsche* (Paris: Seuil, 1971), 199. And elsewhere: "Tropes, *improper designations,* are considered to be rhetoric's greatest artifices. But all words, in themselves and from the very beginning, are, as for their meaning, tropes"; quoted in Pautrat, *Versions,* 205 [trans. D. L.]. See also Pautrat's commentary, 199–207.

8. This Ciceronian stumbling block for the possibility of science has endured. Nearly twenty centuries after its first appearance, Nietzsche reproduces it once again.

9. For more details, see my *Barbarolexis: Medieval Literature and Sexuality* (Cambridge, Mass.: Harvard University Press, 1989), chap. 1.

10. "Scaevola . . . observed, 'Crassus, why do we not imitate Socrates as he appears in the Phaedrus of Plato?'"; *De oratore,* I, vii, 28.

11. It is necessary to emphasize once more the contradiction between the Platonic mimetic ideal and a histrionic thought that is sophistic by nature.

12. See Alain Michel's *Rhétorique et philosophie chez Cicéron: Essai sur les fondements philosophiques de l'art de persuader* (Paris: Presses Universitaires de France, 1960), 197, a work that is essential to any study of Cicero.

13. Quintilian, *Institutio oratoria,* trans. H. E. Butler (Cambridge, Mass.: Harvard University Press, 1920–22). All citations of the *Institutio oratoria* are taken from this translation.

14. *On the Character of the Orator,* III, 12.

15. Alain Michel emphasizes the tension implied by this sublime ideal of the orator: "This desire for fullness and worrying about perfection are united with a search for abundance and complexity." *Rhétorique et philosophie chez Cicéron,* 380.

16. See *De oratore,* II, lxvii, 269–72, and Michel, *Rhétorique et philosophie chez Cicéron,* 281.

17. According to Michel's terminology, *Rhétorique et philosophie chez Cicéron,* 367.

18. Jacques Lacan, *Télévision* (Paris: Seuil, 1974), 39.

19. On the ideal orator's *virilitas,* "masculinity," and *frugalitas,* "asceticism," see *Institutio oratoria,* respectively, I, i, 9 and X, vi, 17. Elsewhere, Quintilian recommends sexual abstinence to strengthen the speaker's voice (XI, iii, 19).

20. See *Institutio oratoria,* I, i, 28; I, viii, 14; I, x, 27. See also the introduction to *Barbarolexis.*

21. Homer the teacher is contrasted with the frivolous (*vacuus,* "empty") Homer of Saint Augustine (*Confessions,* I, xiv). The church father's rejection of the Greek is a sign not of his lack of culture but of his conscious break with the tradition of fiction that runs through all of rhetoric. I will return to this point.

2. THE BREAK

1. With the exception of Georges Didi-Huberman, "La Couleur de chair ou le paradoxe de Tertullien," *Nouvelle Revue de psychanalyse,* no. 35 (1987): 9–49, which is primarily concerned with aesthetics.

2. For more on this idea, see Jean-Claude Fredouille, *Tertullien et la conversion de la culture antique* (Paris: Etudes augustiniennes, 1972), chap. 4. This work is an essential key to Tertullian.

3. See Quintilian, *Institutio oratoria,* trans. H. E. Butler (Cambridge, Mass.: Harvard University Press, 1920–22), VII, v, 2.

4. See Heinrich Lausberg, *Handbuch der literaschen Rhetorik,* 2nd ed. (Munich: Hueber, 1973).

5. See Fredouille, *Tertullien et la conversion,* 233.

6. See Tertullian, *Apologétique,* ed. E. Dekkers, Corpus Scriptorum Christianorum, Series Latina, no. 19 (1954), 120–21.

7. Tertullian, *Apology,* trans. Sister Emily Joseph Daly, The Fathers of the Church, no. 10 (Washington, D.C.: The Catholic University of America Press, 1950), 116.

8. In Alexandre Kojève's strictly Hegelian terms, in *Introduction à la lecture de Hegel* (Paris: Gallimard, 1947), 255–62. Unfortunately, the English translation of Kojève's work omits this key passage [translator's note].

9. Tertullian, *On the Flesh of Christ,* trans. Holmes, The Ante-Nicene Fathers, no. 3 (Buffalo, N.Y.: Christian Literature Publishing, 1885), XIII, 4.

10. See Alexandre Koyré's study "Du monde de l'à-peu-près à l'univers de la précision," in *Etudes d'histoire de la pensée philosophique* (Paris: Gallimard, 1986), 341–62.

11. Tertullian, *On the Soul,* 27, 4.

12. Tertullian, *On Spectacles,* II, 4, trans. Rudolph Arbesmann (New York: Fathers of the Church, 1959), 33–110.

13. I offer these citations from Bede, "Novum Testamentum, qui est Christus"; and from Amalarus, "Evangelium, Christus est"; both drawn from Father H. de Lubac, *Exégèse médiévale* vol. 1, part 1, I (Paris: Aubier, 1959), 322. He comments, "Jesus Christ is the unity of writing because he is its end and its completion. Everything refers to Him. He is, finally, its only object"; possibly the only thing.

14. Isidore of Seville writes, in the seventh century, "The Latins did not consider the numbers as letters, which for them only made up words, except for the letters *I* and *X,* which stand for the sign of the cross, and are used in the number ten" (*Etymologies,* I, iii, 11); and elsewhere, "The letter *X* was introduced to Latin in Augustus' time, which is appropriate, because it stands for the name of Christ and also because it forms the cross" (*Etymologies,* I, iv, 14); [both trans. D. L.].

15. Fredouille, *Tertullien et la conversion,* 30.

16. As Jean-Pierre Mahé has noted, "Tertullian's goal is to write a polemic against the God [of the Marcionites] but, of course, in the manner of Marcion"; *De carne Christi* (Paris: Editions du Cerf, 1975), 167 [trans. D. L.].

17. See the French translation and the rich commentaries of Mahé. In regard to this passage, Mahé notes, "In contrast to his adversaries for whom all language is deceitful and reflects an inferior reality when it attempts to communicate with the divine Eon, Tertullian forcefully affirms the words that the Holy Spirit used when addressing men"; Mahé, *De carne Christi,* 127 [trans. D. L.].

18. Johannes Erigena, *Commentaire sur l'Evangile de Jean* (Paris: Editions du Cerf, 1999) 95 [trans. D. L.].

19. See Tertullian, *On the Flesh of Christ,* V, for Tertullian's comments on the *stultitia,* which, according to Gnostic thought, is the folly of the crucifixion. Tertullian states that this folly is in Christian discourse's favor, as a sign of its impossibility.

20. See the article by H.-C. Puech, "Time and History in Patristic Christianity," collected in *Man and Time* by Henry Corbin, et al. (Princeton: Princeton University Press, 1957).

21. Note that, at least until the Cathars, the hatred of matter and the body is a recurring trait of anti-Catholic heresies. Thus, for Apelles, the world is a sin, and matter and creation are marked with the negative sign of evil; Tertullian, *On the Flesh of Christ,* VIII, 1–4.

22. Mahé has analyzed this; *De carne Christi,* 128ff.

23. See Mahé, *De carne Christi,* 393.

24. See the introduction to my *Barbarolexis: Medieval Literature and Sexuality* (Cambridge, Mass.: Harvard University Press, 1989), 14–16.

25. See Fredouille, *Tertullien et la conversion,* 344ff.

26. Tertullian, *Against the Valentinians* 5, 1. On this point, see Fredouille, *Tertullien et la conversion,* 352–54.

27. Tertullian, *On the Apparel of Women,* trans. Edwin A. Quin (New York: Fathers of the Church, 1959), 111–49.

28. See the study by R. H. Bloch, "Medieval Misogyny," *Representations* 20 (1987): 9–15. "The danger of woman . . . is that of literature itself." *On the Apparel of Women* confirms this conclusion at every point, as we will see. If women are "the Devil's gate," then pagan literature's idolatry, as seen by the church fathers, is also not only on the side of heresy but also on the side of the feminine.

29. See the opening to book II: "Handmaidens of the Lord, my fellow servants and sisters, on the strength of the right of fellow servantship and brother—the right by which I, the very last of you, am counted as one of you—I am emboldened to address to you some words, not, of course, of affection, but paving the way for affection in the cause of your salvation" (*On the Apparel of Women,* II, 1, 1). And of course, "Now, since, by a defect of nature, there is inborn in men because of women (just as in women because of men) the desire to please, the male sex also has its own peculiar trickeries for enhancing their appearance" (II, 8, 2).

30. On the notion of the interpolator, see below.

31. Ovid, *The Art of Love,* trans. J. H. Mozley (Cambridge, Mass.: Harvard University Press, 1979), I, 4. Many critics have noted the antithesis between these two books. For example, see Fredouille, *Tertullien et la conversion,* 53–54.

32. In another of Tertullian's treatises, *Prayer,* he refers to the Gospel of Peter: "As for the modesty of their attire and adornment, the admonition of

Peter, too, is clearly expressed"; trans. Sister Emily Joseph Daly (New York: Fathers of the Church, 1959), XX, 2.

33. Cicero, *De oratore,* trans. E. W. Sutton and H. Rackham (Cambridge, Mass.: Harvard University Press, 1948), III, 199.

34. As, for example, in Quintilian, *Institutio oratoria,* II, x, 11.

35. On this point, see my article "Trois nudités: Adam, le Christ, Mercure," *Lendemains* 51 (1988): 7–10.

36. Geoffrey of Vinsauf, *Poetria nova,* trans. Ernest Gallo (The Hague: Mouton Press, 1971), ll. 916–17.

37. "Vestire atqua ornare," as Cicero writes in *De oratore,* I, xxxi, 142.

38. See Lausberg, *Handbuch der literaschen Rhetorik,* 358.

39. See Didi-Huberman, "La Couleur de chair ou le paradoxe de Tertullien": "It is not enough to write the history of forms, we must also write the history of their theoretical uses—of their conversions"; 46 [trans. D. L.].

40. Tertullian, *De idolatria,* I, 1.

41. We need to compare "the pomp of the Devil" to the pomps of women *[muliebri pompae],* which are denounced in *On the Apparel of Women,* I, 4, 1.

42. See Tertullian's condemnation of the last three artisitic activities in *On Spectacles,* X, 13.

43. The histrions, the devil's minions, not only produce impious gestures inspired by Venus and Liberus (*On Spectacles,* X, 8), they are also the *letters* of the perverse text: "The text of your pantomimes, too, represents all the vileness of your gods" (*Apology,* 15, 2). See also *Ad nationes,* I, 10, 44–45.

44. See Barbara Cassin's excellent commentary, "Du faux ou du mensonge à la fiction (de 'pseudos' à 'plasma')," in *Le Plaisir de parler,* ed. Barbara Cassin (Paris: Minuit, 1986), 10–11.

45. Nietzsche sees in these final pages of *De spectaculis* a simple metaphorical transfer of the pagan problematic of the spectacle, whose ethic and meaning is only a mask (*The Genealogy of Morals,* I, 15). No doubt this reading comes from his basic position that thought and language are essentially rhetorical. As a consequence, it is impossible to introduce any criterion of reality to language. It is also impossible in such a system to think of the notion of the epistemological break. It goes without saying that the docrine of the proper in Tertullian (his philosophical, linguistic, rhetorical, and artistic realism) resists this interpretation.

3. FORNICATION

1. Saint Augustine, *Confessions,* trans. R. S. Pine-Coffin (New York: Penguin Books, 1961). All citations of the *Confessions* are taken from this volume, unless otherwise noted.

2. This view derives from the author himself: "The first ten books were written about myself *[de me scripti sunt];* the last three about Holy Scripture, from the words: 'In the beginning God created heaven and earth' as far as the

Sabbath rest"; Saint Augustine, *The Retractations,* trans. Sister Mary Inez Bogan, The Fathers of the Church, no. 60 (Washington, D.C.: The Catholic University of America Press, 1968).

3. In *The Teacher,* this interior master is Christ (but he is also exterior since he is the incarnate word). As Adeodatus says, "As for me, I have learned, thanks to being reminded by your words, that words do no more than prompt man to learn, and that what appears to be, to a considerable extent, the thought of the speaker expressing himself, really amounts to extremely little. Moreover, as to whether what is said is true, He alone teaches who when He spoke externally, reminded us that He dwells within us"; Saint Augustine, *The Teacher,* trans. Joseph M. Colleran, Ancient Christian Writers, no. 9 (New York: Newman Press, 1950), 186.

4. In this respect, the last three books of the *Confessions,* a commentary on the absolute origin of the world, structurally and cosmologically fill in the hole where the *infans* has its origin.

5. This fitting expression comes from Eugène Vance's article "Le Moi comme langage: Saint Augustin et l'autobiographie," *Poétique* 19 (1973), 163. See also his article "Augustine's *Confessions* and the Poetics of the Law," *Modern Language Notes* 93 (1978): 618–34.

6. See his remarks in *Confessions,* I, 7, which describe the newborn as a sinner.

7. In a way, Monica is only the terrestrial figure of "The Bride of Christ"—the Catholic Church, who made her a saint based solely on her role in the *Confessions:* "You, my God, were my guardian even then, and you saw the fervour and the strength of my faith as I appealed to the piety of my own mother and to *the mother of us all,* your Church, to give me the baptism of Christ your Son, who is my God and Master"; I, 11, (emphasis added).

As for Patricius, he is the exception to the spiritual law that rules the home: "Even at that age I already believed in you, and so did my mother and the whole household except for my father"; I, 11.

8. See my reflections on the *Homo Iesus Christus* and the Incarnation, below.

9. As Alexandre Kojève writes in another context, "This is sin, the crime of desire, that is humanized"; *Introduction à la lecture de Hegel* (Paris: Gallimard, 1947), 261 [trans. D. L.].

10. Saint Augustine, *Confessions,* trans. F. J. Sheed (New York: Sheed and Ward, 1943). I prefer this translation of this passage to Pine-Coffin's.

11. I owe this observation to E. Vance.

12. *The Teacher* (A.D. 389), *The Trinity* (A.D. 401–419), *De doctrina Christiana* (A.D. 398?–426). See E. Vance's study "Augustine: Language and Temporality," in *Mimesis: From Mirror to Method, Augustine to Descartes,* ed. J. D. Lyons and Stephen G. Nichols (Hanover, N.H.: 1982). See also M. Baratin and

F. Desbordes, "Sémiologie et métaliguistique chez saint Augustin," *Langages* 65 (1982), 75–89.

13. M. L. Colish made this point in *The Mirror of Language: A Study in the Medieval Theory of Knowledge* (Reprint; Lincoln, Neb.: University of Nebraska Press, 1983), 17ff. In this sense, there cannot be a "metalinguistics" in Augustine.

14. "If a man therefore purge himself from these, he shall be a vessel unto honour, sanctified, and meet for the master's use, and prepared unto every good work" (2 Tim. 2:21).

15. Here we are closest to Lacan and Freud, two thinkers whom Augustine anticipates constantly—we will see this again below. Only the urgency of defining his relation to God kept the author of the *Confessions,* who is everywhere sensitive to the unconscious aspect of being, from inventing psychoanalysis.

16. On the *gaudium,* see the *Confessions* themselves (X, 32; IX, 10). For more on the *fruitio Dei,* see *De doctrina Christiana,* I, 3, 3. In the latter text, the homonymy of *fruitio* is in the superlative *perfruitio,* which makes it infinite. See Georges Didi-Huberman's "Le Paradoxe de l'être à voir, fragments," *L'Ecrit du temps* 17 (1988): 88–89.

17. This refers to Plato's hierarchy of representations, which is in full force here (no doubt from a neo-Platonist source): (1) heaven of true ideas; (2) the object or the human notion of these ideas; (3) artistic simulacrum (= degradation) of the object; (4) and, in the unique case of Terence, representation (painting) in or of the representation (play).

18. Aristotle, *Poetics* 6, 49 b 24. See the excellent discussion of this notion in R. Dupont-Roc and J. Lallot's edition of the *Poétique* (Paris: Seuil, 1980), 188ff.

19. Augustine, *Against Lying,* trans. Harold B. Jaffee, The Fathers of the Church, no. 14 (Washington, D.C.: The Catholic University of America Press, 1952), 153–54.

20. Ibid.

21. Augustine, *Soliloquies,* vol 5., trans. Thomas F. Gilligan, The Fathers of the Church, no. 14 (Washington, D.C.: The Catholic University of America Press, 1948), 415.

22. Quoted from Henri-Charles Puech's study *Le Manichéisme, son fondateur, sa doctrine* (Paris: Civilisations de Sud [S.A.E.P.], 1949), 68 [trans. D. L.]

23. Among others, there are *Against Adimantus, a Disciple of Mani* (388), *On Genesis, against the Manichaeans* (388–389), *Against Faustus, the Manichaean* (398–404), and *Against Felix, the Manichaean* (404).

24. On this problem, see Puech, *Le Manichéisme,* 66–67; G. Widengren, *Mani and Manichaeism,* trans. Charles Kessler, rev. by the author (London: Weidenfeld and Nicolson, 1965); and K. H. Lutke, *"Auctoritas" bei Augustin* (Stuttgart, 1968), 128ff. Let me say in advance that this apocryphal pretense to authority that Augustine condemns is the very source of the medieval literary text. This places it very clearly in Lucifer's camp. I need only mention one of Guillaume IX of Aquitaine's poems, in which he declares that the text, through

its enunciation, is its own authority: "Et est vertaz, / E puesc en traire.l vers *auctor* / Quant er lassatz" [And it's true / And one can deduce the *author* from the poem / When he leaves it]; *Poème VI,* ed. Alfred Jeanroy (Paris: Champion, 1964) (emphasis added).

25. The *Confessions* do not identify the particular Docetism they are criticizing. Pierre de Labriolle, in his introduction to the *Confessions* (Paris: Les Belles Lettres, 1950), attributes the doctrine to the neo-Platonists. The condemnation is equally applicable to the gnoses attacked by Tertullian as well as to the Manichaeans. We will see below, in the discussion of Guillaume de Machaut (chapter 9), that this logic of disincarnation is at the center of medieval poetic practice.

26. See Puech, *Le Manichéisme,* 72; S. Runcimann, *The Medieval Manichee* (Cambridge, Mass.: Harvard University Press, 1960), 21; and P. Brown, *Augustine of Hippo: A Biography* (Berkeley and Los Angeles: University of California Press, 1967), 46ff. The last work is also a basic work for any study of Augustine.

27. See *Confessions,* V, 4: *copiosissime delirans,* "wildly delirious"; III, 6: *loquaces,* "babble"; V, 6 (concerning Faustus): *gratium et incundum verbis,* "gratuitous and flowing words."

28. *Regula:* a ruler used to draw a straight line or a right angle; figuratively, a standard allowing one to judge. *Regularis* (for Cassiodorus): from the canon, canonical. Labriolle observes that in the *Confessions,* "[W]e have the original metaphor that has given birth to a number of ecclesiastical expressions, *r. fidei, r. pietatis, r. veritatis, r. disciplinae,* etc."; 61, n. 2 [trans. D. L.].

29. In line with the title of François Regnault's essential work *Dieu est inconscient* (Paris: Navarin, 1985).

30. With regard to this, it becomes evident how decisive margins—social margins, of course, but also geographic and, above all, conceptual margins—are to Christian culture. The Roman centrality of the church seems only to play one, papal, role of cohesion. Tertullian and Augustine are Africans, Isidore of Seville is "Spanish." They are the crucial witnesses to the importance of the periphery that is not yet crystallized in centrality.

31. Quintilian, *Institutio oratoria,* X, v, 4–11.

32. P. Courcelle, *Recherches sur les* Confessions *de Saint Augustin* (Paris: de Boccard, 1968) 192, n. 2, identifies some Persian reminiscences in this passage. Augustine, thus, is secretly practicing paraphraxis. We will avoid accusing him of using rhetoric as would a grammarian. This example clearly shows the mercenary nature of rhetoric: Homonymy allows it to be used again.

33. On this episode, read P. Courcelle, "'Le Tolle, lege,' fiction littéraire et réalité," in *Recherches sur les Confessions,* 188–201, which relates the "biographical," "true" event to a literary model. They thus deny precisely the real ("Incarnation") dimension. Although this "rhetorical" reading is always possible, and partly legitimate, the problem has to be shifted. Augustine knows that there is no access to the proof of the angelic voice if one limits oneself to the text alone.

4. KNOWLEDGE AND LACUNAE

1. This mixture of genres forms the basis of such diverse texts as Alain of Lille's *The Plaint of Nature* and the "chantefable" *Aucassin et Nicolette.*

2. All quotations from Martianus Capella are from *The Marriage of Mercury and Philology,* ed. and trans. James Willis (Leipzig: Teubner, 1983). All references to the *Marriage* refer to the paragraph number. I also recommend Fanny LeMoine's detailed and erudite book, *Martianus Capella: A Literary Evaluation* (Munich: Munchener Beitrage zur Mediavistik und Renaissance Forschung, 1972), which pays close attention to the rhetorical and literary resources of the text.

3. This sort of writing is a common feature of late-antique writing. See Alexandre Kojève's analysis "The Emperor Julian and His Art of Writing," in *Ancients and Moderns,* ed. Joseph Crospey (New York and London: Basic Books, 1964), 95–113.

4. Later in this chapter, I will return to this Carolingian rereading of Martianus, to which even modern scholars refer for explanations of the text's many obscurities. Let me say here that Johannes Ereginus, *Annotationes in Marcianum,* ed. C. E. Lutz (Cambridge, Mass.: The Medieval Academy of America, 1939), 165, makes a point of the relation between Silenus's drunkenness and that of the poets.

5. On this point, see Edgar de Bruyne, *The Esthetics of the Middle Ages,* trans. Eileen B. Hennessy (New York: F. Ungar, 1969).

6. This is also the Augustinian definition of the true statement; see chapter 3.

7. See Johannes Ereginus, *Annotationes,* 3; and Remigius of Auxerre, *Commentum in Martianum Capellam,* ed. C. E. Lutz, vol. 1 (Leyden: Brill, 1962), 66.

8. Johannes Ereginus: "Fraud is called thus because she often obeys Mercury. Mercury is the god of eloquence because he uses a great number of tricks and frauds for both good and evil"; *Annotationes,* 39 [trans. D. L.].

9. Johannes Ereginus cosmologizes (naturalizes) the evil essence of Philology's knowledge. Tartare, for him, is "the passage of stars under the earth," the movement of the spheres that escapes astronomical observation but that Philology knows (Ereginus, *Annotationes,* 26). Remigius of Auxerre makes less of neutralizing this diabolic aspect: He glosses *Tartareos recussus* as "the depths of hell," with no further discussion; Remigius of Auxerre, *Commentum,* 96). It is obvious that a positive Christian knowledge cannot incorporate a knowledge of infernal origin, unless it is first radically cathected, as with Saint Augustine and the "river of hell" of rhetoric.

10. For an example, see the excellently researched notes to William Harris Stahl, Richard Johnson, and E. L. Burge's English translation of *The Marriage of Mercury and Philology* in *Martinaus Capella and the Seven Liberal Arts,* vol. 2, bk. 4 (on Dialectic) (New York: Columbia University Press, 1977), which shows

clearly that the *Peri Hermeneias* and Aristotle's *Categories* are particularly mistreated. Stahl, Johnson, and Burge's first volume, a general introduction to Martianus, is necessary to any study.

11. To be distinguished from the letter of the matheme.

12. To see the analogy's reversibility, and thus its universal application, one needs only to look at the book on Music, where the models for the octaves are called tropes. Harmony is thus a mirror reference to Grammar and Rhetoric (935).

13. And also: "The swirling celestial mechanism in the swiftness of its motion, produces a harmony which it recognizes as concordant with the gamut of all proportions" (921).

14. Arithmetic assigns the symbolic number seven to the human (739). Man is thus "mathematizable," that is, "harmonizable," and vice versa.

15. Grammar and Rhetoric also make long references to Harmony in their own books; the former insists on eloquences necessary to euphonia (514–22), and the latter insists on the sound of letters (231–61).

16. For more on this point, see de Bruyne, *The Esthetics of the Middle Ages.*

17. Remigius of Auxerre, *Commentum,* 368.

18. In *Patrologia Latina,* ed. Jacques Paul Migne (Paris, 1844–55), 115, col. 1294. This reference to Saint Augustine is obviously significant. *De civitas dei,* in effect, can be read as the very antithesis of the *Marriage,* insofar as it destroys the edifice of ancient mythology point by point, the same edifice that Martianus constructs. In particular, Augustine presents the gods of the Greek and Roman pantheon as demons acting on Lucifer's orders and their statues as nothing but idols, made by the hand of man. It is clear that in the fifth century, the *Marriage*'s copious descriptions of the pantheon were thought to be idolatrous.

5. A DIVINE HARMONY

1. For more information on the problems discussed in this chapter, I refer the reader to Jacques Fontaine's fundamental study, *Isidore de Seville et la culture classique dans l'Espagne wisigothique* (Paris: Etudes augustiniennes, 1959); see also Pierre Riché, *Education and Culture in the Barbarian West, Sixth through Eighth Centuries,* trans. John J. Contreni (Columbia: University of South Carolina Press, 1976), as well as the pages devoted to Isidore by M. Banniard in *Génèse culturelle de l'Europe, Cinquième à huitième siècles* (Paris: Seuil, 1989), 159–63.

2. In passing, I must do justice to the later compilers. The Romans are those truly responsible for the decline of theoretical knowledge. They were only interested in Greek science's practical aspect, which they codified in large recipe books cut off from all analysis. Roman knowledge, compiled by Varro and Pliny, remained fixed until the twelfth century and the arrival in the medieval West of the Greek texts that had been translated into Arabic and then into Latin. It is an anachronism to accuse Martianus or Isidore of Seville of ignorance

and incompetence. They compiled what they had access to, a "science" cut off from its theory. As we will see, Isidore's incomplete knowledge did not prevent him from taking a decisive step in the progress of knowledge.

3. The quotations from Isidore's *Etymologies* are taken from the edition assembled by W. M. Lindsay, ed., *Etymologiae* (Reprint, Oxford: Oxford University Press, 1987). All translations are those of D. L.

4. On this point and on the "poetics" of the *Etymologies* in general, please see the article by R. Dragonetti, "Propos sur l'étymologie," *Fabrica* 1 (1983): 69–107; and R. H. Bloch, *Etymologies and Genealogies* (Chicago: University of Chicago Press, 1983), 51–56.

5. See letter 6 in Lindsay, *Etymologiae.*

6. Keeping in mind that *Origins* is the other title that the tradition has given to the *Etymologies.*

7. *Patrologia Latina,* ed. Jacques Paul Migne (Paris, 1844–55), 83, col. 9 (hereafter *PL*).

8. In the opinion of Fontaine, *Isidore de Seville et la culture classique,* 38–41.

9. See his etymology of *cosmos:* "[T]he Greeks took this name from the world of the ornament because of the diversity of its elements and the beauty of the stars. For them, in fact, the world is called *cosmos,* which means ornament." However, for Isidore, this ornament (which immediately implies rhetoric) is created (V, xxxix, 1). This makes a difference, and it is crucial. One can now pass from cosmetics (and aesthetics) to metaphysics and, ten centuries later, to science. If one assumes a rational will is at the origin of the whole universe and not just the celestial spheres, then one can easily formulate the laws of the sublunary world, which the Greeks never thought of doing. On this question, see Alexandre Koyré's studies "Les Philosophes et la machine" and "Du monde de l'à-peu-près à l'univers de la précision," both in *Etudes d'histoire de la pensée philosophique* (Paris: Gallimard, 1986).

10. On one level, we hold *Deus* (in the Christian sense) and *physis* to be real synonyms. We must point out, however, that this synonomy does not appear in Isidore, who makes an absolute distinction between the Creator and his creature. What does appear in Isidore is, thanks to the relation between these two, the possibility of synonymy, which will only come about in later centuries.

11. This is how he describes his work in the dedicatory letter to King Sisebut; Lindsay, *Etymologiae,* letter 6.

12. See Heinrich Lausberg, *Handbook of Literary Rhetoric: A Foundation for Literary Study,* trans. Matthew T. Bliss, et al., ed. David E. Orton and R. Dean Anderson (Boston: Brill, 1998).

13. *PL,* 83, col. 685. On this issue, see Fontaine, *Isidore de Seville et la culture classique,* 785–806.

14. Even though Isidore condemns the theater (XVIII, iv) and painting in

terms close to Tertullian's: "Picturs autem quasi fictura; est enim imago ficta, non veritas"; (XIX, xvi, 1).

15. See Fontaine's detailed commentary in *Isidore de Seville et la culture classique,* 174ff.

16. See Isidore's different etymologies of *diabolus;* VII, xi, 18–23.

17. See Jean-Claude Fredouille, *Tertullian et la conversion de la culture antique* (Paris: Etudes augustiniennes, 1972), 174.

18. As E. R. Curtius has emphasized in *European Literature and the Latin Middle Ages,* trans. Willard R. Trask (Princeton: Princeton University Press, 1953); however, Curtius mistakenly holds Isidore's hermeneutics to be original. The same idea can already be found in Tertullian; see Fredouille, *Tertullian et la conversion,* 185. Isidore's "invention" is to make hermeneutics an indispensable key to the system of encyclopedic knowledge.

19. In this way, Isidore prefigures Martianus's legitimation by the Carolingians.

20. Jacques Fontaine opens his great work with a quotation from a professor whom I will not name—"Dans quelle mesure et pourquoi Isidore a-t-il été un imbécile?" [To what degree and why was Isidore an imbecile?]—and then presents an eight-hundred-page refutation of this idea.

6. "SANCTA SIMPLICITAS"

1. This is how Prudence conceived of the articulation of the imperial structure and the spread of the evangelical message; see later in this chapter. A previous version of this chapter appeared in *Romania* (1988): 447–71.

2. See L. Musset, *The Germanic Invasions: The Making of Europe, A.D. 400–600,* trans. Edward James and Columba James (London: Elek, 1975); P. Courcelle, *Histoire littéraire des grandes invasions germaniques* (Paris: Etudes augustiniennes, 1964), particularly the account given by Rutilius Namatianus.

3. I refer the reader to the work by Renée Balibar, *L'Institution du français: Essai sur le colinguisme des Carolingiens à la République* (Paris: Presses Universitaires de France, 1985), 11–91. It demonstrates convincingly that the Roman language of the Oaths is an artistic language, incorporating various dialectical traits in a way that covers the entire area of political domination under Charles the Bald. Balibar allowed me to see her observations for a previous version of this chapter, for which I give her my deepest thanks. On the philological problems involved in establishing the text, see R. H. Bloch's study "842: The First Document and the Birth of Medieval Studies," in *A New History of French Literature,* ed. Denis Hollier (Cambridge, Mass.: Harvard University Press, 1989), 6–13.

4. One need only read Einhard's *Life of Charlemagne* to see the living presence of Greek in the Carolingian court. For a general overview of the culture of the epoch, please see P. Riché, *Daily Life in the World of Charlemagne,* trans. Jo Ann McNamara (Philadelphia: University of Pennsylvania Press, 1978).

5. See Paul Zumthor's remarks in *Langue et techniques poétiques à l'époque romane, ouzième–treizième siècles* (Paris: Klincksieck, 1963), 82ff.

6. Once again, see Balibar's analysis in *L'Institution du français,* upon which these paragraphs are based.

7. Salic law reserved royalty uniquely to male heirs.

8. This repeats, in a different context, Augustine's notion of the *parlar materno.* The maternity of spoken language was thus a topos well before the creation of the expression "mother tongue" *(maternus sermo),* which dates from Guibert of Nogent (twelfth century); see J. Batany, "L'Amère maternité du français médiéval," *Langue française* 54 (May 1982): 29–39.

9. On the break between popular and educated cultures and its Merovingian origins, see J. Le Goff, *Time, Work, and Culture in the Middle Ages,* trans. Arthur Goldhammer (Chicago: University of Chicago Press, 1980).

10. See C. Tagliavini, *Einführung in die romanische Philologie* (Munich: Oscar Beck, 1973), 376, which emphasizes the literary significance of the *Sequence of Saint Eulalia* but does not develop it. See also his bibliography on the question (471–72).

11. Excepting the pages that Zumthor devotes to the *Sequence* in *Langue et techniques.* To my knowledge, this work is the first to examine the *Sequence* from the angle of literary analysis. My point of view, however, is profoundly different. Much closer to my reading is the article by Renée Balibar, "Eulalie et Ludwig: Le génie littéraire," *Le Gré des langues* 2 (1993): 172–87.

12. The medieval conception of writing, which either pays little attention to the problems of attribution or puts them into play in the fiction, does not permit us to distinguish between author and copyist or even to guess at how many people participated in the creation of a text. Nevertheless, I will call these artisans of language by the singular noun "maker." We can guess, with a reasonable degree of certainty, that the maker was a cleric, and therefore a man who was educated and chaste (in theory) and also linked to the political power of Charles the Bald's son, Louis II (846–79), and that of his son Louis III (863–82).

13. The poem was found during the nineteenth century in a manuscript of Gregory of Naziance. It is now conserved in the library of Valenciennes. The Germanic poem that it also contains is devoted to Louis III's victory over the Normans at Saucourt (A.D. 881). Louis III died in 882, and had the manuscript been made after this date, it would doubtless have contained a funerary poem. From this, the sequence is dated to 881. I accept the conjecture Tagliavini presents in *Einführung in die romanische Philologie,* which I hope to present in a coherent manner. See also J. Batany's recent edition, *Français médiéval* (Paris, Montreal: Bordas, 1972), 51–53, which has the double advantage of printing the Latin sequence after the French and of giving an exact transcription, without corrections, of the Old French text.

14. The argument for linguistic know-how is not destroyed by the hypothesis that there were three different (monolingual) copyists. The master craftsman

of the work and its putative recipient could both have been able to play with two regional languages and one international language.

15. "Copista (se pur era solo copista—[this is, in fact, the question]) perfettamente trilingue" [A perfectly trilingual copyist (if there were but one copyist)], writes G. F. Contini in "La posizione di 'Eulalia,'" in *Studi in onore Italo Siciliano* (Florence: Olschki, 1966), 249.

16. It is anachronistic to speak of a linguistic norm in the ninth century. French as the norm and as a language of the court and of literature did not yet exist. Paris and the Ile-de-France would not achieve their political and linguistic preeminence until sometime between the tenth and the twelfth centuries. On the other hand, Old French was not a language of instruction codified by grammarians. The modern minister of education, ruling by decree over the spelling of schoolchildren and their teachers, had no counterpart in ninth-century institutions. Centralizing French Jacobinism did not yet exist.

17. "Every poetics, at its roots, is part of a linguistics," Zumthor writes in *Langue et techniques* [trans. D. L.]. I reverse this proposition: "Linguistics, in the opening moments of the French vernacular, is part of a poetics." I also refer the reader to Zumthor's commentary on Saint Fleury in *La Linguistique fantastique,* ed. S. Auroux et al. (Paris: Denoel, 1985), 291.

18. "La Séquence de sainte Eulalie," in *Français médiéval,* ed. Jean Batany (Paris: Bordas, 1972), 1. Numbers refer to line numbers; all quotations from the *Sequence* are from this edition, trans. D. L.

19. Balibar justly emphasizes that the edict of the council of Tours uses *transferre,* "transpose, change," instead of *traducere,* "carry across in its integrity." The word "translation" changes meaning depending on whether one addresses it to the *literati* or the *idiotes; L'Institution du français,* 38.

20. Bernard Cerquiglini has dispensed with this interpretive prejudice in another field, that of dialogues in the *romans,* by showing that the "word" obeys not the logic of the stenographer but the calculations of writing and rhetoric; see *La Parole médiévale* (Paris: Minuit, 1981) and *In Praise of the Variant: A Critical History of Philology,* trans. Betsy Wing (Baltimore: The Johns Hopkins University Press, 1999). All that remains is to extend his hypothesis to the oldest monuments of French literature (which are, always and obviously, monuments of writing) and to link it with Balibar's demonstration.

21. Walter von Wartburg, whose point of view is representative, dates the submission of linguistic evolution—which was, for him, more or less unconscious until then—to the explicit constraints on writing in the sixteenth century.

22. We must stop moralizing over the phenomenon of writerly constraints on the development of language, often labeled "artificial" and said to slow the "natural" development of the language (which favors, no doubt, a populist and naturalistic mysticism).

23. "Séquence de sainte Eulalie: Texte latin," in *Français médiéval,* ed. Jean Batany (Paris: Bordas, 1972), ll. 15–16.

24. Prudence, "A Reply to the Address of Symmachus," bk. II in *Prudentius,* trans. H. J. Thomson, vol. 2 (Cambridge, Mass.: Harvard University Press, 1953), 586ff. All quotations from the "Reply" are from this edition. Saint Ambrose also emphasizes the combining of the temporal empire and the spiritual kingdom in the *Enarratio in psalmis,* XLV, 21.

25. Prudence, "Crowns of Martyrdom, III," in *Prudentius,* ll. 76–85.

26. In the "Peristephanon liber," he makes this metaphor the exhortation of the hymn to the martyrs Emeterius and Chelidonius: "Written in heaven are the names of the two martyrs; Christ has entered them there in letters of gold, while on earth he has recorded them in characters of blood"; *Prudentius,* l. 99. Thus, there are two writings that reflect one another: one divine, that of the spirit, and the other human, that of the body, which is a second, faithful transcription of the former.

27. See E. R. Curtius, *European Literature and the Latin Middle Ages,* trans. Willard R. Trask (Princeton: Princeton University Press, 1953), "writing in blood." Just as in Augustinian martyrology, testamental writing assumes a bleeding to death, in the tradition of Saint Paul; Heb. 9:13–17; see chapter 5.

28. The first vernacular monuments (French and Provençal) share these roots. It is sufficient here to list their supposed dates and their titles: *Life of Saint Leger* and *Passion* in the Clermont-Ferrand manuscript (tenth century), *Sermon on Jonah* (circa 940), *Life of Saint Alexis* (eleventh century).

29. On these points, see S. Lusignan, *Parler vulgairement: Les Intellectuels et la langue française aux treizième et quatorzième siècles* (Paris: Vrin, 1987).

30. See Curtius, *European Literature,* "affected modesty," 83–85.

31. See Zumthor's comments in *Langue et techniques,* 10.

32. Please see the exposé by H. de Lubac, *Medieval Exegesis,* trans. Mark Sebanc (Grand Rapids, Mich.: W. B. Eerdmans, 1998). One quotation cited there from Gregory of Naziance (whose manuscript contains the text of the sequence) serves as a program for the production of *Sequence:* "That which is old has passed, and all has become new! The letter gives way, and the Spirit takes over; shadows disappear, and the Truth enters"; I, 1, 353.

33. This is another point in favor, not of the disdain for history, but of the skill of the maker. In this substitution, he uses Christian speech to confront directly the speech of the master of pagan discourse, thus going directly to the heart of the conflict.

34. See Paul Zumthor, *L'Inventio dans la poésie française archaïque* (Paris: Groningue, 1952); and my *Barbarolexis: Medieval Literature and Sexuality* (Cambridge, Mass.: Harvard University Press, 1989), chap. 2. After Prudence, the church fathers keep the memory of the martyr alive; for example, Gregory of Tours (sixth century), *The Book of Miracles,* and Aldhelm of Malmesbury (seventh century), *Carmen de virginitate.* The profound originality of the *Sequence* on every level (except that of prosody) rapidly frees it from a comparison to its "sources."

35. Quintilian, *Institutio oratoria,* trans. H. E. Butler (Cambridge, Mass.: Harvard University Press, 1920–22), IV, ii, 57–58.

36. See the play on *A/lexis* in *The Life of Saint Alexis,* ed. Christopher Storey (Paris: Droz, Geuève, 1968), which, in this respect, maintains a close relation to the *Sequence.* See also *Barbarolexis,* chap. 2.

7. AXIOMATIC FICTION

1. In *Patrologia Latina,* ed. Jacques Paul Migne (Paris, 1844–55), 210, col. 321 (hereafter *PL*).

2. See the distinction introduced in Alain of Lille's *De fide catholica, contra hereticos, valdenses, iudaeos, et paganos* (in *PL,* 210) between deceitful (magical) appearance and Christian (enigmatic) appearance. In *The Plaint of Nature,* sleight of hand is related to Venus's *ars magica,* that is, her poetic art. All references to *The Plaint of Nature* are taken from Alan of Lille, *The Plaint of Nature,* trans. James J. Sheridan (Toronto: Pontifical Institute for Medieval Studies, 1980). (Although the author's name is most often spelled "Alain," this edition of *The Plaint of Nature* spells his name "Alan of Lille" [translator's note]).

3. *Rhythmus de incarnatione Christi,* ed. M. T. d'Alverny, in M. T. d'Alverny, "L'Homme devant Dieu," in *Mélanges de Lubac* (Paris: Aubier, 1964), 126–28 [trans. D. L.].

4. Alain of Lille, prologue to *Distinctiones,* in *PL,* 210, col. 687 [all trans. D. L.].

5. This must be distinguished from profane rhetoric's *peregrinatio,* in which there is an infinite migration; see Heinrich Lausberg, *Handbook of Literary Rhetoric: A Foundation for Literary Study,* trans. Matthew T. Bliss et al., ed. David E. Orton and R. Dean Anderson (Boston: Brill, 1998); Geoffrey of Vinsauf, *Poetria nova,* trans. Ernest Gallo (The Hague: Mouton, 1971), ll. 765–68; and my commentary in *Barbarolexis: Medieval Literature and Sexuality* (Cambridge, Mass.: Harvard University Press, 1989), 24–28.

6. "The *Regulae* of Alan of Lille represents a nearly unique attempt in the West to weave the free will of God and the disparate moments of man's salvation into a deductive and axiomatic system—a system which related the creative extension of the divine Unity to the multiplicities of created realities and the causal reintegration of all these realities in Christ and the sacraments"; M.-D. Chenu, *Nature, Man, and Society in the Twelfth Century,* trans. Jerome Taylor and Lester K. Little (Chicago: University of Chicago Press, 1968), 290. "It contains the idea of a possible theology, reduced to the state of abstract formulas and proceeding through a series of rigorously deduced propositions"; Etienne Gilson, *La Philosophie au Moyen Age* (Paris: Payot, 1962), 315. [trans. D. L.]

7. See Alverny's remarks in "L'Homme devant Dieu," and in particular note 9, page 113.

8. Alain of Lille, *Theologicae regulae,* in *PL,* 210 [all trans. D. L.].

9. See Aristotle's *Posterior Analytics,* I, ix, 75b and 76a. Thomas Aquinas reproduces this impasse when he separates theology and philosophy.

10. Gilson, *La Philosophie au Moyen Age,* 312.

11. "Alain seems to have been one of the first to use [philosophia naturalis] to indicate the knowledge accessible to human reason"; Alverny, "L'Homme devant Dieu," 35; also, "The final part of the *Regulae* seems to be a very original attempt to contrast *'naturalis philosophia'* and sacred science"; Alverny, "L'Homme devant Dieu," 67 [both trans. D. L.].

12. Kojève was entirely correct when he stated that the medieval conception of philosophy was simply a restatement of authentic (which is to say, pagan) Platonism and Aristotelianism—which I have called the schizophrenic structure of medieval culture. Alain of Lille, despite his neo-Platonism, here serves as an exception. On the other hand, the case of Alain proves that there is no contradiction between Christianity and modern science. Let me nuance this: Alain is not always exempt from pagan knowledge; in particular, his *Anticlaudianus,* in which he sets out to produce the perfect man in the heaven of theology, smacks of paganism. Why should he want a perfect man, if there is Christ? Please see the commentary by G. R. Evans, *Alan of Lille: The Frontiers of Theology in the Later Twelfth Century* (Cambridge: Cambridge University Press, 1983), for an appreciation of the heterodoxy of Alain's project. Christian knowing never appears in a pure state.

13. Alain of Lille, *Summa* [all trans. D. L.].

14. Quintilian, *Institutio oratoria,* trans. H. E. Butler (Cambridge, Mass.: Harvard University Press, 1920–22), X, i, 28.

15. See *Barbarolexis,* chap. 3. The enunciation of the text, which gives way before everything that it denounces as hermaphroditic, provokes the return of the literary exception *in* a theology that is otherwise completely orthodox.

16. Alain of Lille, *Expositio prosea de Angelis,* ed. M. T. d'Alverny, in *Mélanges de Lubac,* 196, 198.

17. Alain of Lille, *De miseria mundi,* in *PL,* 210, col. 579 [all trans. D. L.].

18. *Sermo in die Cinerum,* ed. M. T. d'Alverny, in *Mélanges de Lubac,* 267.

19. "And I saw the dead, small and great, stand before God; and the books were opened: and another book was opened, which is the book of life: and the dead were judged out of those things which were written in the books, according to their works"; Rev. 20:12.

20. "Jesus is the book of life. . . . Happy is he to whom it is given to read from this book. Christ must be the model, the model and the example *[forma et exemplar]* of clerics and peoples. But, O misery, the clerics of our time [which can thus be assimilated to Alain's sophistic pseudography] are as blackened coals, the book has been erased"; Absalom of Springkirsbach, quoted by J. Leclercq, "Aspects spirituels de la symbolique du livre au douzième siècle," in *Mélanges de Lubac,* 65 [trans. D. L.].

21. Leclercq, "Aspects spirituels."

22. Ibid.

23. "We who call ourselves knights of theology"; "Quoniam hominess," ed. P. Glorieux, *Archives d'histoire doctrinale et littéraire du Moyen Age* 20 (1953): 120 (trans. D. L.). This spiritual militia is in opposition, on the one hand, to worldly knighthood "that harbors theft" (*Sermo de cruce Domini,* ed. M.-T. d'Alverny [Paris: Vrin, 1965], 283 [trans. D. L.]), and on the other hand, to the "knighthood of letters" proclaimed by Jean de Meun in the *Romance of the Rose.*

24. In *PL,* 210 [all trans. D. L.].

25. There is an excellent example of this in *The Autobiography of Guibert, Abbot of Nogent-sous-Coucy,* trans. C. C. Swinton Bland (Westport, Conn.: Greenwood Press, 1979).

26. On this point, see the essential study of heresy by Jean Duvernoy, *La Religion des cathares,* vol. 1 (Toulouse: Privat, 1976), 84 [trans. D. L.]. The Albigensians had an excellent knowledge of the biblical text; they differed from the church canon only in their interpretation of it. The texts in question are, among others, Matt. 24:26, Luke 4:30, and Luke 24:31.

27. *The Autobiography of Guibert, Abbot of Nogent-sous-Coucy.*

28. Ibid.

29. See Duvernoy, *La Religion des cathares,* 81.

30. Alain formulates it in this manner: "Flesh is that carnality that always contradicts the spirit, which is to say, reason"; col. 310. We must, then, distinguish between the rejection of and disgust for the flesh that belongs to Gnosticism and Catharism, on the one hand, and the Christian vision that sets the flesh between the good of creation and the desire for evil, on the other.

31. Duvernoy, *La Religion des cathares,* vol. 1, 190.

32. Quoted in ibid., 191.

33. A. Lecoy de la Marche, *Anecdotes historiques, legends, et apologues tirés du receuil inédit d'Etienne de Bourbon* (Paris, 1877), 311. Cited in Duvernoy, *La Religion des cathares,* vol. 1, 191.

34. Duvernoy, *La Religion des cathares,* vol. 1, 28–43.

8. THE COUNTERFEIT

1. Quotations in the Old French are taken from Mario Roques's edition of the *Roman de Renart* (Paris: Champion, CFMA, 1970); numbers in citations are line numbers. Unless otherwise noted, English translations are from D. D. R. Owen, *The Romance of Reynard the Fox* (Oxford: Oxford University Press, 1994), which translates Dufournet's edition. This book's translator, D. L., has altered Owen's translation only where the original texts differ widely enough to affect interpretation. Such modifications are placed between square brackets within the translations. Also, the spelling of the fox's name has been changed to "Renart" in order to maintain consistency with the original Old French.

The spelling of *ess'art,* "and his art," reinforces the negativity of the art of Renardy (as I will define it in this chapter), for it is also *essart,* "destruction." A solid analysis covering all the branches, along with a complete bibliography, can be found in Jean Scheidegger, *Le Roman de Renart; ou, Le Texte de la derision* (Geneva: Droz, 1989).

2. The narrator seems to be espousing Alain of Lille's Catholic position by associating Renart with the devil and condemning his acts as "against nature": "Cest essample vos ai mostré / Por Renart qui est si maufé / Et qui ovre contre nature" [This moralizing of mine is aimed at Renart, that [devil] who acts against nature] (14,203–5).

3. Ernest Gallo, *The* Poetria nova *and Its Sources in Early Rhetorical Doctrine* (The Hague: Mouton, 1971), 19–21.

4. See Alain of Lille, *The Plaint of Nature,* trans. James J. Sheridan (Toronto: Pontifical Institute for Medieval Studies, 1980). From the very beginning of the treatise, sodomy is an "excessive amplification" of the natural laws of grammar and of logic. Its addition makes of it a disfigurement, deformation, discoloring, and deflowering of the tropes of Christian rhetoric. It is also a degeneration into the most irrational bestiality inspired by the elephantine leprosy of debauchery. Since Tertullian, the devil has always been seen as acting by adding to and interpolating within true creation, a supplementarity that pretends to be original.

5. See Isidore of Seville, *Etymologies,* in *Etymologiae,* ed. W. M. Lindsay (reprint, Oxford: Oxford University Press, 1987), XI, i, 97.

6. "Fous est qui croit sa fol pense; / Mout remaint de ce que foux pense. / Fox est qui croit fole esperance / Que toz li monde est en balance" [It is foolish to believe one's idle thoughts. What a fool thinks rarely comes about. To trust in vain hope is folly, for the whole world hangs in the balance] (14,167–70). Note the subtle play of assonances where thought *(pense)* is associated with a maw *(panse),* the place where gluttony begins. The reader will also notice the reference to English (attested to in the branch of *Renart the Minstrel*), which associates the *fou,* "foolish, insane," with "fox," the name of the animal. *Fous* also has resonances with *foutre,* "fuck," upon which the branch plays by making it a simple past form of the verb *être* ("to be," and thus insisting upon the being of the sex; this cannot be a mere accident). For example, Renart says, "Biau saignor, je fout bon guglere" [Good mister . . . Me savvy good song] (2858).

7. See my article "Le Ressassement," *Le moyen âge* 2 (1983), 239–68.

8. Trans. D. L.

9. I take this quotation from Jean Dufournet's edition, *Le Roman de Renard: Branches I–V, VIII, X, XV* (Paris: Garnier-Flammarion, 1970 [trans. D. L.]), which follows a different manuscript from that of Roques. If there is to be a "new philology," it can only have meaning if it rids itself of the fictions created by nineteenth-century positivism. What is to be rejected are the notions of the "author" and the "copyist," which must be replaced with an interpretation

that takes all the versions of the same text into account, in the absence of an authentic manuscript. This method is entirely pertinent to the case of the *Roman de Renart,* which is written in a flowering of branches but has no central trunk.

10. Trans. D. L.

11. Isidore of Seville calls the testicles "witnesses" and the penis the "writer's pen": "In the diminutive, testicles are called 'witnesses' *[testibus],* and there must always be at least two. They produce the sperm through a pen [*calamo,* 'the penis']," *Etymologies,* X, i, 104.

12. Trans. D. L. Compare to this the emblems of writing in Alan of Lille's *Plaint of Nature,* which one can use for good or for evil: The hammer and anvil of spelling, and those of adultery, the plough in a sterile field of falsigraphy, and finally the pen/penis and the page/womb.

13. Trans. D. L.

14. Roques, *Roman de Renart,* branch 8, line 8195.

15. Roques, *Roman de Renart.*

16. Rutebeuf points out this relation in the opening lines of his poem to Renart: "Renars est mors: Renars est vis! / *Renars est ors, Renars est vils:* / Et Renars regne!" [Renart is dead. Renart is alive! / *Renart is sewage, Renart is vile.* / And Renart rules] [trans. D. L.]; *Renart le bestourné,* ed. Faral Bastin, vol. 1 (Paris: Picard, 1969), p. 537; emphasis added. Please note the subtle play of echoes. The fox is at one and the same time *or,* "gold," and *ors,* "sewage." This is literature's dirty little secret.

17. "Se fust or ci icist Renart, / Ja fust il pandu a l'art" [If that there Renart was here, then he be stringed up on the gibbet] (2579–80). The *art,* "rope," is also Ren-art's art.

18. "Ce fout si sol, tot fout portez / Et tot fout desfigurez" [And if me alone, me get carried away, [And I would be torn apart]] (2565–66).

19. Dufournet, *Le Roman de Renard,* vol. 2, 346ff.

20. Roques, *Roman de Renart.* Owen does not include this branch in his translation of the Renart cycle. All trans. D. L.

21. See Alain of Lille, *The Plaint of Nature,* 69; and E. R. Curtius's commentary in *European Literature and the Latin Middle Ages,* trans. Willard R. Trask (Princeton: Princeton University Press, 1973).

22. The work is paradoxically "biblical." The four animals can be associated, in medieval numerology, with the four Evangelists.

23. This theme is known in the *fabliaux* as well. For an example, see *Le Con qui fist fait a la besche;* and R. H. Bloch's commentary, *The Scandal of the Fabliaux* (Chicago: University of Chicago Press, 1986), 105.

24. *Renart the Magician,* branch 23, ed. Ernest Martin (Paris: Leroux, 1882–87). In manuscript M (Turin), this branch immediately precedes *How Renart Perfected the Twat.* Here we have a copyist who understood perfectly the coherence between these two branches. All translations of this branch by D. L.

25. See Roques, *Roman de Renart:* "Cil Diex, s'i li vient a plaisir, / Puet

encore bien consentir / A parler les bestes sauvages, / Et les usuriers faire larges" [This God, should he feel like it, could still agree to make wild animals speak, and to make usurers generous] (3959–62).

26. *Renart le contrefait,* ed. G. Reynaud and H. Lemaître (Paris: Champion, 1914). All translations by D. L.

27. See the moral description of acedia, line 35,321. In the Middle Ages, depression is prohibited. We do not know whether this commandment cured any actual occurrences of depression. Medical treatises link acedia with erotic and artistic activities; see Giorgio Agamben, *Stanzas: Word and Phantasm in Western Culture,* trans. Ronald L. Martinez (Minneapolis: University of Minnesota Press, 1993).

28. Renardy is the thus the inverse of the Alain of Lille's conception of the gloss, which always refers to a Real; see chapter 7. Guillaume de Machaut defines his poetics in a manner that is almost identical to Renart's; see chapter 9.

29. See Roger Dragonetti's remarks in *Le Mirage des sources* (Paris: Seuil, 1987), 17–27.

30. *Renart le contrefait,* ed. Reynaud and Lemaître, para. 45, p. 247.

31. Also mentioned in *Renart le contrefait,* ed. Reynaud and Lemaître, para. 138, pp. 286–87.

32. *Renart le Contrefait,* pp. 229–31.

33. Thus, there is no "chronological progress."

34. Roques, *Roman de Renart.*

35. A variant from Dufournet, *Le Roman de Renart,* vol. 1.

36. Geoffrey of Vinsauf, *Poetria nova,* trans. Ernest Gallo (The Hague: Mouton, 1971), ll. 765–68 and 801–4. See my *Barbarolexis: Medieval Literature and Sexuality* (Cambridge, Mass.: Harvard University Press, 1989).

37. "Mais besoin fait vielle troter" [Need makes the old wife trot] (3372). In this line, the poetic hurdy-gurdy *(vielle)* reappears in a homophone for desire (*vielle,* "want" and "old woman").

38. "Toutes les foiz c'Adans feri / En la mer, que beste en issi, / Cele beste si retenoient / Quel que el ert, si l'aprivoisoient: / Celes que Eve en fist issir / Ne pot il onques retenir: / Si tost con de la mer issoient, / Après le leu au bois aloient: / Les Adam bien aprivesoient, / Les Evain asauvagisoient. / Entre les autres en issi / Li gorpis, si asauvagi; / Rous ot le poil conme Renarz. / . . . Icil gorpis vos senefie / Renart, qui tant sot de minstrie; / Tot cil qui sont d'anging et d'art / Sunt mes tuit apelez Renart." [Adam struck the sea so much that beasts emerged. These beasts retained what they had and domesticated it. What Eve caused to emerge, they could not keep. Soon twats came from the sea and from there ran to the woods. Thus Adam's beasts were tame, but Eve's were wild, and from these the wild fox sprang. Their hair is red, like Renart's. . . . Thus the fox means Renart who knew so much of trickery. Ever since, those who are crafty and clever are all called Renart.] (3817–33). Once more, literature is associated

with the feminine; Renart and Ysengrin are born from the stick Eve uses to strike the sea. From their very beginning, they escape all mastery, which is specifically masculine. See R. Dragonetti, "Renart est mort, Renart est vif, Renart regne," *Critique* 375–76 (1978): 797.

39. This recalls the lines by Bernard de Ventadour, for whom the lady's eyes are the mirror and fountain of Narcissus in which the poet loses himself: "C'aissi.m perdet com perdet se / Lo bels Narcissus en la fon" [So I am lost just as the handsome Narcissus was lost in the fountain] [trans. D. L.]. For Alain of Lille in *The Plaint of Nature,* the writing of the same is obviously associated with the mythological character: "Narcissus, when his shadow faked a second Narcissus, was reflected in a reflection, believed himself to be a second self, and was involved in the destruction arising from himself loving himself" (136).

40. On this point, see Claude Reichler, *La Diabolie: La séduction, la renardie, l'écriture* (Paris: Minuit, 1979).

41. See Quintilian, *Institutio oratoria,* trans. H. E. Butler (Cambridge, Mass.: Harvard University Press, 1920–22), IX, 3, 33, 85, 95; and Heinrich Lausberg, *Handbook of Literary Rhetoric: A Foundation for Literary Study,* trans. Matthew T. Bliss et al., ed. David E. Orton and R. Dean Anderson (Boston: Brill, 1998); see the headings *commutatio, distinctio, regressio, reversio, tropus,* and *tropologia.*

42. For more details, see Robert E. Lerner, *The Heresy of the Free Spirit in the Later Middle Ages* (Berkeley and Los Angeles: University of California Press, 1972); Jean-Claude Schmitt, *Mort d'une hérésie* (Paris and New York: Mouton, 1978); Raoul Vaneigem, *The Movement of the Free Spirit,* trans. Randall Cherry and Ian Patterson (New York: Zone Books, 1994).

43. Saint Bernard, *Sermo 64.*

44. Gautier of Coincy, *Life of Saint Leocade,* ed. Vilamo-Pennti (Helsinki, 1950), 179.

9. DISINCARNATION

1. All citations of the *Voir Dit,* and their translations, are taken from *Le Livre dou Voir Dit (The Book of the True Poem),* ed. Daniel Leech-Wilkinson, trans. R. Barton Palmer (New York and London: Garland, 1998). Unless otherwise stated, references are to line numbers. Jacqueline Cerquiglini has also provided a definitive French edition of the *Voir Dit,* along with a translation (Paris: Le Livre de Poche, 1999).

2. The asterisk represents a place in the text where what I call a "hovering dot" was used. This appears to have been a punctuation mark, and it seems to indicate a desired vocal pause or an emphasis. It is ubiquitous throughout the published text. *Trans.*

3. For an example, see the opening formula of Letter 27, "Mon tresdoulz

cuer, ma douce suer, ma douce amour" [My very sweet heart, my sweet sister, my sweet love].

4. "Et aussi vostre livre avera nom le *livre dou Voir dit.* Si ne veuil ni ne doit mentir." [And so your book will be named the *Book of the True Poem.* It does not wish to lie, nor must it.] See Jacqueline Cerquiglini's remarks, "Syntaxe et syncope: Langage du corps et écriture chez Guillaume de Machaut," *Langue française* 40 (1978): 60–74.

5. Translation modified; D. L.

6. On this subject, see K. Brownlee, *Poetic Unity in Guillaume de Machaut* (Madison: University of Wisconsin Press, 1982), 126–27.

7. In courtly poetry, the *losangier* is a third person who is jealous of the poet and the Lady. He also suffers from envy with respect to the poetic virtuosity that structures their relations. This is the case here.

8. On adultery as a metaphor for truth, see R. H. Bloch, *Medieval Literature and Law* (Berkeley and Los Angeles: University of California Press, 1977), 56ff, and my *Le Graal et la littérature* (Lausanne: L'Age d'Homme, 1982), 174ff. For Alain of Lille, *adulteration* of "natural" language is one of the fundamental transgressions of sodomite writing; see *The Plaint of Nature,* trans. James J. Sheridan (Toronto: Pontifical Institute for Medieval Studies, 1980), 157.

9. Translation modified; D. L.

10. We must remember that for Isidore of Seville, Erichtonios is an eminently diabolical character: "As the fables report, he was the son of Minerva and Vulcan, procreated from the fruit of his pleasure fallen to the earth, a demoniacal monster, or better yet, a devil who was the first to dedicate horse races to Juno"; *Etymologiae,* ed. W. M. Lindsay (reprint, Oxford: Oxford University Press, 1987), XVIII, xxxiv, 2. This etymology is almost a word-for-word quotation of Tertullian, *On Spectacles,* trans. Rudolph Arbesmann (New York: Fathers of the Church, 1959), IX, 3.

11. Guillaume de Machaut, *Le Remede de fortune,* 3883 [quotations trans. D. L.].

12. Guillaume de Machaut, *Le Confort d'ami,* 46 [quotations trans. D. L.].

13. Paulin Paris's observation on this point deserves mention here: "Machaut is quoting Josephus here (*De antiquitabus Judoreum,* I, xviii) instead of the Bible, so as not to be accused of giving the same authority to the holy scripture and to Ovid's *Metamorphosis*"; Paulin Paris, ed., *Le Livre du Voir-Dit de Guillaume de Machaut où sont contées . . . ladite Peronnelle* (Paris: Société des Bibliophiles François, 1875), 326.

14. In accord with Freud's reading of the story of Medusa, which is entirely pertinent here: "The hair upon Medusa's head is frequently represented in works of art in the form of snakes, and these are once again derived from the castration complex. It is a remarkable fact that, however frightening they may be in themselves, they nevertheless serve actually as a mitigation of the horror, for they replace the penis, the absence of which is the cause of the horror. . . .

The sight of the Medusa's head makes the spectator stiff with terror, turns him to stone. Observe here that we have the same origin from the castration complex and the same transformation of affect! For becoming stiff means an erection. Thus in the original situation it offers consolation to the spectator: he is still in possession of a penis, and the stiffening reassures him of the fact"; Sigmund Freud, *The Complete Psychological Works of Sigmund Freud,* trans. James Strachey, vol. 18 (London: Hogarth Press, 1955), 273.

15. Both lovers have the key to this treasure, but the text remains silent with regard to it. The "treasure" implies a sexual relation but should not be reduced to it.

16. Polyphemus is also a figure for the half-blind poet who becomes blind: Guillaume de Machaut.

17. See Machaut's own comments on *soufisance,* "sufficiency," 1063–82.

18. See the *Voir Dit,* 4194–4285. I owe this reference to an article by Jacqueline Cerquiligni, "La Chose médiévale et la question de l'identité," unpublished.

19. See *Le Remède de fortune,* where lines 407–8 are identical.

20. "Mais quant amours .I. amant point / Il nest pas tous iours en .i. point / Eins a des pensees diverses / Et des douces et des parverses" [Yet when Love wounds a love, / The man is not every day the same, / But thinks many different thoughts, / Some sweet, others perverse] (1331–34).

21. *Le Livre dou Voir Dit,* ed. Leech-Wilkinson, pp. 94, 295, 250.

CODA

1. Poem 39, *The Life and Works of the Troubadour Raimbaut d'Orange,* ed. and trans. Walter T. Pattison (Minneapolis: University of Minnesota Press, 1952).

Index

Alexandre Leupin is Gregorie Professor in French Studies at Louisiana State University. He is the author of *Barbarolexis: Medieval Literature and Sexuality, La Passion de idoles,* and *Phallopanies,* and the editor of *Lacan and the Human Sciences.* He has also written numerous articles on literature, theory, art, epistemology, and psychoanalysis.

David Laatsch is a Ph.D. candidate in the Department of French Studies, Louisiana State University.